SALMON

The World's Most Harassed Fish

Anthony Netboy

SALMON,
The World's Most Harassed Fish

WINCHESTER PRESS

First published 1980 by
André Deutsch Limited
105 Great Russell Street London WC1

Library of Congress Cataloging in Publication Data

Netboy, Anthony.
  Salmon, the world's most harassed fish.

  Bibliography: p. 296
  Includes index.
  1. Salmon. 2. Salmon fisheries. 3. Salmon fishing.
I. Title.
QL638.S2N488   333.95'6   80-6207
ISBN 0-87691-335-4

Winchester Press
1421 South Sheridan Road
P. O. Box 1260
Tulsa, Oklahoma 74101

1 2 3 4 5 6 7 8 9   88 87 86 85 84 83 82 81 80

To the Memory of
My Father and Mother

Contents

List of Plates

List of Figures

Introduction

N o family of fishes has received more attention from man, their greatest predator, than the torpedo-shaped, silvery-coppery salmon who roam over the vast expanses of the Atlantic and Pacific Oceans in the northern hemisphere. Descended from primordial salmonid stock probably about a million years ago, they may have preceded man on this planet, and now man in his greed and determination to destroy the habitat of his food animals, and the animals as well, has already exterminated the Atlantic salmon (*Salmo salar*) in many countries and reduced the stocks to token populations in others. Canada, Scotland, Ireland, Norway, and Russia now produce the bulk of Atlantic salmon. While the Pacific salmon (*Oncorhynchus* species) have fared much better, they too have been pressed hard in many countries and some races, notably those who inhabit the upper Columbia River watershed in the United States, are now being considered for listing on the Endangered Species list. Eminently desirable for food as well as sport, no piscatorial group has been so greatly harassed except perhaps the whales.

This book is a chronicle of the salmon's fate from the Stone Age to the present, from the times when they lived harmoniously with man, supplying him, as Nature intended, with sustenance, to the Industrial Age, when their immemorial haunts were steadily invaded by factories, hydroelectric dams, weirs, and other barriers to their migration to and from their spawning grounds, by pollution of rivers with toxic wastes, by withdrawal of water flow in summer for agricultural purposes, and other antagonistic developments. As populations swelled in salmon-producing countries demand for the savory fish zoomed and huge flotillas of fishing boats, towing nets miles long, scoured the seas for them while other flotillas dragged the tidal reaches of the rivers for them.

The story in essence is a drama of the salmon fighting for survival in the face of reckless exploitation and inadequate conservation and compensation measures on all three continents, Europe, North America and Asia where they are found.

Thus the latest report on the condition of the Atlantic salmon, published by Restoration of Atlantic Salmon in America, Inc. (RASA), reveals that catches in home waters, excluding Greenland, Norwegian and Baltic fisheries, dropped by 47 percent between 1967 and 1979, indicating a serious decline in the health of the species which is being fished hard on their feeding grounds in the mid-Atlantic by Greenlanders and Danes and in the Baltic Sea by Danes and other fishermen, as well as by Scottish, Irish, Norwegian and Canadian fishermen off the coasts of their homelands. "It is not unrealistic to assume," says Richard Buck, chairman of RASA, "that, unless the long downward trend is sharply reversed, the species will become, in the not too distant future, not necessarily extinct, but of little practical use to man, as a source of recreation or food."

To stave off such a calamity, the United States, Canada and England, with the encouragement of the European Common Market nations, are attempting to negotiate a treaty that would bring a measure of protection to the Atlantic salmon in international waters, such as is provided to other wide-ranging species like tunas, herring and whales. As the year 1980 moves to a close, however, such a treaty is still in the distant future and meanwhile the bells toll for *Salmo salar*.

The six species of Pacific salmon are far more numerous than their Atlantic cousins. Landings of Pacific salmon average 300,000 to 400,000 metric tons a year compared with no more than 10,000 to 12,000 tons of Atlantic salmon. Russia, Canada and the United States now produce the bulk of the Pacific salmon. However, Japan in some years harvests more salmon than any of these countries, mostly fish that emanate from eastern Russia, and are taken on a quota basis, with Russia's consent, in the mid-Pacific. Japan has permitted the greater portion of its wild stocks to disappear in the frenzied pursuit of industrial success which gives industry supreme rights on rivers and fish very little consideration. To compensate for this loss, Japan has become the world's greatest salmon culturist.

Demand for the flavorsome fishes in the world's markets has increased steadily as supplies declined, thus giving birth to a new industry to fill the gap. This industry, the production of salmon that never go to sea but are bred in saltwater cages, burgeoned in Norway and is now a going business in Scotland, the United States, and other countries. In 1979 quantities of such salmon were sold in Billingsgate wholesale fish market in London. The outlook for this industry is said to be bright as the product is gaining consumer acceptance wherever it is available.

This book is based on material drawn from three continents where salmon are found, including scientific journals, official reports and unpublished memoranda, books on various phases of the subject, and discussions with many people who have devoted their professional lives to the propagation, management, conservation and enhancement of the salmon in many lands. I have visited all the countries where salmon was, or still is, an important resource, with the exception of Soviet Russia, Korea and China in the Far East, and Finland, Poland, and Switzerland in Europe.

I met not only people who spent a lifetime working with the salmon, but also many men and women who make a living as fishermen and others who are dedicated anglers seeking the prince of game fishes. These are invariably a happy and cohesive group and I am delighted to acknowledge their cooperation and hospitality; I learned much from them. If I have succeeded in imparting to my readers some of the pleasure derived from pursuing the salmon around the world and visiting the magnificent scenery amidst which they live, as well as outlining the problems we face in saving what is left of the resource, my task will be well rewarded.

There is a sticker on my study wall, provided by the Salmon Conservation Association of South Brittany, which says, "Quand le Poisson Meurt, l'homme est menace." "When the fish become extinct, man is endangered."

We are beginning to realize that man is no longer the kingpin of the animal world, and that he does not have, as the Old Testament alleges, "dominion over the fish and the sea, and over the birds of the air, and over all the earth, and over every creeping thing that creeps upon the earth." This Judeo-Christian concept has wrought immense harm to the animal world, and must be rejected out of hand. Man must learn to co-exist with the fishes and

other animals that feed and clothe him, and only then will Nature, to whom, as Alexander Pope says in his "Essay on Man," there is
...no low, no high, no great, no small,
be able to restore the balance. The alternative is disaster.

For complete bibliographies on the salmon see my two previous books *The Atlantic Salmon: A Vanishing Species?* and *The Salmon: Their Fight for Survival*, both published by Houghton Mifflin, and the forthcoming *The Columbia River Salmon: Their Fight for Survival*, University of Washington Press.

The poems on pages 138–39 and 238–39 are used with the kind permission of the Atlantic Salmon Association, publisher of *The Atlantic Salmon Journal*, and the University of Washington Press, respectively.

I am grateful to Mr. Samuel H. Bryant for permission to use the maps from *The Salmon: Their Fight for Survival*.

Anthony Netboy
Jacksonville, Oregon
October 1980

Part One

THE LIFE OF THE SALMON

CHAPTER I

Marine or Freshwater Species?

SALMON are cold-water anadromous fishes; like the shad and sturgeon they are born in freshwater and spend part of their lives in the ocean, returning to freshwater to spawn. The origin of this complicated existence is difficult to fathom and has intrigued ichthyologists for centuries, some arguing like A. Günther, author of a monumental nineteenth-century *Catalogue of Fishes*, that the salmon are freshwater species who acquired over a long period of time the habit of going to sea where they found an abundance of food, while others, like his contemporary Francis Day, believed that they originated in the ocean and eventually discovered a more protective spawning environment in the rivers.

The theory of a freshwater origin now seems to be generally accepted. According to the Russian ichthyologist G. V. Nikolsky, the change from a freshwater to an anadromous life began in the northern hemisphere about a million years ago, when enormous masses of freshwater significantly lowered the salinity of parts of the ocean around glaciated lands, thus enabling the fishes to develop biological mechanisms for adjusting from one environment to the other. We may conjecture that at the height of the glaciation food became scarce for the Salmonidae in their frozen riverine environments. Many species died off along with other animals and plants. But a few salmonids managed to venture out of the rivers into the ocean where there was a relative abundance of food, at least in summer.

At that time continuous ice caps covered most of northern Europe and northern North America. The landscape was a panorama of densely packed ice with occasional granitic 'nunataks' projecting through the white mass. There was a scarcity of animal life in this bleak world, and man probably lived only at the fringes of the glaciated areas. Inland waters were no longer free from ice even in summer. Perhaps flocks of ducks came down to rest on the open waters as they migrated across the globe. Terns, puffins, cormorants and other sea birds soared over the purple horizon on their way to milder climates. It is believed that at the peak of the Ice Age the only signs of life in the deeply frozen regions were the spiders and other insects which found morsels of food in the sparsely vegetated nunataks.

The ocean-going Salmonidae began to wander farther and farther from their home streams, grew fat, and instead of remaining in the sea when reaching sexual maturity, found their way back, by means of uncanny mechanisms, to the rivers where they were born. There they spawned and nowhere else. This life cycle evolved over an immense period of time as the fishes colonized new regions of the globe. The original stock, it is believed, was the Atlantic salmon (*Salmo salar*); from it evolved the six Pacific species belonging to the genus *Oncorhynchus*. The salmon remain native only to the northern hemisphere, though they have been successfully planted in some rivers of South Island, New Zealand, and are being introduced to the waters around southern Chile.

The theory we have sketched is accepted by such authorities as the Swedish zoo-geographer Sven Ekman, who says that in distant geologic epochs the North Pacific was favourable to the creation of new species of fish. Evidence for this belief is that among many genera common to both the Atlantic and Pacific Oceans the latter have more species. Professor J. H. Macfarlane in his book *The Evolution and Distribution of Fishes* argues against a possible marine ancestry for the Salmonidae that 'it is difficult to imagine genera like *Salmo* . . . which show few or no truly marine species, becoming dispersed as they are over land areas of the northern hemisphere, if they were marine – or even coastal – derivatives. A considerable number, further, show the anadromous or "homing instinct", in that though often migrating seaward to feed, they return to rivers or lakes to spawn . . . The swim-bladder is highly developed in primitive and freshwater types, but gradually becomes smaller and [is] even absorbed in marine species. These with other strong reasons compel the writer to accept a freshwater origin for the family to which salmon and trout belong.'

Along with the question of how the salmon evolved there has been much speculation about the relationship of the Atlantic to the Pacific species. Dr Ferris Neave of the Canadian Fisheries Research Board, in a paper published in 1958, offers a plausible theory. He says that the six Pacific species are relatively recent offshoots of *Salmo salar*. Millions of years ago some individuals may have wandered from the Atlantic to the Pacific Ocean via the Arctic at a time when there was no Bering land bridge connecting North America and Asia, nor solid ice to prevent such marine penetration. There they became isolated when an impassable barrier formed and, by adapting themselves to the new environment, evolved into the genus *Oncorhynchus*, which colonized rivers on both the Asian and American continents.

Species that become isolated, as Darwin illustrated with the finches of the Galapagos Islands, acquire unique biological characteristics. Neave thinks that *Oncorhynchus masu*, the cherry salmon found only in Asia, may be the earliest offshoot of *Salmo salar* because it is the closest to it biologically, especially in blood composition. All Pacific species are morphologically alike; they die after spawning, while a small proportion of the Atlantics survive this ordeal (the spent fish are called kelts), recuperate and return to the sea; some kelts manage to return to the river for a second spawning and even a third.

Neave places the separation of *Oncorhynchus* from the parent stock at about one million to 500,000 years ago. Probably at the end of the Pleistocene, 15,000 to 25,000 years ago, all Pacific salmon possessed their present characteristics and were dispersed over the vast area of the Pacific rim. The original range of the Atlantic salmon was much greater than it is today.

CHAPTER 2

Unravelling the Mysteries

FOR countless centuries the mysterious life cycle of the salmon intrigued men. They saw the females bury their pink eggs, and the miniscule fry emerge from the gravel to grow into parr and silvery smolts a few inches long. They headed for the ocean and disappeared from view, only to reappear in a year or more as husky adults determined to push their way upstream against the current and all obstacles in an endeavour to reach their spawning grounds. This phenomenon occurred with such clocklike regularity every year that the primitive peoples ascribed it to supernatural powers.

The first mention of the salmon in a scientific work is in the *Natural History* of Pliny the elder, written in the first century AD. Here we encounter for the first time the fish's name, *Salmo*, the leaper. 'In the rivers of Aquitaine,' he says, 'the salmon surpasses all other fish [in taste].'

There are many references to the plentitude of salmon in English medieval chronicles and histories, as in the Venerable Bede's *Ecclesiastical History of the English People* (eighth century) and Giraldus Cambrensis' twelfth-century *Description of Wales* but the first fairly accurate account of their life cycle is found in the *History of Scotland* by Hector Boethius, Principal of the new University of Aberdeen, written in Latin in 1517 and translated into English in 1585. Boethius probably based his account on the lore of the nearby countryside, since salmon abounded in the Rivers Don and Dee. He says:

> Salmon is more plentiful in Scotland than in any other region in the world . . . Because the nature of this fish is strange, I will set down so much as I do know hereof at this present time, as followeth.

The salmon in harvest time cometh up into the small rivers, where the water is most shallow, and there the male and female rubbing their womb one against another they shed their spawn, which forthwith they cover with sand and gravel and so depart away. From henceforth they are gaunt and slender, and in appearance so lean that they appear naught but skin and bone . . .

The aforesaid spawn and milt being hidden in the sand . . . in the next spring doth yield great numbers of little fry but so nesh and tender for a long time, till they come to be so great as a man's finger. If you catch any of them you shall perceive them to melt and their substance to dissolve and fade even as it were jelly or as ice laid forth against the sun. From henceforth they go to the sea, where within the space of 20 days they grow to a marvellous greatness, and then returning again toward the place of generation, they show a notable spectacle not unworthy to be considered . . . Finally there is no man knoweth readily where this fish liveth, for never was anything yet found in their bellies, other than a thick slimy humor.

Boethius was wrong only about the length of the fishes' sojourn in the sea. Since the salmon do not eat when they return to the river but live on the fat stored up in the ocean, their bellies are empty – this Boethius did not understand. The mystery of their whereabouts at sea would not be solved for centuries.

Konrad von Gesner in his *Historiae Animalium* (1585), a copy of which may be seen in the library of Magdalen College, Oxford, refers to Boethius and supports his description of freshwater spawning with reference to reports from correspondents who had observed this phenomenon in the upper waters of the River Elbe and the little Alpine tributaries of the Rhine in Switzerland.

False scientific information dies hard. As late as 1755 the Dane Pontoppidan in his *Natural History* offered a detailed description of salmon mating in the sea and three-quarters of a century later a witness before a Parliamentary Committee on Salmon Fisheries testified that there was no doubt that salmon bred in the ocean. He was promptly refuted, however, by another witness who said that juvenile salmon develop in fresh water. Even as late as 1882 Thomas Henry Huxley, Inspector of Salmon Fisheries, wrote to a Scottish correspondent who had sent him a smolt found in the stomach of a whiting captured in the ocean that 'it raised the novel and interesting question whether salmon spawn in the sea'.

Although the life cycle of the salmon was known by many people in the seventeenth century, the presence of the fish in its various freshwater stages confused observers. For example, Izaak Walton in the *Compleat Angler* speaks of 'little salmons called skeggers, which abound in many rivers relating to the sea', and says they are the offspring of sick and stunted adults who were prevented from descending to salt water by flood gates or weirs. The skeggers were probably small grilse who had spent only a short time in the ocean.

The bulk of our scientific knowledge of both the Atlantic and Pacific salmon has been acquired only in the last century. For example, the epochal discovery that every salmon normally carries a record of its life history on its scales, as a tree does on its rings, was made by H. W. Johnstone in 1904. Previous investigators had reported scale readings on the eel, carp and cod, a technique which dissipated many fallacies and solved some biological problems. Tagging of fish to test the theory that they return to the home stream to spawn is first mentioned, in England at least, by Walton. He speaks of an experiment in which 'a ribbon, or some known tape or thread' was tied to the tails of young salmon taken in weirs as they swam towards the sea and were recaptured six months later at the same place, thus proving 'that every salmon usually returns to the same river in which it was bred, as young pigeons taken out of the same dovecote have also been observed to do'.

Systematic tagging of smolts began in Scotland around 1825 and was continued intermittently for the next forty years by river owners like the Duke of Atholl on the River Tay and others on the Tweed. The earliest experiments on a rigidly scientific basis are credited to P. H. Malloch of Perth who started tagging salmon in 1906. Subsequent studies in Ireland, Norway, France and other countries firmly established that Atlantic salmon invariably return to their natal waters and will spawn nowhere else. If their migratory routes are blocked they die without spawning. Similar results were obtained in large-scale experiments with Pacific salmon, although individuals of some species have a tendency to stray into alien rivers.

The high value attached to the salmon wherever they abound led to ever-expanding programmes of scientific research and the creation of laboratories for this work. The information thus acquired has served as a basis of management in many areas. No family of fishes has been so intensively studied. Thus the *Pacific Salmon Literature Compilation – 1900–59* which includes only publications reporting original scientific research, comprises 1,406 articles and 17,895 pages of text. Since 1959 this mass of material has substantially increased.

The feeding grounds of Atlantic salmon remained a mystery until the late 1950s when it was discovered that fishes from both North America and Europe congregate in the rich waters off Greenland, but even now we do not know where they feed in their first year at sea – perhaps around the Faroe Islands. Similarly the migrations of Asian and North American Pacific salmon began to be extensively charted in the 1950s and the wanderings of most of the species are now fairly well known. However, though many of the mysteries of the salmon's life cycle have been uncovered, much remains to be known.

CHAPTER 3

Life Cycle

THERE is only one species of Atlantic salmon, *Salmo salar*, but there are six of Pacific salmon: chinook (*Oncorhynchus tshawytscha*), pinks (*O. gorbuscha*), sockeye (*O. nerka*), chum (*O. keta*), coho (*O. kisutch*), and cherry (*O. masu*) found only in Asia.

The Atlantic and Pacific species have generally similar biological characteristics and behaviour patterns although they vary considerably in the length of their freshwater and marine existence, life spans, spawning seasons and migratory habits, as the table on page 29 shows. All adult salmon look more or less alike except for size, weight and colouration. Among Pacific species only chinook attains or exceeds the weight of *Salmo salar* – all the others are smaller.

The salmon's life is divided into three distinct phases: (1) freshwater existence or juvenile phase; (2) feeding migrations in the ocean; and (3) return to the home stream to spawn. This kind of cycle is called 'anadromous' and is found in some chars, whitefish, and trouts, lamprey, sturgeon, shad, smelt and others.

Freshwater life

Salmon begin life as fertilized orange-red eggs about the size of a buckshot buried in the gravel of a swift-flowing stream. After an incubation period of fifty to 110 days, depending on the climate – the longer period is needed in Arctic or subarctic areas – the eggs hatch out as tiny translucent fishes with black eyes and spotted backs, and huge yolk sacs attached to their bellies. These alevin, as they are called, nestle in the redds for several weeks until the yolk sacs on which they feed are absorbed, then they emerge as fry and begin to forage for food. Some species, like chum, pinks and some of the chinook, descend to the sea as fry. In the rivers a plethora of food awaits them such as microscopic plankton, insect larvae and nymphs clinging to rocks. Growth is quickest in summer when planktonic and insect life is abundant and slow in winter, especially in waters that freeze and ice over.

The fry develop into parr when they are a couple of inches long. Atlantic salmon parr have brownish backs with black spots running down the sides and a few red spots in the vicinity of the lateral line. Their bellies are light grey, creamy or silvery, depending on their habitat. The most unusual feature of the parr are thirteen dark bars, called parr marks, clearly visible on each side. Among the males there are individuals (as among the trout and cherry salmon) who become sexually mature as parr, never leave freshwater, and participate in the mating of adults.

Some species of Pacific salmon also have parr marks but among those who migrate to the sea as fry these are either faint or obscure. Parr feed on mayflies, stoneflies, other insects and insect larvae, worms, tiny mussels and snails.

The first year of a salmon's life is the most precarious. In British rivers fry and parr are eaten by larger salmon, trout, pike, perch, eel, chub, roach and other fish; water birds and snakes devour them. In British Columbia lakes where sockeye spend part of their juvenile life, char, prickly sculpin and squawfish feed on them. Squawfish, whose populations have increased enormously in the Columbia River since it has been almost completely dammed and converted into a series of lakes, account for a considerable mortality of young salmon. Moles, muskrats, great horned owls, herons, fish hawks, even sandpipers devour baby salmon.

Mergansers and kingfishers are addicted to salmon. The large white, green-headed male merganser and his red-headed mate may live off salmon as they follow the winding course of a river or gather on a lake or reservoir. The Canadian biologist H. C. White reported in 1957 that of the 1,200 mergansers shot in a duck-control experiment on the Miramichi River in New Brunswick, 86% had been devouring salmon at a rate amounting to 1,900,000 parr annually. Dr Arne Lindroth found that half the food of mergansers shot in an experiment on the Indal River in Sweden consisted of salmon and trout parr; in one year they

destroyed a substantial portion of the juvenile stock on this
stream.

After the parr stage comes the smolt (or fingerling) stage when
the fishes adapted for life in freshwater are metamorphosed for
survival in the sea. Marked body changes can be seen. They acquire
a silvery hue, scales become prominent and easily rubbed off,
and tails lengthen and are more deeply forked in preparation for
their oceanic odysseys. Just before the start of seaward migration
they become more buoyant by filling the swim bladder with
air. Smolts are four to six inches long; they may be one to
two years of age, and much older in cold climates such as
Greenland.

They descend in stages, usually in the spring, in shoals led by a
scout, their heads turned upstream, the water pouring over them,
into their mouths and passing through their gills. In the river the
current carries them down but when it slackens they will actively
swim. The timing of their migration is probably dependent on
changes in light and temperature as well as water flow in the river.
Thus migration of sockeye smolts in Babine Lake in British
Columbia, 100 miles long and up to five miles wide, usually
starts soon after the ice has melted. They move at dusk – 5 to 60
million in a year in this lake – along direct routes which lead
them into the river, travelling mostly between dusk and dawn, a
time when they are invisible to aerial predators.

The tiny fish move with unceasing speed, up to five miles a day,
sliding over rocks and weirs, occasionally snapping at a fly or
other prey, eating greedily. Some streams offer obstacles in the
form of moving rafts of undissolved human or other organic
wastes, effluents from pulp mills or chemical plants, and the like.
On certain Siberian rivers the tiny travellers must contend with
mountains of bark dust left by the log rafts. In the Columbia-
Snake river system they are confronted by high dams which
can only be passed by going through the turbines at the power
houses or over the spillways.

In the headwaters of the great salmon rivers of the world
there is an enormous stirring in April and May as the spring
spates alert the smolts to begin their downstream journey. Some
major American and Asian streams send down 100 to 200 million

or more each year. On lakes where sockeye dwell it has been suggested by investigators that the smolts may use the sun as a beacon or react to the polarization of light from the sky, although they manage to find their way to the river even when the sky is overcast. As Dr Margaret Brown says, 'the direction of migration in relation to celestial clues appears to be inborn', and this may also be true, as we shall see, when they move on well-directed routes in the ocean.

Nothing can stop these hardy wanderers. When they reach the estuary, where they spend some time getting acclimatized to saltwater, they follow paths taken by their ancestors for countless generations. 'Where does this memory of sea water, inherited by the little fishes from their parents, reside?' asks Louis Roule in his book *Journeys and Migrations of Fishes*. 'And how does it come into existence in the little creatures who still know only the fugitive, flowing waters of their native torrent?' Scientists have attempted to answer these questions with the help of extensive tagging experiments, monitoring the fish with ingenious electronic instruments, and tracing their movements over thousands of miles in the oceans. Nevertheless we know little about their navigational mechanisms. That they follow preordained routes with the fidelity of ocean liners is indisputable. Their itineraries are perhaps part of 'folk' memories; put in another way, they may be imprinted on the chromosomes.

Only a minuscule portion of each year's crop reaches the sea. Dr R. E. Foerster, who spent a lifetime studying the sockeye in British Columbia, sets up a hypothetical mortality table, drawn from data on several rivers and lakes, which probably offers clues applicable to other species. Assuming that 1,000 adults enter the river, 500 males and 500 females each bearing 4,000 eggs, he estimates that their fate might be as follows under normal conditions:

1. A 5% loss of adults in the upstream migration, resulting in a total of 1,900,000 eggs.
2. A 50% loss of the eggs, leaving 950,000 to be incubated and become alevins.
3. A 75% loss of alevins during emergence from the redds

and while migrating into the lakes where young sockeye are reared, resulting in 237,000 fry.

4. A 97% kill of the fry, leaving 7,000 smolts to accomplish the journey to the sea.

In order to maintain a run of wild fish in a river – without adding hatchery stock – every pair of adults who mate must produce at least one pair of progeny who will survive all the hazards of their juvenile and adult lives and spawn successfully. No population of wild fish can survive unless this ratio is maintained, and there will be no surplus unless it is exceeded.

Life in the sea

One of the most critical periods of the fishes' existence occurs when they reach the ocean. 'Since several freshwater functions are contrary to their marine counterparts,' says Professor Lynwood S. Smith of the College of Fisheries of the University of Washington, 'optimum adjustment is impossible during the period. Additional stress such as high temperatures, low oxygen levels in the water, pollutants . . . further complicates the situation and can lead to fatal consequences. And finally, in sea water there are a number of other changes – new food to recognize and catch, different predators to avoid and unknown large bodies of water to traverse. It's a rough transition.'

In the estuaries the fish may hang around for days, swimming back and forth with the tides while getting acclimatized to saline waters. Fishermen report seeing them near the surface during daylight hours, in May and June, with much jumping in slack water. They start life as zooplankton feeders and as they develop strong jaws and sharp teeth devour crustaceans such as shrimp (who give the salmon flesh its red or pink colour), anchovies, pilchards and small herring. Typical of the food found in the stomach of smolts caught in the sea are shrimps, copepods, amphipods, pteropods, and squid. Predators are numerous: remains of salmon have been recovered from the stomachs of pollack, tuna, whiting, swordfish and seals.

Where do the juvenile salmon, scarcely larger than a man's finger, go after they leave the rivers?

Table 1 BIOLOGICAL DATA ON SALMON OF THE WORLD

Scientific names	Salmo salar	Oncorhynchus masu	O. tshawytscha	O. gorbuscha	O. nerka	O. keta	O. kisutch
Common names	Atlantic salmon	Cherry	Chinook, King, Spring, Quinnat, Tyee	Pink, Humpbacked, Humpy	Sockeye, Red, Blueback	Chum, Dog	Coho, Silver
Length of freshwater life	1–4 yrs.	1 yr.	few days to 2 yrs.	few days	few days to 3 yrs.	few days	1–2 yrs.
Length of ocean life	1–4 yrs.	1–2 yrs.	1–5 yrs.	16–20 mos.	½–4 yrs.	½–4 yrs.	½–1½ yrs.
Average length at maturity	30 in.	NA	36 in.	20 in.	23 in.	25 in.	24 in.
Range of length at maturity	22–38 in.	NA	16–60 in.	14–30 in.	15–33 in.	17–38 in.	17–36 in.
Average weight at maturity	10½ lb.	9 lb.	22 lb.	3–4 lb.	6–8 lb.	8–9 lb.	10 lb.
Range of weight at maturity	5½–25 lb.†	8–20 lb.	2½–125 lb.	1½–12 lb.	2–12 lb.	3–45 lb.	1½–30 lb.
Principal spawning months	Nov.–Jan.	NA	Aug.–Sept.	July–Sept.	July–Sept.	Sept.–Nov.	Sept.–Dec.
Fecundity of female (average no. of eggs)	600–800 per lb. of weight	NA	5,000	2,000	4,000	3,000	3,500

NA – not available   † Record sport catch 70 lb. and net catch 103 lb.

Systematic tagging in European countries gradually uncovered some of their migratory routes. The late W. J. M. Menzies thirty years ago postulated a theory, based on his study of tagging results, that salmon from some European and North American areas have common feeding grounds in the North Atlantic. His assumption was shown to be true when shoals of salmon appeared rather suddenly in the 1950s off the south-west coast of Greenland and in Davis Strait thus setting off a profitable fishery. Recovery of tagged fish in Greenland fishermen's nets showed that they came chiefly from Canada and the British Isles, including Ireland, with contributions by the United States, Norway, Sweden and France. These were fish who had spent at least one winter in the sea, as evidenced by their scales.

Salmon from the Baltic countries pasture in the Baltic Sea, accomplishing marine journeys of 700 miles or more to obtain the nutriments they like. Rarely do they move out into the more turbulent North Sea. Norwegian salmon feed mainly in the Norwegian Sea, sometimes accompanied by companions from Sweden and Iceland.

In his Buckland lectures published in 1949, *The Stock of Salmon*, Menzies described the general pattern of migrations from Norway and Scotland. Fish tagged at Titran in northern Norway went around the North Cape and were netted in the White Sea, some 800 miles distant. Others marked at Brevik, about 100 miles south of North Cape, were found in the Arctic Ocean off the Finnish coast and in the White Sea; one of these indomitable creatures landed in the Pechora River in Russia, 1,200 miles from Brevik. The general movement of fish from the north-west coast of Scotland, according to Menzies, was through the Sea of the Hebrides and the Minch towards the east coasts of Scotland and England; some of the tagged specimens were recovered in the Tweed and others off the Yorkshire coast.

Tagging of thousands of Irish smolts and kelts has produced an almost complete picture of their wanderings. The bulk of the recoveries were made less than 100 miles from home waters, while a small number had circumnavigated the island and clocked 200 to 300 miles before being recaptured. A few of the tagged salmon went much further; they were netted in the rivers Tay

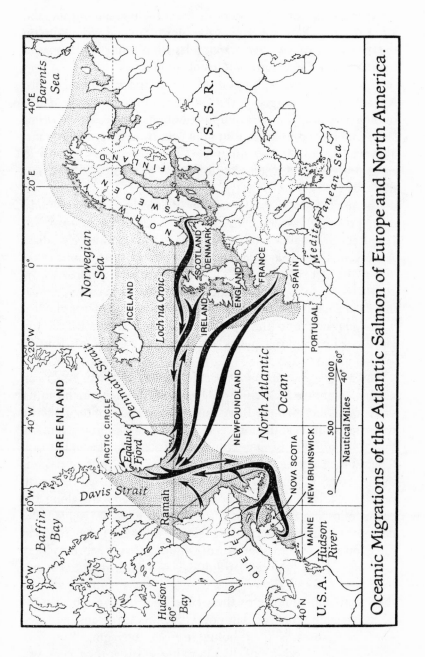

Oceanic Migrations of the Atlantic Salmon of Europe and North America.

and Aberdeenshire Dee, 800 miles from the tagging station, and a few hardy individuals crossed the North Sea and wound up on the west coast of Sweden, 1,200 miles from home. Others went west and met their deaths in Greenland nets.

The longest ocean migration of an Atlantic salmon on record is that of a smolt tagged in the Gulf of Bothnia, a northern arm of the Baltic Sea, who was recaptured on the west coast of Greenland, some 3,300 miles in a straight line from its starting point. This was one of the rare fishes from a Baltic country known to enter the North Sea and one of the few whose journey was traced as far as Greenland.

The migrations of Pacific salmon often eclipse those of *Salmo salar*, probably because they have a vaster ocean to roam in. Hundreds of thousands of smolts have been tagged by Canadian, American, Russian and Japanese scientists in their home rivers during the past two decades. These activities were inspired by the 1953 treaty between Canada, the United States and Japan delimiting Japanese salmon fishing at an abstention line of 175 degrees west longitude, and the 1956 convention between Russia and Japan setting annual quotas on Japanese catches of Russian salmon in the ocean.

The general movement of Pacific salmon of North American origin is counterclockwise while that of Asian is in the other direction. Dr William F. Royce and his colleagues of the Fisheries Research Institute at the University of Washington tracked many thousands of pinks issuing from south-eastern Alaska and British Columbia. They found that after spending three to five months in the estuaries, inner bays and channels, they reached the ocean proper in July and headed northward and westward along the coasts following the Alaskan Gyre, averaging ten to twelve miles daily for months on end. In late fall and midwinter they reversed direction and moved southward; in January and February they were spread out between latitudes 41 and 45 degrees north and longitude 140 and 160 degrees west, gaining weight rapidly. In the spring and summer of the second and final year of life the pinks, weighing three or four pounds, left these regions and raced northward towards their home streams, averaging forty-five miles per day. The size of the migrating shoals at their peak was estimated on the basis of sample catches with purse seines as 750,000 fish passing daily, for thirty to sixty days, any given line of latitude in south-east Alaska. When the fishes finally arrived in their home streams in Alaska or British Columbia they had covered an elliptical orbit of some 2,000 miles.

Chum and sockeye, who spend up to four years in the sea, may complete two or three similar circuits of even greater amplitude, sometimes totalling as much as 10,000 miles before returning to their natal rivers. Royce and his colleagues estimated that every day from late June to late August some 500,000 sockeye, or 30 million fish who had been at sea one year, passed Adak Island in the Aleutians. So precise and punctual are their movements, thanks to their biological clocks, that one can predict their arrival in Bristol Bay, Alaska, with considerable accuracy, a fact that is of immense importance to the fishing and canning industry. While the size of the runs may fall below or exceed predictions, based on sample fishing of the smolts who left freshwater three or four years earlier, their arrival in the rivers is rarely more than a few days or a week off. This knowledge enables the fleet of fishermen to gather in Bristol Bay to await them and the canneries which process the bulk of the catches to marshall their work forces and prepare the machinery and supplies. Sometimes, of course, there are not enough fishermen fully to exploit the bountiful run, as in 1970, while at other times there are too many and the pickings may be slim.

Chinook and coho, the largest in size and least abundant in numbers of Pacific salmon, do not generally travel as far in the ocean as the other, smaller species. Many of them stay in protected waters like Puget Sound while others make longer marine treks. Columbia River chinook and coho may move southward towards the coast of California, or northward as far as the Queen Charlotte Islands – thus contributing to the sport and commercial catches in both areas – before returning to their home rivers to spawn.

The circuits of some Asian salmon such as chum and pinks, moving in a clockwise direction, may overlap those of American fish. For example, salmon from the East Kamchatka Peninsula follow the East Kamchatka current south-westward along the coast and then turn eastward into the open sea, sometimes going as far as the western part of the Gulf of Alaska. American purse seiners catch them in the foulest weather as they migrate through the Aleutian passes and along the islands. At times shoals of American and Asian fish intermingle but each eventually returns to its own continent.

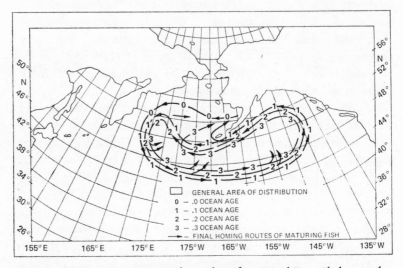

2 *During their oceanic migration, sockeye salmon from Bristol Bay, Alaska, complete these circuits before heading back to home waters to spawn*

In similar fashion sockeye from Bristol Bay wander far westward, beyond the 175 degrees West abstention line which delimits Japanese high-seas salmon fishing, and are taken in Japanese gillnets by the millions. Only rarely has a salmon of American origin been caught in Asian waters, such as a pink tagged in the Gulf of Alaska south of Anchorage which was recovered in the Sea of Japan near Korea, 3,500 miles away, and a sockeye tagged south of Adak in July 1972 which was found a year later in Lake Pekulneiskoe on the Chukotka Peninsula.

Like their American cousins, some Asian pinks have set unusual speed and distance records, clocking some 4,000 miles in twelve to fifteen months. Chum and sockeye may cover 2,000 miles in less than a year.

Until recently the marine life of steelhead trout, a Pacific 'cousin' of Atlantic salmon, was quite obscure. It is now known that many of these silvery fishes, who average twelve pounds in the river and may weigh up to thirty pounds, roam the ocean extensively, while others stay within estuarial tides and return to freshwater in less than a year (as in the Rogue River in Oregon) weighing only half a pound. The longest known migration of a steelhead was made by a smolt tagged in the Wynooche River in the state of Washington which was caught by a Japanese research vessel south of Kiska Island in the Aleutians, some 2,000 miles from home.

Guidance mechanisms

How do fishes accomplish their herculean journeys? Many theories have been advanced to account for their navigational feats, some based on controlled experiments in laboratories or in lakes or rivers. Dr Arthur D. Hasler in his book *Underwater Guideposts: Homing of Salmon* concludes on the basis of his studies that the fishes 'set a compass course, using celestial features, as birds do, to guide them', but he admits that they also employ other methods which we cannot fathom. In considering Hasler's theory we must remember that some salmon swim in the top ten to fifteen feet of water, or deeper, and would find it hard to take measurements from the sun. Moreover, in the north Pacific ocean there is little clear weather from one year's end to the next during which they could take celestial bearings, as birds do. The skies are frequently overcast except in summer, gales and storms roil the seas and fog is frequent. Even merchant ships sometimes find it difficult to keep to their course. In the days of sail the north Pacific coast of the United States was a nightmare to mariners and a graveyard of ships.

In the outer parts of Bristol Bay, which teems with salmon, the average weather in June, when the sockeye come back, is characterized by fog, mist or haze over 40% of the time and the mean cloud cover is 80%. In the central Gulf of Alaska the average June weather consists of fog, mist or haze and there is persistent cloud cover, yet the fishes find their way to their particular river and into the lake, rivulet or creek where they spawn.

Dr Royce and his colleagues in their report, 'Models of

Oceanic Migrations of Pacific Salmon and Comments on Guidance Mechanisms', conclude that as they swim around half the globe salmon have the help of small electrical voltages generated by the ocean currents, but 'their response to all migratory cues is inherited, not memorized'. Some species of fish have electric organs as well as electro-receptors but so far as we know the salmon do not – and there the puzzle remains. All we are sure of is that the delicate perceptiveness of these fishes guides them in the ocean and to the river of their origin. Probably they identify the stream, which may be only a slender brook far up in the mountains branching off from a tributary of a larger river, by a unique sense of smell, or 'chemical memory' as Roger Caras calls it. Some straying occurs but as Dr Harry Wagner of the Oregon Department of Fish and Wildlife asserts, 'It appears that adult fish retrace in sequence a trail of stimuli that is the reverse of that imprinted in young fish on their seaward migration.'

Return to the river

The salmon spend varying periods of time in the sea, feeding ravenously, and return weighing four or five pounds (pinks and sockeye) and up to a hundred or more in rare instances (Atlantic salmon and chinook). Many of them return prematurely as precocious adults after one winter in the ocean; these are called grilse if they are Atlantic salmon and jacks if Pacific, and they are usually males. Grilse may weigh from one and a half to nine pounds, and in some rivers constitute at times as much as 50 to 90% of the run. Some countries like Norway and Scotland seem to breed heavier Atlantic salmon than the average. The largest Atlantic known to have been caught weighed 103 pounds and was taken from the River Devon in Scotland.

Jacks are commonly found among chinook, coho and sockeye populations and occasionally steelhead trout. They mature at one to three years of age instead of three, four or five, and are rarely more than twenty inches long. Like the sexually mature Atlantic salmon parr, jacks and grilse are created by nature seemingly to provide a reserve of males to mate with the superfluous females, although biologists tell us they do not often have a chance to spawn if larger males are around. It is not known if jacks and grilse reproduce their own kind (precocious males) – they seem to be sports.

In the sea the streamlined salmon are magnificent fishes. Their backs are silvery green, sides silvery and bellies white, with small x-shaped and rounded spots above the lateral line. Sockeye in their spawning livery turn red and their heads green. Upon entering freshwater the fishes shed their sea lice and lose some of the silvery sheen, turning greenish or brown mottled with red or orange, and develop large dark spots edged with a lighter colour. The males develop hook jaws as they come close to spawning and in the case of the pinks a humpback as well.

No longer do the fishes desire to eat, though they will snap at an angler's fly. They live off the fat stored in their bodies during their marine period in proportion to the journey that lies ahead of them. Thus the heaviest salmon in the Columbia River before Grand Coulee dam was built were the fifty to seventy pound chinook, called 'June hogs', who spawned in the upper part of the watershed. After their mating and rearing grounds were inundated, they disappeared. There are short streams that harbour large chinook but their fat reserves are usually less than those of the long-distance travellers.

The early fish in the river are in prime condition; their bodies are solid with fat and muscle, they are well proportioned, and their flesh is pink and firm. Fixed or floating gear awaits them in the estuaries or along the coast as well as in the river, and take a proportion of the runs. Seals and porpoises follow them. Their coming may be so stealthy at first as to be unobserved. Anglers may reconnoitre the tidewater area and hardly notice them. They doggedly seek to return to their natal waters, or to a stream where they were released as hatchery fish. Many of them die in the attempt. Numerous experiments have proven that salmon rarely spawn in alien streams unless their paths are blocked; usually they will just keep trying until they expire from exhaustion.

They may linger for days or even weeks around a waterfall, and when the opportune time comes with an increase in flow they climb or jump from rock to rock until they reach the top of the obstruction and go over. Patiently they push themselves up fish ladders at dams and move into the slack waters of the reservoirs. On some of the great rivers of the world, like the Loire in France and the Fraser in British Columbia, the ascent may take weeks, or months. In their travels certain signposts probably guide them to their natal stream and always the chemical memory of the flowing water which they knew as juveniles, no matter how remote it may be or difficult of access.

Even when man does not snare them in his nets in the sea, ocean life takes a heavy toll of each generation. Dr Foerster estimates that 90% of the sockeye who left the river in his hypothetical run fail to return to freshwater. Usually the timing of the run is arranged by nature to coincide with the most favourable environmental conditions. For example, spring chinook return to the Columbia River when the vine maples and alders are budding and the mountain snows are beginning to melt. In June and July come the summer chinook and in August and September the fall chinook, each adjusted to the temperature of the water at that time, the volume and velocity of flow, and with enough dissolved oxygen to sustain their migration. If man alters these environmental conditions by damming or polluting the river he immensely complicates the fishes' migration and sometimes kills them off, as we shall see in later chapters.

A heavy rain or spate is needed to lure the newly arrived fishes upstream, a siren call as it were from their ancestral spawning grounds.

Salmon enter British rivers at all seasons of the year. Those who arrive from December to March ascend at a more leisurely pace than those who come later and have less time before the spawning season – November to January – arrives. If the water is very cold they may loiter in the deeper layers of the estuary until river temperatures rise. Those who arrive with severe infections like ultradermal necrosis (UDN) which has been rampant in British, Irish and some French and Spanish streams in recent years, may not ascend at all and die without spawning unless the stream is treated with some antidote.

In British rivers summer or fall fish have a different migration pattern than spring fish; also they seem to prefer to travel at night when the water is cooler. In contrast, salmon of the semi-arid rivers in the San Joaquin valley of California do not migrate in the summer at all because the flow is at an ebb. They come back from the ocean late enough in the year, between October and January, to enjoy an adequate supply of cool water.

For successful spawning anywhere the water must be below 58 degrees Fahrenheit. 50 to 52 degrees is ideal. In colder climates spawners may not arrive until the ice breaks up in the river. Forty-five degrees Fahrenheit is believed to be good water to lure fish upstream providing the river is in flood – that is, running eighteen inches or more above normal winter level.

Salmon are said to have the stamina of race-horses, and this has been verified both in the field and in laboratory tests. For example, Dr J. B. Brett of the Canadian Fisheries Research Board found in his laboratory that sockeye can be made to swim at speeds of 1.8 miles per hour against a simulated normal river current for almost thirteen days without stopping, the equivalent of 660 miles. Field observations corroborated these results as biologists followed a school of sockeye from the mouth of the Fraser River to Stuart Lake, a distance of 640 miles which they covered in over six days. If the river's mean velocity was three miles per hour, the six-pound fishes made the journey at an average speed of 4.4 mph. Upon arrival at Stuart Lake they had just enough energy left to spawn and die; the females had expended about 96% of their body fat and 53% of their protein reserves.

Studies at the National Marine Fisheries Service's Bonneville, Oregon, Laboratory revealed the amazing ability of the salmon to climb fish ladders. One sockeye continued on an endlessly moving simulated fishway for five days without interruption, achieving a 'climb' or altitude of 6,648 feet or more than a mile, and was still going strong when the test was terminated. Examination of its tissues showed that it was not unduly tired! It is the dissolved oxygen in the water that permits them to push onwards: if it falls below five parts per million they may die; if the water is too warm they may succumb to furunculosis; and if it is supersaturated with nitrogen gas – as often happens at the reservoirs on the Columbia and Snake Rivers – they develop bubble disease, resembling the bends which afflict divers, and die.

The pace of upstream travel in some instances is almost unbelievable. Charles H. Gilbert of the US Bureau of Commercial Fisheries followed the chinook upstream from the mouth of the Yukon to their destination in the headwaters. When they arrived at Whiskey Creek, 622 miles from the ocean, they had been moving against a consistently rapid current at an average speed of fifty-two miles per day; at Fish Creek (851 miles) at seventy miles per day; and when they reached Dawson City, almost 1,500 miles from the sea, they were still going at the rate of fifty miles per day. By then they were but pale shadows of the jaunty fish coming in from the Bering Sea and, said Gilbert, 'contained no more oil than is needed to furnish satisfactory dog food'. The natives dwelling along the banks of the Yukon took the fish in their nets or wheels and fed them to their dogs.

The much smaller chum salmon moved into the Yukon ten days behind the chinook. They covered the first 800 miles at an average speed of ninety miles per day and the next 700 miles at fifty-five miles per day. These are the longest freshwater journeys of salmon on record.

In the short placid English rivers which are unpolluted the salmon have a much less difficult ascent to their spawning grounds. We can follow them, for example, on the lovely sixty-five mile Eden, a border stream, as they emerge from the Solway Firth moving towards the ancient city of Carlisle, past green pastures and picture-book villages with red brick houses, a church nestling under the hills, manorial dwellings surrounded by neatly-clipped lawns and avenues of venerable yews and larches. The flow is gentle, the water sparkles in the summer sun, the fish move into the headwaters in the Yorkshire Pennines where spawning takes place. They move only when water conditions are favourable, resting in pools or lie for days at a time; here the lucky anglers may get them to rise to an artificial fly. A nocturnal downpour will propel them upriver. Sometimes they may be seen leaping out of the water as if to feel the warmth of the sun on their backs.

What proportion of each year's run reaches the spawning grounds is an important question because the amount of reproduction determines whether the stock will be depleted, enhanced or stay at a given level. There are predators to contend with. In the River Tweed, for example, grey seals kill or injure many salmon around the estuary. In the Alaskan rivers bears wait in the bush with their cubs to feast upon the fish. Gulls sometimes peck at their eyes and take live fish but generally they gnaw at the carcases.

Dr Foerster estimates that there is a 5% loss during upstream migration for the sockeye who returned from the sea in his hypothetical table. Studies on the Columbia-Snake system indicate a much higher mortality of upstream migrants owing to the blockades of the high dams and supersaturated nitrogen gas in the reservoirs. In Scotland there is also a significant mortality of adult salmon at the dams, particularly in the Gary-Tummel system.

It is thrilling to watch a huge run come up from the sea and move on to their spawning grounds. In 1970 some 40 million sockeye crowded the rivers of Bristol Bay, Alaska, of which 21 million were caught by fishermen and 19 million were permitted to escape.

We followed the spectacle from the air. The gleaming fish, some of whom had already acquired their red spawning livery, were moving up the pellucid rivers like armies on the march, hugging the shores. Once they passed into nontidal waters, beyond the set nets on the banks, there was nothing to interfere with their journey. No human habitations could be seen, no boats. In the towers biologists were counting the migrants as they passed, while on the ground others were taking samples to determine their biological characteristics. The sockeye run lasted three weeks, and there were so many fish that a fisherman in a boat could take 4,000 in a day. In the Atlantic salmon world there are no such spectacles; the runs have been reduced to a comparative trickle, except for a small number of rivers.

Mating and survival

When the salmon reach their spawning grounds they pair off. The female digs the redd by scooping out the gravel with her powerful tail while the male tries to establish territorial dominance. The female may join the male in driving away intruders.

Courtship precedes mating. The male swims back and forth over the female as she rests near the bottom of the redd, often touching her dorsal fin with his body, or nudging her with his snout. He may even pretend to dig. Finally he curves his body around her and induces her to drop some of the tiny pink eggs into the redd while he simultaneously deposits a cloud of milt over them. Sperm is viable in water only a very short time and the eggs have a lifespan, so to speak, of one and a half minutes. After an egg has been in the water for several minutes the shell has changed so much that the sperm may not be able to enter the minute pore called the micropyle.

After fertilization the female moves slightly upstream, turns on her side and repeats the digging in such a manner that the current will sweep the disturbed gravel over the eggs and safely bury them. This is repeated until she has shed all her eggs. Sometimes more than one male can be seen mating with a single female.

All Pacific salmon die within a few days after spawning. Their rotting carcasses litter the banks of the streams or lakes, gnawed by wild animals or birds, disintegrating to provide the nutrients which fertilize the waters and give sustenance to aquatic life in the spring. Thus the new generation subsists on the remains of the old. In a few weeks the rivers and lakes are generally clear again, although the skins and skeletons of the fishes may still be around in the spring.

Among Atlantic salmon and steelhead trout a certain proportion of spawners, known as kelts, survive their ordeal, usually more females than males. They drop downstream, usually tails first, and find pools to rest in. They do not eat, although they may rise to an angler's fly. Patiently they await the spring spates that will reanimate them and take them down to the sea. Then they resume their ocean travels.

Dr J. W. Jones in his book *The Salmon* divides the kelts into three groups: (1) those who return to the river in about six months – the fall following their descent; (2) those who spend an entire summer and winter in the sea; and (3) those who stay away about eighteen months. When they reappear in the rivers they are again glistening creatures with muscles taut and fat-content about as high as when they were virgin fish. Their scales are golden rather than silvery and usually they have many more spots on their backs and gill cover than clean fish. Not more than 5% of the kelts who go to sea ever come back to the river.

Not much is known about the migrations of kelts. The late A. G. Huntsman in a study published in 1945 found that they tend to linger in Canadian estuaries but if they are driven out by floods and lose touch with the river they wander far. A kelt tagged in the Blackwater River, Ross-shire, Scotland, was recovered on the west coast of Greenland, 1,730 miles away. Invariably they return to the home river even if they are released in an alien stream.

Sometimes it is difficult to differentiate the kelts from clean fish, as many anglers know. T. W. Pennington, whose angling career spanned a half-century, wrote in *Trout and Salmon* (January, 1975): 'On the Wye, at any rate, they enliven the scene in the early months of the season, particularly in February, when clean salmon are few and far between.' On the Miramichi River in New Brunswick there is a regulated spring fishery for 'black salmon', as kelts are called there, with many thousands taken by anglers each year.

The proportion of kelts in a run seems to vary greatly. According to Dr Derek Mills, a four-year study on the Conon River system in Scotland showed that of an average run of 333 on the River Meig, 14% were kelts and at Tor Achilty dam 26% of a 2,300 run were kelts. J. A. Hutton examined 36,000 salmon on the River Wye over a number of years and found that out of every thousand fifty-five had spawned once and two thrice. Dr Arthur Went reported that kelts constituted, on the average, about 5% of the catches in various Irish rivers he sampled, with the Corrib setting a record of 17%. The record spawning for *Salmo salar* is that of a fish caught on Loch Maree on the west coast of Scotland which had marks on its scales indicating it had mated four times and was thirteen years old.

In many countries kelts were commonly fed to indentured servants and apprentices before the Industrial Revolution, thus giving substance to the tales that they often rebelled at being fed such tasteless fish and refused to work unless the salmon ration was reduced. However, despite extensive searches no documentary proof of these tales has ever been produced.

In Britain and Ireland efforts are made to protect the kelts, which are regarded as valuable fish, at power dams and other obstructions. Grids or screens are sometimes provided to keep them from going through the turbines – instead they are shunted around them at some installations by means of bypasses. Nevertheless many are stranded in eddies or at weirs while others fail to find the bypasses. In periods of high water kelts will sometimes descend safely over the spillways. Kelts invariably return to their home streams, even if released in an alien waterway.

In the dammed Columbia River no attempts are made to facilitate the downstream migration of steelhead trout kelts over the dams. However, some tributaries are closed to fishing at the end of February, at least in the upper reaches, in order to protect the ascending spawners and descending kelts.

How long do salmon live? Atlantics that spawn once may live from two to eight years, but those who mate more than once and make two or more trips to the sea live much longer. Chinook salmon may live up to seven years, sockeye as much, coho up to four, chum up to five, and pinks only two. In comparison, the anadromous white sturgeon (*Acipenser transmontanus*), their companions in the Columbia River (but not their wandering equals), may live up to a hundred years and attain a weight of 1,000 pounds. Damming of the rivers, however, has decimated the sturgeon as well as the salmon, and only relatively small specimens remain.

CHAPTER 4

Salmon Culture

As the stocks of Atlantic and Pacific salmon declined in the past century or more, efforts were made to supplement them by increasingly intensive artificial propagation. Fish breeding is a very ancient art. It was practised by the Chinese as long ago as 2000 BC. They succeeded in breeding artificially many species of fish in their ponds and passed their knowledge on to the Japanese who are now the world's foremost fish culturists.

The Romans had some knowledge of fish culture, but it was lost with the decline of their civilization. A fourteenth-century monk, Dom Pinchon, rediscovered the art of fertilizing fish eggs and hatching them by burying them in sand or wooden boxes. Several centuries later a Westphalian landowner, Stephan Ludwig Jacobi (1711–1784), repeated Dom Pinchon's experiments. He spread the fertilized eggs over a bed of gravel at the bottom of oak boxes, permitted water to flow over them, and in due time saw them incubate and emerge as fry which he released in a stream. Jacobi published an account of his experiment in a Bavarian scientific journal in 1765 and sent it to the great naturalist Buffon who had it translated into French and published in 1783. Jacobi's method is essentially the basis of artificial salmonid propagation to this day.

It was not until the nineteenth century, as the stocks of Atlantic and Pacific salmon declined, that extensive attempts were made to breed salmon artificially; the earliest in Britain dates from 1838. The objective was to increase abundance by planting ova or fry in waters inaccessible to adults, or where it was believed juveniles would thrive. The next step was to breed the fishes to the parr stage in order to augment the number of survivors available to go to sea. It was recognized that parr were not a separate species but the young of salmon. Enthusiasts believed that salmon populations, which were perceptibly declining in many English and some Scottish rivers, could be rebuilt in this way.

The first English salmon hatchery was established in Troutdale, Cumberland, in 1868 but was abandoned in 1883 because of a faulty water supply. In 1884 the Scottish Fishery Board reported that the experiments at Stormontfield 'demonstrated not only the practicability but the profitableness of rearing salmon artificially'. By the end of the century there were eighteen salmon hatcheries in Scotland, some of which raised parr on a liver diet. Francis Francis' *Fish Hatching*, published in 1863, gave impetus to the movement.

In England, Frank Buckland, Inspector of Salmon Fisheries from 1867 to 1880, was the most ardent of fish culturists. Through his journal *Land and Water*, his lecture tours, and his quaint Museum of Economic Fish Culture in South Kensington, he aroused much interest in fish cultivation, especially by great landowners. He used to roam the country in search of spawning salmon and maintained a kind of hatchery in the kitchen of his London home, where, he told a lecture audience, he had hatched 30,000 fish 'and as natural history books told that salmon always returned to the places where they were hatched, he had a very cheering prospect before him'. The Thames Angling Preservation Society planted fertilized salmon eggs in the heavily polluted Thames but, needless to say, no adult fish ever appeared.

The first salmon hatchery in North America was built in 1866 by Samuel Wilmot on Wilmot Creek, a tributary of Lake Ontario. It was quite successful until the lake's salmon population dwindled away and the station was closed.

In 1871 the Craig Brook salmon hatchery was opened at Orland, Maine, on the Penobscot River – it is still in existence. In 1872 the US Fish Commission received a small appropriation from Congress for the propagation of food fishes and some of this money was used to build a salmon hatchery on the McCloud River in northern California under the supervision of Livingstone Stone, an ordained minister who had taken up fish culture as a hobby. The purpose was to produce fertilized chinook eggs for restocking Atlantic salmon streams. At that time it was not generally known that the Atlantic and Pacific salmon were

separate species with unique biological and ecological requirements. The Baird hatchery, as it was called, was a failure and was
closed in 1884.

In subsequent years many salmon hatcheries were built in
California, Oregon, Washington and British Columbia; a few
were constructed even in Alaska which then had the largest
salmon stocks on the North American continent. As in England,
there was a prevailing illusion that little more was necessary to
augment the fishery than to plant fertilized ova or fry in the
streams. This idea also fired the imagination of the Japanese who
in 1889 established their first salmon hatchery, modelled on the
Craig Brook plant, at the headwaters of the Ishikari River in
Hokkaido. This facility was designed as a central station to
supply eyed eggs for other hatcheries and became the nucleus
of the Hokkaido salmon hatchery system, now the world's
largest.

By 1900 the state of Washington had fifteen stations and
Oregon as many, producing chiefly chinook; sockeye hatcheries
were operating in British Columbia. Some of the stations had
enormous capacities; the one at Ontario, Oregon, could incubate
15 million eggs and the central hatchery at Bonneville on the
Columbia River four times as many. 'It was assumed,' said Tom
Barnaby of the US Fish and Wildlife Service, 'that one adult
fish could be produced from nearly every egg that hatched. But
the truth was that in the absence of scientific knowledge artificial
propagation was in the trial and error stage, with ample evidence
that many of the trials were errors.' Little or nothing was known
about salmon genetics, dietary requirements, disease control,
survival possibilities in the ocean, etc. There were negligible data
on the rate of adult returns to the hatcheries, without which
superintendents were operating in the dark. Many of the establishments were closed when results did not meet expectations. The
Canadians abandoned their efforts to breed Pacific salmon.

The next step in the development of salmon culture was the
discovery that larger, or older juvenile fish have a better chance
of surviving the hazards of the ocean. Instead of turning them
loose as fry they are reared to the smolt or fingerling stage. Thus
fall chinook were kept in the hatchery until they reached a

weight of 100 to the pound and coho until they reached seventeen to the pound.

Two of the basic needs in fish culture are clean water and proper food. If you had visited a Pacific Northwest hatchery as late as the early 1950s you would have seen a kind of butcher shop on the premises. The diet fed the fish consisted largely of ground-up horse meat, liver, fish cannery and packing house scrap, condemned pork and beef, tripe, hearts, etc. 'It was an unbalanced diet,' says Ernest Jeffries, Chief of Hatcheries for the Oregon Fish and Wildlife Department, 'sometimes productive of diseases like tuberculosis which come from infected meat. Much of the feed leached into the ponds was lost, and the decomposed food particles actually deprived the little fishes of oxygen they needed.'

A breakthrough was achieved in salmonid culture as a result of studies dealing with the nutrition, pathology and physiology of the fishes. The major factor was the development of pasteurized feed in pellet form, among which the Oregon moist pellet is the best known. It was a product of Oregon State University scientists working with biologists of the Oregon Fish Commission. The pellet consists of 30% fish meal, 30% ground up raw fish, and 40% water, with vitamins added. It produces healthy fish who survive quite well in the sea.

Salmon hatcheries almost everywhere went on a pelletized diet in the 1960s, thus vastly increasing their productivity. Other inprovements include the building of automated, antiseptic hatcheries where the fish receive precise amounts of food instead of having it broadcast by hand; water purity is constantly monitored and disease is reduced, sometimes with the help of a resident fish pathologist.

Atlantic and Pacific salmon, and steelhead trout *Salmo gairdneri* can now be produced in almost unlimited numbers by artificial means. Among the leaders in recent developments in salmon culture are Dr Loren Donaldson, formerly with the College of Fisheries at the University of Washington, Roger Burrows of the US Fish and Wildlife Service, Dr David Piggins of the Salmon Research Trust of Ireland, and the late Dr Borje Carlin of the Swedish Salmon Research Institute.

There are now some forty modern Atlantic salmon smolt hatcheries in Europe, of which Sweden has about twenty, Russia fifteen, and Finland, Iceland, Norway and Ireland the rest. Some fifteen Atlantic salmon smolt hatcheries are found in eastern Canada and New England. The capacity of a modern European hatchery like those in Sweden is 100,000 to 200,000 smolts while that of some American plants producing Pacific salmon is much larger. The Cowlitz hatchery on the Cowlitz River in Washington cost $10 million to build, can incubate 28 million eggs and produce 18 million salmon fingerlings annually. It is designed to replace the wild fish in the Cowlitz River whose spawning grounds were wiped out by Mayfield dam. Dworshak hatchery in Idaho, which produces steelhead trout for restocking the Snake River (whose runs have been severely damaged by high dams), is probably the most completely automated fish-rearing plant in the world. A computer regulates not only the flow of water in the ponds but its temperature and quality as well as the feeding operation. Dworshak has the capacity to rear 3,500,000 seagoing fish and much of the rearing of juveniles is on an accelerated growth basis, requiring only a year to reach smolt stage instead of two.

Pacific species are bred on a far larger scale than Atlantics since the economic benefits are much greater and artificial propagation is now recognized as an essential tool of fishery management. There are over a hundred Pacific salmon and steelhead rearing plants in the United States alone, operated by the federal and state governments. British Columbia has embarked on an ambitious programme. In 1973 the United States produced 275 million salmon and steelhead for release in Pacific Northwest rivers, mostly in the Columbia-Snake River system which has suffered enormous losses of wild stocks. Without the hatcheries the runs would have plummeted even more than they have done in the last three decades.

Japanese salmon culture, which should really be called salmon farming, dwarfs even that of the United States. Having polluted and ruined the bulk of their salmon rivers, the Japanese depend almost entirely on artificial propagation. There are some fifty field stations and eighty egg-collecting stations on the island of

Hokkaido and about the same number on Honshu. In 1974 the Hokkaido system released almost 500 million fry, the bulk of which were chum salmon. The domestic salmon industry now operates on the basis of 97% artificial production and 3% natural spawning. Many streams are set aside as 'salmon culture rivers'.

As the following chapters will reveal, both the Atlantic and Pacific species have been mercilessly exploited and their populations drastically reduced in many countries through overfishing and destruction of habitats. Advances in artificial propagation have not only helped to slow down or stem the tide of depletion in many watersheds in Europe, Asia and North America, but have formed the basis for creation of new salmon fisheries by means of transplantation, as for example in the Great Lakes of the United States.

Saltwater rearing

The revolution in salmon culture has generated considerable experimentation with saltwater rearing. 'Only a decade ago,' Dr J. I. W. Anderson told the annual meeting of the British Salmon and Trout Association in November 1973, 'informed opinion in the salmon world expressed doubt about the feasibility of farming *Salmo salar* at all . . . With the benefit of hindsight one can see that the full grown adult salmon raised entirely in captivity has been the natural outcome of developments in knowledge and understanding of the salmon in captivity which began in the early part of the nineteenth century.'

Reports of successful saltwater rearing emanated from Norway in the 1960s where the Vik brothers claimed they could raise these fishes for the market on a large scale. Their work petered out after initial successes, but they were succeeded by the Mowi Company in Bergen, organized in 1969, which has four plants, two for breeding smolts and two for fattening them to market size in saltwater. Two hundred tons of small salmon were produced in 1972 and an ultimate output of 1,500 tons was then envisaged by the company.

The fish are incubated in freshwater and transferred to saltwater pens when smolt livery appears. The saltwater plant on the island of Sotra, west of Bergen, consists of pens that enclose the ocean waters with barriers of iron or aluminium gratings in a concrete framework. The water is recycled, as in an aquarium, and the fish are fed pelletized food, fortified with vitamins. While the freshwater phase is fraught with difficulties because the young fish are vulnerable to disease and parasites, especially when temperatures rise in summer, the saltwater phase presents even more problems because little is known about saltwater rearing and its array of diseases. Sea birds are a menace and so are 'outsider' fish who may steal into the cage to feed on young fish. There is also a certain amount of cannibalism among the salmon.

Despite these difficulties, Atlantic salmon saltwater culture is making impressive headway in many countries. For example, the Unilever Company operates a plant on a sea loch on the west coast of Scotland. Here it was found that after one year in salt-water pens some of the fish reached two kilograms (4.4 pounds) and were ready for the market; others were kept until they weighed four kilograms and occasional specimens, eight kilograms.

The sheltered sea lochs around western Scotland offer ideal waters for aquaculture. Dr Anderson said he envisaged a national production of some 10,000 tons annually and possibly as much as 20,000 tons, or five to ten times the current harvest of wild salmon in Scotland. However, 'many problems still need to be solved before the potential of large-scale salmon farming is realized. More research in key areas is essential, particularly in nutrition and diseases, as well as in engineering and hydrography.'

There is a movement on foot to introduce coho salmon culture in Scotland but it is strongly opposed by the Atlantic salmon industry.

Salmon farming is making headway in France, where wild stocks are now at a minimum. A government agency, the Centre National Pour L'Exploitation des Oceans, operates four experimental plants and produced fifty tons of coho in saltwater in 1977, with expectation of a tenfold increase within five years.

In North America, saltwater culture of both Atlantic and Pacific salmon is rapidly increasing. Coho are being produced on the Sheepscot River in Maine; the first batch of 'tasty, plate-sized fish' weighing three-quarters of a pound were harvested in 1974; the company hopes ultimately to produce 250,000 pounds a year. Other companies have entered the business in recent years in New England. There are many salmon farmers on the west coast of the United States. Some of them produce pan-size salmon, where the fish are captive from egg to harvest, as in Newport, Oregon, an establishment of the Weyerhaeuser Timber Company. Others follow the 'ranching' techniques where after release, the fish migrate to the ocean, feed on ocean pastures, accumulate high quality protein and return to the point of release. Before their recapture by ocean ranchers, both the sport and commercial fishery have an opportunity to catch them.

Summing up the status of these developments, Anthony J. Novotny of the National Marine Fisheries Service said in the *Marine Fisheries Review* (January 1975, Volume 37, No. 1):

> Through the efforts of past technology, we have been able to establish the beginnings of a sound farming system in salt water with the coho salmon . . . However, a great deal of scientific information relating to salmon is needed by growers. We are probably on the threshold that the poultry industry confronted fifty years ago . . . Expansion of this industry will be limited to the technological effort that is applied to it, either by private enterprise or by the government.

CHAPTER 5

Species Transplantation

North America

THE breakthrough in salmon culture has accelerated the efforts, begun in the nineteenth century, to transplant these fishes to regions in the temperate zones of both hemispheres where they never existed before. One of the most successful species transplantations has occurred in the Great Lakes of North America. Except for Lake Ontario, which originally harboured large numbers of landlocked Atlantic salmon that were exterminated in the nineteenth century, the lakes had not been known as salmon habitat. By the 1950s Lake Michigan seemed doomed to become a biological wasteland owing to pollution and eutrophication. Many of its sandy beaches were deserted because of pollution and high bacteria levels, and to compound the problem the opening of the St Lawrence Seaway introduced the parasitic sea lamprey, a species that lives in saltwater but breeds in freshwater. Within a few years the lamprey had decimated the abundant lake trout; with the disappearance of the trout another problem arose. Without the predatory trout to keep them in check, the alewife population exploded and resulted in millions of dead alewives littering and fouling the lake beaches.

Introduction of salmon along with lamprey control measures was the means of keeping the alewife population in check. In 1966 and 1967 coho and chinook from Oregon and Washington hatcheries were introduced in upper Lake Michigan and Lake Superior streams, and in subsequent years into the streams flowing into Lakes Erie, Ontario and Huron. The results have been spectacular. The salmon forage around the lakes, subsisting on alewives and smelt, and then return in August and September to spawn in the streams into which they had been released as juveniles. At the mouths of the rivers there is now a booming sport fishery which encompasses the five Great Lakes. Salmon hatcheries have been built in the state of Michigan and elsewhere to meet the demand for planting stock because the streams are not suitable for propagation.

In 1974 the state of New York planted some 4 million juvenile coho in Lakes Michigan and Huron; Wisconsin released 650,000 chinook and 300,000 fingerlings in Lakes Michigan and Superior; and Illinois 700,000 chinook in Lake Michigan. The 1974 fall run to New York tributaries of Lakes Ontario and Erie was the largest since Pacific salmon were first stocked there in 1968; the adult coho and chinook averaged several pounds heavier than the year before, a fact attributed to better lamprey control. New York now plans to build a hatchery to produce 3 to 4 million salmon smolts annually and has reintroduced Atlantic salmon in Lake Ontario.

Great Lakes salmon have created an important recreational industry, for these are now the largest freshwater fishes available to sportsmen. To the amazement of older inhabitants around the lakes – as in Chicago – who never dreamed of seeing salmon in these waters, the fishes are being caught off the city's beaches, including chinook of twenty-five pounds and coho of twenty pounds. However, the plenitude of salmon in the lakes has led to gross abuses. It seems to be impossible to control snagging (foul hooking) in some rivers, as along the Muskegon in Michigan. These snaggers were so thick in the fall of 1974, said the Michigan Department of Natural Resources, 'they look like a picket fence, and every one is fishing illegally. If they catch a male chinook they toss it back. When they snag a female they almost have to fight to keep its eggs.' A fisherman can snag as many as fifty a day, giving him as much as $300 in eggs. Fishery officials say it is futile to arrest snaggers as they quickly return, in defiance of the law. Unhappily, serious pollution of Lake Michigan with deadly industrial chemicals has greatly reduced the excitement about salmon fishing. The fish are said to be mostly poisoned and people are warned not to eat them. See an article in *Chicago* magazine, August, 1977.

Further transplantation activity in North America includes

five transplants of eyed eggs of pink salmon from British Columbia, totalling 15 million, made between 1959 and 1966 in North Harbor River, Newfoundland. At first adult returns were fairly large, peaking at 8,500 in 1967, but they fell to 2,425 the next year and declined steadily after 1969. The reasons for the failure of this experiment, according to W. H. Lear of the Canadian Fisheries Marine Service, are (1) 'predation of the fry by brook trout, herring and possibly eels'; (2) unsuitability of donor stocks; (3) inadequate numbers of eggs were transplanted to produce populations required to maintain the runs; and (4) unfavourable surface temperatures in the river for the fry.

Pacific salmon have been introduced in a few New England rivers in the hope of filling the gap left by the disappearance of Atlantics and providing sport for anglers. In 1967 the state of New Hampshire released 750,000 coho juveniles into the Lamprey and Exeter Rivers and followed it up with additional plantings, but returns were so low that the state abandoned the programme in 1976. Massachusetts has planted coho in the North River with greater success and here the experiment is being continued, with the federal government, as elsewhere, providing most of the funds on a matching basis.

Flyfishermen who believe that New England rivers should be reserved for Atlantic salmon object strongly to these schemes. According to Richard Buck, chairman of the Atlantic Salmon Restoration Association, they fear that the success of the coho and chinook plants will endanger efforts to restore *Salmo salar* to rivers in Maine and on the Connecticut and Merrimack.

Southern hemisphere

The dream of having salmon in the southern hemisphere led to the colonization of *Salmo salar* in New Zealand in 1868 with eggs from the British Severn and Tay Rivers. Shipment of Atlantic salmon eggs from Europe and North America continued spasmodically until 1911. How many fish were reared to the seagoing stage is not known but in 1908 the New Zealand government took control of the work and began confining liberations of fry to the Upukerora River, a tributary of Lake Te Amu on South Island. According to R. T. Hutchinson of the

New Zealand Wildlife Service, Atlantic salmon became established as a landlocked fish throughout the lake drainage, ranging in weight from eight to fifteen pounds, but the introduction of brown and rainbow trout and continued trapping of spawners for egg collection caused a decline in the stocks. Very few Atlantic salmon are left in New Zealand.

Much greater success was attained with 'quinnat' (chinook) salmon, with eggs imported from California in 1875. Planting fry in the semiarid drainages of North Island was a failure but in South Island the fish became firmly established in the Hakatarama River and spread to other east coast glacial streams – the Waimakariri, Rakaia, Ashburton, Rangittata, Opoki, Waitaki, and Clutha Rivers – where they now offer good sport for anglers. The fish weighing up to forty pounds return to the rivers from their oceanic migrations from December to March, the antipodean summer. Liberation of hatchery stock also established runs in the Moeraki and Paringa Rivers on the west coast.

An ambitious scheme is under way to establish chum and cherry salmon in the province of Aysen in southern Chile, with eggs and technologists imported from Japan. A modern hatchery has been constructed on the banks of the River Claro, a tributary of the Simpson. Over 4 million eggs were flown from Japan and hatched. The fry descended to the Pacific Ocean and were expected to return in two to four years. The first returns of adult fish were due in 1977, and according to the official announcement, it was hoped to establish a commercial fishery, thus 'creating a new source of employment and foreign exchange'. No adult fish had returned in 1977, thus somewhat dampening the enthusiasm of the project's sponsors.

An even more ambitious scheme is suggested by Dr Colin E. Nash, of the Oceanic Institute of Waimanalo, Hawaii and Dr Timothy Joyner, formerly of the National Marine Fisheries Service in Seattle, to seed salmon in the Southern (Antarctic) Ocean where there is a rich supply of krill (tiny shrimp). With the colossal slaughter in this ocean of the whale populations, who subsist largely on krill, a gap has been left in the food chain which, it is believed, salmon could fill.

'Salmon, of all marine species,' says Joyner, 'seem to offer the best prospects for early development of an aquacultural system capable of taking advantage of the natural productivity of ocean ranges.' The reasons are: (1) The early stages are spent in fresh water which is both accessible and can be protected by man; (2) There is a considerable body of knowledge of its life history 'and a proven hatchery and nursery technology that can be applied to a rational system of management'; (3) 'After they migrate to the sea, the far-ranging salmon can efficiently seek out productive feeding grounds'; (4) 'After fattening for several years at sea, salmon return to their native rivers without having to be herded,' and can be easily harvested with traps; and (5) The fecundity of salmon, though far less than that of cod or herring, is high and the rate of growth rapid.

Thus Joyner and his colleagues envisage the possibility of a tremendous increase in the supply of protein food as salmon fill up the gaps in the Antarctic; but the enterprise will be immensely difficult compared to the Aysen venture. There are ideal breeding conditions in southern Chile, where there are cold freshwater streams, flowing into saltwater inlets much like those in Alaska and Norway. From there fish will have access to the ocean. Trial sites for ocean seeding might be found near the Straits of Magellan, an area which is 'great for salmon but tough on people,' admits Joyner, 'but once a self-sustaining salmon population is established [as is hoped for in Aysen], the yield of protein would be prodigious'. At the beginning of 1978 this project was at a standstill as the Government of Chile appeared reluctant to undertake it.

European transplantations

There have been many attempts to introduce Pacific salmon in European waters. From 1933 to 1938 the Russians incubated millions of chum eggs brought from Sakhalin Island in a station at Murmansk, and released the fry into streams flowing to the White and Barents Seas. There were some returns from this plant but the experiment was a failure. In 1957 a similar experiment was launched with pink salmon on a much larger scale, and in 1960 adults began to appear in European Arctic streams in considerable numbers. Altogether about 80,000 adults were counted in Russian territory. Strays showed up along the coasts of Norway, Iceland, Spitzbergen and Scotland. Encouraged by these results, additional plantings were made in 1961 but there were almost no surviving progeny from the returning spawners. It seems that many eggs died during the severe cold in the Murmansk hatchery and some of the fry were misshapen or had watery yolk sacs. Thus ended one of the most ambitious programmes to stock Atlantic salmon rivers with Pacific salmon.

Part Two

THE ATLANTIC SALMON

———

WHEN man first entered western Europe and North America, probably at the end of the last Ice Age, the Atlantic salmon were abundant in thousands of rivers on both continents. We have no way of knowing the magnitude of the runs. The American anthropologist Erhard Rostlund in his study *Freshwater Fish and Fishing in Native North America* concludes that 'there is theoretical reason for thinking that Atlantic salmon, per unit area, was at least as plentiful as Pacific salmon'.

If we accept this reasoning it seems clear that Industrial Man in both North America and Europe has destroyed by far the greater part of his Atlantic salmon heritage. World landings of this species in the decade 1964–1973 averaged only 13,000 metric tons annually, compared with about 365,000 tons of Pacific salmon in the years 1967–1975. In other words, for every Atlantic almost thirty Pacifics were landed.

The range of *Salmo salar* has been greatly constricted in the past two centuries. The fishes have been driven out of Portugal, the Low Countries, Germany, Switzerland and Czechoslovakia, and reduced to token populations in Denmark, Spain, France, the United States and Poland. In all other countries, including the Baltic nations, they are now much less numerous than at the end of the nineteenth century. Rivers once famous for their savoury salmon which are now depopulated include the Rhine, Seine, most of the Loire, Douro, Gudenaa, Oder, Elbe, Weser, Connecticut, Kemi and many others. About 70% of the Atlantics are produced in six countries, Norway, Canada, Scotland,

Ireland, Russia and Sweden. About 30% of the catches are made by Danish fishermen and their Greenland colonists.

The six nations mentioned, particularly Sweden, Russia and Canada, spend substantial sums of money to sustain their stocks, by building and maintaining extensive hatchery systems, conducting stream improvements, and taking other measures to protect habitats, and in some instances by preventing excessive fishing.

CHAPTER 6

Great Britain

FROM the beginning of recorded history the British Isles, blessed with abundant rainfall and numerous rivers, have been renowned for the variety and abundance of their freshwater fisheries, especially salmon. 'It is on record,' says A. Courtney Williams in his delightful book, *Angling Diversions*, 'that Roman soldiers, set to guard the ford at Laleham, near Staines, saw many big salmon leaping the ford on their way to the spawning beds higher up the river.' Salmon then thronged the Thames probably as far as Lechlade in Gloucestershire. The report of the Thames Migratory Fish Committee issued in 1977 says, 'The freshwater fisheries of the Thames were probably heavily exploited and there are records of many weirs across the river which were not only a nuisance to navigation but which also supported nets and other fixed engines to catch fish.' Reference to such weirs is found in the Magna Carta and subsequent legislation. This 'indicates that the salmon stock was of a size to warrant conservation measures and went some way to preserving the fisheries for salmon . . . until the beginning of the 19th century'.

The *Domesday Book*, the survey of England's wealth made in 1086 by William the Conqueror's agents, lists scores of eel and salmon fisheries on the coasts and in the valleys. In the twelfth century Giraldus Cambrensis (Gerald the Welshman) in his *Description of Wales* describes salmon fishing with coracles (small boats) on the Teifi and other Welsh streams, and Ranulf Higden, a monk attached to St Werburgh's monastery in Chester in the fourteenth century notes in his *Polychronicon* that salmon were so abundant they were fed to the sows.

British rivers

British rivers, with some notable exceptions, are relatively short

3 *Major salmon rivers of Great Britain*

judged by American standards. 'In such a country as America,' says the novelist H. E. Bates, 'not more than a dozen . . . would be called rivers at all.' Yet even 'twiddling little streams' produced crops of salmon every year in Saxon times and down to the Industrial Revolution. The larger rivers like the Thames, Tyne, Trent and Severn, can command even an American's respect.

The 215-mile Thames, England's longest river, rises on the steep slopes of the Cotswold hills in Gloucestershire and runs eastward across south-central England, gathering the flow of thirteen tributaries before emptying through a long estuary into the North Sea. The present pollution-racked, canalized river hardly resembles the original. The Elizabethan poet Edmund Spenser called it 'silver-streaming Thames'. He could see salmon leaping under London Bridge and if he went up to the villages of Chelsea and Fulham he observed fishermen netting salmon, their horses drawing the boats up the steep banks. The fish spawned in some of the upper tributaries like the Lea, which Izaak Walton liked to fish.

The northern arm of the eighty-mile Tyne issues out of the Cheviot Hills near the Scottish border while the southern arm comes out of the Durham-Cumberland border. Like north-eastern rivers generally, which rise in limestone formations or flow through such outcrops in their upper reaches, they are naturally prolific salmon and trout waters, and, where they are pure, remain among the best fishing streams. The Tyne, however, is now one of the most polluted waterways in Britain, at least in its lower reaches.

The 220-mile Severn runs down the spine of the heavily scarred Midlands, acquiring the flow of such delightful tributaries as the Teme, Stour and Warwickshire Avon. Salmon have to make one of the longest journeys in the British Isles to reach their spawning grounds in this watershed. In the distant past, as Brian Waters, historian of the Severn, says, many townsmen dwelling along its banks 'enjoyed the savage festival of poaching the spawning fish, when hooligans with torches and blackened faces speared and gaffed the salmon'. Ironmongers, bridge builders, potteries and other industrial operators have sorely abused parts of the Severn but there are still small runs of salmon.

The Trent has not fared so well. Its source is in north Stafford-shire, about thirty miles east of the Irish Sea, and in the words of E. E. Hunter-Christie, it 'curls like a whiplash across the backbone of England,' emptying in the Humber estuary. Many little streams flow into the Trent, some of them so shallow they can barely support a paper boat, yet at one time they all held salmon. Trent's waters were then so pure they supported a considerable brewing industry. The river is now connected by a network of canals with all the major industrial and shipping centres of the Midlands.

Typical of north-west rivers is the Eden which, born in the bleak Yorkshire Pennines, near the source of two other prominent salmon rivers, the Ribble and Lune, flows through the undulating Westmorland and Cumberland fells. In its sixty-five-mile course the Eden passes a countryside once soiled with the blood of victims of Scottish and English warfare; it passes picturesque villages like Armathwaite and Corby, and after receiving the flow of the Irthing, reaches the city of Carlisle and then disappears into the Solway Firth.

Not many miles south is the Border Esk which comes in from Scotland and after crossing the Solway marshes meets the Irish Sea. The firth is frequented by many shore birds, some of whom feed on salmon smolts; black-headed gulls nest here, herons live on the high moors, and cormorants perch and roost in the trees around the estuary.

Moving into Wales we meet the Wye, an Anglo-Welsh river which springs from the desolate bogs of Plinlimmon, not far from the source of the Severn, The 'sylvan Wye', as Wordsworth called it, evokes happy thoughts in anglers because it now has more salmon than any stream south of the Scottish border. Augustus Grimble described it as 'white, foaming Wye, racing between the hills and hanging woods of the Welsh border . . . Its banks are hemmed with vivid lines of flowers, and great salmon leap suddenly from dark swift channels.' The Wye runs for 130 miles to the Bristol Channel.

Some South Wales rivers have been ruined by gross pollution from mills and factories, but the British Field Sports Society lists almost a score of Welsh rivers where salmon may still be caught by hook and line. In addition to the Severn and Wye, there are the Elwy, Ledr and Conway in Carnarvonshire; the Dee and Ceirog in Denbighshire; the Mawdoch and Dovey in Merionethshire; the Teifi and Ystwyth in Cardiganshire; the Towy and Taf in Carmarthenshire; and the Usk in Breconshire.

The Dee is typical of these Welsh streams. It comes out of the Merionethshire mountains and placidly follows a corkscrew path for over a hundred miles in north-eastern Wales and England; for some distance it is used as an aqueduct to carry water to Liverpool. Its estuary is about twenty miles below Chester.

The Dart is one of the supreme Devon rivers. In Chaucer's day it teemed with merchant ships as far as Dartmouth and also with salmon. Although it is now a lonely and somnolent river, the Dart remains a gem among English streams. Other renowned West country rivers are the Tamar, Tavy and Plym which discharge into the English Channel, and the Taw and Torridge which empty into the Irish Sea.

Chalk streams are numerous in southern England. They harbour trout and coarse fish as well as salmon. The Frome is such a river, slow and deep in its lower stretches, frequented by ravens and hawks and wading and song birds of many kinds. Salmon were once so plentiful in the Frome, said Augustus Grimble, that 'the officials of Wareham made a law that the apprentices of the town were not to be fed salmon more than three times a week'.

The Itchen and Test, running into the English Channel, are more famous for trout than salmon, but the neighbouring Avon was once more notable for its salmon than trout. At the Nag's Head pub just outside Ringwood you can still see a sign recording the fact that in 1928–1929 anglers caught salmon weighing from forty-two to forty-eight pounds on the Avon, a rarity now anywhere in England. Unlike the east coast of Scotland, the east coast of England has few salmon rivers. South of the Tweed we meet the still productive Coquet, and then the longer Tyne, Tees and Trent, all emptying into the North Sea. These once-opulent streams are now virtually deserted and in fact hardly recognizable as waters that could support such sensitive fish as salmon. Yorkshire too has several rivers which formerly were respectable salmon streams, such as the Ouse, Derwent, Wharfe, Aire and Don.

It is noteworthy that eighteen out of twenty-five English cathedral towns were built on salmon rivers; among them are Canterbury on the Stour, London on the Thames, Rochester on the Medway, Winchester on the Itchen, and Salisbury on the Hampshire Avon.

With few exceptions British rivers are privately owned. The water and fish belong to the riparian owners and the right to fish must be obtained from them; in some estuaries there is a public right to fish but a licence must be purchased.

Salmon enter British rivers at all seasons of the year. Those that arrive between December and March move upstream with greater deliberation than those which come later. If the water is very cold they may loiter in the deepest layers of the warmer estuary and when they start their ascent are inclined to hurry. If a snowstorm occurs they may turn round and go back down to the estuary. A mild winter may bring more fish than a cold one; they quickly leave the lower waters, reaching the middle and upper reaches as early as February or March, to the delight of anglers. Fish arriving in summer have a different migration pattern. The sudden rise of the river's level will send them upstream quickly. Fall fish usually enter the rivers with their reproductive organs fully developed and move fast in order to reach their spawning grounds before it is too cold.

For the most part the short west coast rivers have summer and autumn runs only, while east coast streams may have spring and winter fish as well. These population patterns are not constant, however. Similarly, some rivers at times have more grilse than full-size salmon, and vice versa.

In the south of England the young fish tend to grow fairly rapidly and may migrate to the sea at one year of age. However, the majority of British salmon stay in the river two years, and a small proportion even longer. Fish returning after two years of ocean life may weigh nine to twelve pounds, and after three years eighteen to twenty-five pounds. The proportion of kelts (mainly females) also varies considerably.

The oceanic migration of English salmon is generally in a

north-west direction. Returns from the Greenland fishery reveal that many of the fish came from the rivers Usk, Axe, Wye, Severn, Wear and Ribble. They had increased enormously in weight during the eighteen or twenty months which had elapsed between the time of release as smolts and capture in Danish nets.

On the whole Scotland has a more rugged terrain than England and some of the highest mountains in the British Isles. The heather-clad, and often peaty Highlands form an imposing land mass that occupies the northern part of Scotland. The Great Glen, once the hideaway of fierce clans, forms a natural trench running north-east to south-west and dividing the region into two parts. To the west there is a mountainous area drained by short, swift and cold rivers, many of which flow through lochs to the sea. These sea lochs penetrate the entire coastline of north-west Scotland and are sometimes of considerable length, like Loch Maree and Loch Torridon. The offshore islands of the Hebrides, separated from the mainland by deep sounds and kyles, are veined by numerous rivers and lochs; salmon are found in some of them, as in the Grimersta on the Isle of Lewis.

While Scotland may have fewer rivers than England and Wales, it has always, as we know from medieval historians, produced more salmon. The major producers are the Tweed, part of which forms the border with England, and the Tay, Dee, Don and Spey, all flowing from west to east. Before the Industrial Revolution the Clyde, flowing in the opposite direction, would probably have been numbered with them. Each has many tributaries, sometimes including lochs, and are complex river systems. Several of the west-flowing rivers rise in the high plateau west of the Tweed; these include the Clyde, descending from the central Lowlands, Annan, Nith and Esk which empty into the Solway Firth. In the far north of Scotland the Oykel and Thurso, among others, still contain substantial numbers of salmon.

The Spey is a classic type of Highland river, coursing through a rugged, picturesque valley. It is about 110 miles long, compared with ninety-six miles for the Tweed, 120 miles for the Tay, ninety miles for the Dee and sixty-two miles for the Don. In its headwaters the Spey is a slender stream but as it flows down the valley, fed by lochs and burns, it gathers considerable volume and below Grantown becomes what William B. Currie in *Fishing Waters of Scotland* calls 'a streamy river with a gravelly, boulder-strewn bed'. Its current is so swift that it can tumble an unwary angler and fill his waders with ice-cold water.

The Don and Dee come out of the Cairngorm mountains and follow parallel courses until they empty into the sea at Aberdeen. Now that the city is becoming the centre of the North Sea petroleum industry serious difficulties threaten the long-established fishing industry. The Tay, the longest river in Scotland, traverses Loch Tay and a large part of the wild and majestic southern Highlands before dropping into the North Sea below Dundee.

Inverness is regarded as the capital of the Highlands; as you drive to Fort William, following Loch Ness and Loch Lochy and Loch Linnhe, the empty waters glisten in the sunshine. There is little traffic on the road in the fall, stands of young spruce march up the hills, sheep graze the dried grass. There may be snow on the highest peaks and as you near the sea the breeze freshens. Ben Nevis towers over the landscape of purple mountains in the distance. This is a fisherman's country, and to the salmon and sea trout angler it is paradise.

There are many lesser rivers in Scotland prized by salmon fishers, such as the Beauly, Deveron, Ythan, South Esk, Findhorn, and Nairn. Every Scottish river has one seasonal run of fish and sometimes two. The main run may be grilse, which return to the rivers after one to one and a half years at sea, weighing from three to ten pounds, while full-grown salmon come early in spring to some rivers and in summer to others. On the Tweed, salmon may appear as early as January. The fish spawn from September to January and in these months the rivers are alive with thrashing fish ploughing up the gravel beds. The early comers usually spawn in the upper reaches of the rivers and the later ones lower down. Some streams produce thirty- to forty-pound fish; the largest specimen ever caught on a rod in Scotland weighed seventy pounds.

Scottish salmon tend to move northward and westward after leaving the home river. Some of them circumnavigate the island

and are found along the Yorkshire coast; others continue south-ward and come round to the waters of northern Ireland, while an unknown proportion seem to head straight for Davis Strait or Greenland as they enter the sea. One smolt, tagged in the Tummel River, travelled at least 1,420 miles before it was caught in the second year of its sea-life at Iqalikofjord in the Julianehaab district of Greenland; yet another journeyed 2,135 miles from the river Conon in Ross-shire to Aqigsserniaq in the Egedesminde district of Greenland.

Use of the resource

In the Middle Ages salmon rivers were valuable properties belonging to the lords of the manor, municipalities and monastic institutions who acquired them directly from the crown or from pious donors. After the Reformation many fisheries passed from the religious houses to laymen as rewards for services rendered to the Crown. For example, Sir Walter Raleigh obtained the valuable fishings on the Munster Blackwater River in Ireland but later sold them to Richard Boyle who became the first Earl of Cork.

The fish were usually taken for local consumption but by the thirteenth century there was already a considerable export of salmon from Aberdeen, Glasgow, Berwick and Perth to England and the Continent. At the Restoration of Charles II in 1660 some £200,000 worth of Scottish salmon was being exported annually, suggesting that catches were of huge proportions. Rentals for salmon water were often quite high; the lower Don, for example, was bringing its owner £30,000 annually in the early eighteenth century.

Travellers in the British Isles noted the prodigality of some of the rivers. Richard Franck, a soldier in Cromwell's army, who wrote his angling memoirs towards the end of the seventeenth century, said that at Stirling the river Forth 'relieves the country with her great quantity of salmon'. Here the burgomasters 'are compelled to reinforce an ancient statute that commands all masters not to compel any servant, or an apprentice, to feed upon salmon more than thrice a week'. Similar tales were reported in Spain, Sweden and the American colonies.

The intrepid Celia Fiennes, who toured much of England and parts of Wales on horseback at the end of the seventeenth century, gives us in her diaries glimpses of the salmon fisheries and methods of fishing on the Severn, Yorkshire Derwent, the Kent at Kendall, the Swale, Eden and Exe. Almost everywhere the rivers were prosperous and landings substantial.

Daniel Defoe, who was a merchant as well as journalist, gives an account of the salmon fisheries in many rivers in his *Tour Through the Whole Island of Great Britain*, published in 1724–1726. In Caithness and the north of Scotland, he said, there were 'salmon in such plenty as is scarce credible and so cheap that, to those who have any substance to buy with, it is not worth their while to catch it themselves. This they eat fresh in the season and for other times they cure it by drying it in the sun [as did the American Indians], by which they preserve it all the year'. The fish sold for a penny a pound in Inverness.

'The fish taken at Perth and all over the Tay,' said Defoe, 'is extremely good and the quantity prodigious. They carry it to Edinburgh, and to all the towns where they have no salmon, and they barrel up a great quantity for exportation.' In 1786 George Dempster, a Scottish merchant, began to ship salmon in ice from the Tay to London, a distance of about 400 miles. This method was soon copied by his competitors in Scotland. By 1817 over 700,000 pounds of iced salmon were reaching London yearly from the rivers Dee and Don. If the fish arrived in good condition they could be kept fresh for ten days in cool weather and a week in summer.

James R. Coull, who made a study of the literature pertaining to north-east Scottish fisheries before 1800, says, 'All streams, down to the smallest, appear to have been fished.' Outstanding were the salmon catches on the Dee and Don (owned by the borough of Aberdeen) and the Spey (owned by the Priory of Pluscarden and afterward by the Duke of Gordon). Of lesser importance were the fisheries on the Findhorn, owned mostly by the Priory of Pluscarden and after the Reformation by the royal burgh of Foress; the Deveron, which belonged to the town of Banff; the Ness, owned by the burgh of Inverness; and the Ythan, held by the local lairds. The fishings on the Ugie, a small river, once belonged to the Abbey of Deer, on the Nairn to the burgh of that name, and on the Lossie to the Bishop of Moray and later to the town of Elgin. All these rivers were exploited almost to the headwaters but most of the landings occurred in the lower rivers and estuaries, for the charters often specifically conveyed to the proprietors the right to fish 'in fresh and salt water'.

The Tweed at its peak probably produced more salmon than any other Scottish river. The naturalist Thomas Pennant stated that, in his time, the last quarter of the eighteenth century, a boatload of salmon, and sometimes two, could be taken on a single tide at Berwick, and as many as 700 fish were swept into one net by the waves. According to the Reverend Richard Warner, around the year 1800 twenty-five to eighty boats were constantly employed on a few miles of the Tweed between January 10 and October 10, and as many as 40,000 kits, weighing in the aggregate about 1,600,000 pounds, were dispatched to markets annually. The farmers in the Vale of Tweed, said Richard Kerr in his *General View of the County of Berwick* (1809), depended upon the salmon for a considerable portion of their winter's food.

In Defoe's time, some of the best English rivers were still producing prodigiously. The Tamar, he reported, 'is so full of fresh salmon, and these so exceedingly fat, and good, that they are esteemed in both counties [Devon and Cornwall] above the fish, of the same kind, found in other places; and the quantity is so great, as to supply the country in abundance . . . The fish have a secure retreat in the salt water for their harbour and shelter, and from them they shoot up into the fresh water, in such vast numbers to cast their spawn, that the country people cannot take too many.'

Martin's *Natural History of England* (1785), noted that the Mersey 'greatly abounds with salmon, which in spring strive to ascend the arm of the sea, and with difficulty evade the nets of the fishermen before they reach Warrington bridge, where the river becomes narrower.' Manchester, Warrington and Stockport were well supplied with fish from this river and the surplus went to London by stage, or was carried on horseback to Birmingham and other inland towns. The Mersey no longer contains salmon.

The north of England also yielded bumper crops. For example, Pennant, writing in 1775, said that on the Tees at Dinstall the nets worked night and day, and the landings were enormous. Fishermen were paid five shillings for a dozen salmon.

By the beginning of the nineteenth century most of the productive rivers in the United Kingdom were still unimpaired. *The Driffield Angler*, published in 1806 as a guide for sportsmen, listed as prime salmon water many of the streams which were in high repute in Elizabethan times: the Thames, Severn, Mersey, Trent, Medway, Exe, Usk and Wye. Yet within a century the Industrial Revolution, moving at a rapid pace, was to transform the face of much of England beyond recognition and destroy many of the ancient and valuable anadromous fisheries.

Protection of the fisheries

Almost from the very beginning, the Crown in both England and Scotland adopted a protective attitude towards the inland fisheries. The law usually concerned the salmon because it was the largest and most valuable of the fishes, and also one of the easiest to catch. A riparian owner in the lower reaches of a river, for example, could (and sometimes did) trap the bulk of the run, thus robbing upstream owners of their share.

One of the earliest statutes, promulgated by King Edward I in 1285, stipulated that in 'the waters of the Humber, Ouse, Trent, Dove, Aire, Derwent, Wharfe, Nid, Swale, Tees, Tyne, Eden and all other waters [where salmon are found] they shall not be taken nor destroyed by nets, nor by engines at mill pools, from the middle of April until the Nativity of St John the Baptist (June 24)'. First offenders faced losing their nets and engines, second offenders three months in jail, and third offenders a year's incarceration. 'As their trespass increases, so shall the punishment,' wisely declares the statute.

A century later Edward II re-enacted the law of 1285 and extended it to all salmon waters in Lancashire and other rivers not mentioned in the original, set the closed season from Michaelmas Day (September 29) to February 1, and banned the use of 'stalkers' and other devices for taking the salmon fry for pig feed. A parallel law created conservators to protect the fisheries and made the Justices of the Peace responsible for enforcing the legislation. These men continued to have such authority until after the middle of the nineteenth century.

In Scotland the earliest salmon law dates from 1030, in the reign of Malcolm II. It established a closed season from Assumption Day (about the end of August) to Martinmas Day (November 11).

In succeeding centuries such statutes came in a steady flow in both England and Scotland, they altered closed seasons to harmonize better with the timing of the runs, introduced weekend closures, banned fixed gear in tidal waters, and stipulated that weirs and other obstructions must have a gap, sometimes called the 'King's gap', to permit the fish to reach their spawning grounds. For example, a twelfth-century decree of Richard the Lion-Hearted stipulated that every dam or dyke that affected migratory fish must have a gap large enough to allow 'a well-fed pig to stand sideways in the stream, not touching either bank'.

In 1499 the sheriffs in Scotland were given authority to destroy illegal nets and other gear, and in the next century James III created a system of conservators, as in England, for all the major rivers, with full power to enforce the conservation laws, jail offenders or fine them up to £200 (a stupendous sum). What was probably the first anti-pollution law in the British Isles was passed by the Dublin Corporation in 1466, stipulating that no tanner, glover nor any person might use the river Liffey for washing leather work or limed ware.

That the conservation laws, at least in England, were often defied or simply ignored may be inferred from works like Leonard Mascall's *Booke of Fishing* published in 1590. It offers a long list of abuses against the salmon, such as the use of 'fire, handguns, cross bows, oils, ointments, powders and pellets . . . to stun and poison the fish'. He pleads that no waters should 'be let to any fisherman without order what mesh, what nets, he or they shall use to fish, and in what months of the year to refrain from fishing, upon pain to forfeit his lease and all such engines'. He laments that England does not have 'more preservers, and less spoilers of fish out of season and in season,' for then 'we should have more plenty than we have through this realm'. He wishes that 'all stop nets, and drags with casting nets, were banished in all common rivers throughout this realm for three months; as in March, April, May, wherein they take fish out of season as well as others, with great spoils of spawn, both of great and small fish, for they use such nets with small mesh, that kills all fish afore they come to any growth'.

Further, he informs us that water bailiffs appointed to guard the rivers shut their eyes to the use of illegal small-mesh nets because the fishermen say that since they pay high rents they must take whatever they can get. 'None cares for the preserving of the common wealth,' a remark that echoes down the ages. He winds up his peroration with the hope 'that careful men were put in office, and such as favours the common wealth, and all other put out that seeks for their own profit only. Then should we have within few years, much plenty of river fish'. This too has a topical ring.

Some of the salmon conservation statutes of later centuries begin with the lament that, the runs having declined, new legislation is needed to arrest the tide of depletion. The latest statute of this kind was promulgated in England in 1714 to protect the runs in the Severn, Dee, Wye, Teme, Wear, Ribble, Mersey, Don, Aire, Ouse, Swale, Wharfe, Calder, Eure, Derwent and Trent, proclaiming that anyone who takes spawn or small fry of salmon, 'or any salmon not being in length 18 inches or more from the eye to the extent of the middle of the tail,' or sets up 'any bank, dam, hedge, or stank net or nets across the said rivers, or any part there of' whereby the salmon may be taken or prevented from passing or going up the rivers to spawn, or 'shall fish in closed seasons or with other nets than those allowed' will be fined £5 for every offence and the fish and nets will be confiscated. Furthermore, the justices of the peace are empowered to demolish illegal obstructions at the owner's expense.

This statute also stipulated that no salmon under six pounds, taken from any of the seventeen rivers named, could be sold in London – a great step forward in conservation. There was already a statute on the books giving the authorities the right to confiscate salmon taken out of season, and a reward was paid to anyone who brought the sale of such unseasonable fish to the attention of the Lord Mayor, the amount to be paid determined by the Fishmongers Company. How well these laws were enforced we do not know.

Impact of the industrial revolution

The second half of the eighteenth century saw the growth of the mining and smelting industry, especially in South Wales, but it was in the nineteenth century that industrialization and urbanization advanced at a geometric rate. Cotton mills and other textile works, potteries and other manufacturing plants mushroomed and blighted the Midland counties; iron and steel mills scarred the green Welsh valleys. The invention of the steam engine, spinning jenny, and other textile machines, the growth of the metallurgical industries and intensification of coal mining, the new chemical and related industries, usually situated on once-sparkling rivers – all helped to seal the fate of the anadromous fishes in numerous watersheds. Canalization, which reached a peak in the early nineteenth century, further imperilled the fish runs. The mining of china clay defiled parts of Cornwall and Devon. Later came electric power stations, drawing heavily on the coal resources of the nation, and a multitude of other types of manufacturing which drew off the river water, returning it as poisonous waste.

One by one, many of the noblest streams were poisoned and blockaded, so that in time the runs were depleted or wiped out. Manchester usurped the rivers Irk and Irwell, Liverpool the Mersey estuary, Leeds the Aire, Sheffield the confluence of the Sheaf and Yorkshire Don, Newcastle the Tyne. The pottery towns of Staffordshire sprawled along the valley of the Trent. Birmingham, situated on the Tame, a small, sleepy city in the days of Dr Samuel Johnson, who frequented it as a young man, became the centre of a vast industrial complex in the nineteenth century. In Scotland industrial development and accompanying urban growth centred on the rivers Clyde, Forth and sections of the Tweed. Charles Reade describes the fate of such rivers in his novel *Put Yourself in His Place*:

Hillsborough and its outlying suburbs make bricks by the

million, spin and weave both wool and cotton, forge in steel the finest needle up to a ship's armour, and so add considerably to the kingdom's wealth.

But industry so vast, working by steam on a limited space, has been fatal to beauty: Hillsborough, though built on one of the loveliest sites in England, is perhaps the most hideous town in creation. All ups and downs and back slums . . .

More than one crystal stream runs sparkling down the valleys, and enters the town; but they soon get defiled and creep through it heavily charged with dyes, clogged with putridity, and bubbling with poisonous gases, till at last they turn to mere ink, stink, and malaria, and people the churchyards as they crawl.

The men who governed England with few exceptions seemed indifferent to the rapid changes that were affecting the land. They trusted to the beneficent properties of flowing water to dilute and carry out to the sea the washings from the coal mines, dyes from bleaching and dyeing plants, sludge from metallurgical works, and untreated garbage from the cities and towns.

Governments exercised no restraints on industrial operations or the economy in general, least of all on polluting industries or jerry builders. There was no planning of these industrial cities, nor was much attention paid to the amenities; sanitary facilities and public hygiene were so rudimentary that outbreaks of deadly diseases were common in early Victorian days.

The typical Victorian capitalist, usually a self-made man like John Rylands of Manchester, was not concerned about the environment nor the conditions among which his workers lived. Rylands took children out of workhouses and sometimes worked them to death. Industrial accidents were frequent. Rylands died a millionaire and left his fortune to his wife who used it to endow the famous John Rylands Library in Manchester. He had no interest whatever in nature and least of all in the fishes of the rivers he and his fellow capitalists putrefied.

'Whenever I am in Manchester,' says Walter Greenwood in his book *Lancashire*, published in 1951, 'I make my customary pilgrimage to the bridge to apologize to the river [Irwell] for its treatment at the hands of my fellow men, who have poured into it such filth and chemical poison that not even primitive slime, from which we are told all of us have derived, can support an instant of life . . . Though the river is dead to life it is still a river, and though its pace is as slow as the wheels of God yet it has a pace, it moves inexorably towards the tumbling waters of the sea a few miles away. Here I know it loses itself and is cleaned.'

Many years before this passage was written an unknown writer penned an epitaph for the Irwell which might be applied to other industrialized streams in Britain and America:

> If with a stick you stir well
> The poor old river Irwell
> Very sick of the amusement
> You will soon become
> For fetid bubbles rise and burst.
> But that is not the worst.
> For little birds can hop about
> Dry-footed in the scum.

It took a long time for governments to institute some kind of controls on pollution for the sake of protecting public health. It took much longer to pass laws to safeguard the purity of the rivers in order to protect the fish and other aquatic life. In fact, this effort continues to this day. A few men like John Ruskin and William Morris raised their voices in defence of the environment and pleaded restraint. In the Prologue to the *Earthly Paradise* (1865) Morris urged his countrymen to

> Forget six counties overhung with smoke,
> Forget the snorting steam and piston stroke,
> Forget the spreading of the hideous town;
> Think rather of the pack-horse on the down,
> And dream of London, small, and white and clean,
> The clear Thames bordered by its garden green.

His plea went unheeded.

In 1877 Archibald Young's *The Salmon Fisheries* presented to the nation for the first time a list of English and Welsh rivers which were seriously affected by pollution:

River	Kind of pollution
Axe	Sewage
Camel	China clay, mines
Dart	Chemicals, mines, paper works, wool washings
Dee	Oil and alkali works, petroleum, paper works, wool washings
Dovey	Mines
Eden	Sewage, tanneries, mines
Exe	Sewage, paper works
Fowey	China clay works, mines
Kent	Manufactures
Ogmore	Coal, tanneries, sewage
Rhymney	Various pollutions
Ribble	Sewage, factories, chemicals
Severn	Sewage, mines, tanneries, dye works
Tamar and Plym	Mines and clay works
Taw and Torridge	Sewage
Tees	Mines, sewage
Teifi	Mines
Teign	Mines, chemicals
Towy	Mines, chemicals
Trent	Sewage, factories
Tyne	Chemicals, mines, coal washings

Nearly all these rivers supported salmon stocks, and many of them have never been restored to anything like their pristine condition.

High among the factors that contributed to the decline of the salmon in Britain was the multiplication of weirs to divert water for millraces or industrial operations. Sometimes these barriers had no gaps to permit the fish to pass, were operated six days a week, and occasionally were left high and dry. The Royal Commission on Freshwater Fisheries of 1861 discovered that the Ouse, Wharfe, Ure, Derwent and other Yorkshire streams were studded with weirs, and the Severn, Dee, Cumberland Derwent, Taw, Torridge and Test were 'also conspicuous for the deterioration of their fisheries since weirs have come into common use'.

In 1866 every one of the seventeen rivers protected by the Act of 1714 was partly or substantially blockaded by weirs or damaged by pollution.

Canalization also affected the fish stocks. By converting a river into a navigable waterway spawning beds were destroyed. As the Inspector of Salmon Fisheries said in his 1869 report, 'The salmon's nest becomes a pike pond, and the capabilities of the river, as a salmon-producing stream, is enormously lowered.' When a stream is polluted there is not enough oxygen to meet the demands of organic life. Part of the organic matter dumped into the water that is not entirely purified then sinks to the bottom to form a layer of sludge or mud in which nothing will grow. Instead, bacteria attack this mass and generate gases that are carried downstream for several miles, forming an impenetrable blockade to fish migration until rendered harmless by chemical reaction with some other substance. Salmon require water that has at least five parts per million of dissolved oxygen – when the DO drops below that level they cannot survive.

H. D. Turing, editor of the *Field*, made an extensive survey of polluted English rivers in the 1940s. 'To see the effects of pollution at its worst,' he said, 'one must as a rule go to the estuaries and tidal waters.' It was generally assumed that the sea, or the mixture of salt and fresh water in the lower tidal sections, would break up the heavy flow of untreated sewage and factory wastes floating downstream. It was believed that the sea cleansed everything, dissolved everything coming down the rivers; but often the materials are too formidable for sea water to break them up so that the estuaries become open sewers. Dark, odoriferous walls of sludge are wafted downstream and washed back and forth with the tides until they finally disappear. Sometimes they form bars at the mouth of the river and have to be dredged far out to sea.

Heavy pollution makes it difficult for the hardiest fishes to reach their upstream destination; to the smolts going downstream it may be lethal. They are extremely vulnerable at the time when they are transformed from a freshwater to a marine environment. In some cases they are stupefied and sucked into saltwater un-willingly so that the sudden change of habitat kills them, or they

are gobbled up by gulls. 'If the smolts did not instinctively select
flood time to make their way to the sea,' said Turing, 'there
would be years when, in a contaminated estuary, hardly any
fish would return to the river.'

The first phase of Scotland's industrial development centred
mainly around textiles, an industry located in Renfrewshire and
Lanarkshire. Cotton mills arose at Neilston, East Kilbride,
Glasgow and at Deanston and Stanley in Perthshire in the last
two decades of the eighteenth century. Because of the need for
water power they were usually built on or near limpid waterways,
rich in salmon and trout and other fish, such as the Clyde, Leven,
etc. Later, mills appeared on the east coast around Dundee on the
Firth of Tay while another cluster sprang up in north Ayrshire.
The rise of the cotton industry inspired the growth of subsidiary
processes – bleaching, dyeing, printing and embroidering. Jute
and woollen textile manufacturing became prominent. Bleaching
was concentrated in the Vale of Leven and the Cart Valley,
making full use of lime-free waters of rivers and lochs like the
fabled Loch Lomond, to the detriment of the fish runs.

The beautiful Scottish countryside was blighted by the spread
of ugly towns which bourgeoned around the mills. Steel and
machinery manufacture arose in the central lowland belt stretching from central Ayrshire to Midlothian and mid-Fife. Here
were good harbours, estuaries and canals. Around Glasgow,
where the Clyde was deepened and a channel cut to the sea,
smelting works, furnaces, steel mills and shipyards cluttered and
corroded the landscape; later came automotive and locomotive
works. Fishermen's huts on the banks of the river disappeared.
Glasgow became a typical Victorian slum, with families living
in one- or two-room houses lined back to back on dingy streets
marked by columns of smoking chimneys. Refuse piled up on
the streets was flushed down a ditch or creek. In time a piped
water supply was provided to supplement local wells and a
sewer system was built, but they merely carried the raw sewage
straight into the nearest body of flowing water.

Whisky distillers poured into the Spey and its tributaries
enormous quantities of organic wastes inimical to aquatic life.
In 1850 there were eleven distilleries using 2,270 barrels of malt a

week; by 1900 the number had risen to twenty-seven and the weekly consumption of malt to 50,000 barrels. A peculiarly toxic effluent known as 'burnt ale' or 'pot ale' killed many fish in the main river and one of its tributaries before it was brought under control by a court action taken by one of the principal landowners.

Some of the tributaries of the Tweed were often 'blae' with the dyes and wastes of woollen mills, though much of the stuff was nontoxic. Many fish were also killed by coal washings in the river Nith, by discharges from collieries and ammonia works on the Don, and by effluents of bleaching works on the Tay. Raw sewage contaminated the Forth, where many dead salmon were picked up below Stirling at times of low water and more were probably washed away by the tides. Pollution practically exterminated the salmon on the Clyde and Irvine Rivers in the Victorian era.

As an example of the destructive effects of industrialization and urbanization the river Forth was typical. It acquired the untreated sewage and miscellaneous wastes from the cities of Stirling, Alloa, Kincardine, Grangemouth, Queensferry and later the town and naval station of Rosyth. When the estuary was reasonably clean it was heavily fished by hang nets and sweep nets. 'But the deposition of sewage and rubbish, of coke and cinders from the increasing shipping in its waters, and from the gas works and coal pits along its shores, have played havoc with the fauna,' said James Ritchie, writing shortly after World War I. 'The large numbers of the fauna have departed; the oyster beds are ruined; the cockles and mussels are not what they once were; but the most rapid changes have taken place amongst the shore animals, for in many places the fine old stretches of sand and rocks whereon the people of the towns once spent happy hours are buried beneath many inches of filthy cinders which have altered the courses of the streams and blotted out all traces of life.'

In 1877 Archibald Young reported that 'although a majority of Highland streams are uncontaminated by pollutions, the lowland rivers and several in Perthshire, Forfarshire, and Aberdeenshire are much polluted.' There were ninety-three mills and

factories in the four counties through which the Tweed and its
tributaries flowed and most of them dumped refuse of a more or
less injurious nature into the waters. Relatively few of these
establishments had tanks or other means of purifying their waste
water. 'The sources of pollution are yearly growing in number
and magnitude,' said Young. In addition to the toll taken by
pollution, 95,000 salmon, grilse and sea trout were killed by
disease in the Tweed from 1879 to 1892.

In the Forth watershed the rivers Devon, Almond, Avon,
Carron, Leven and Esk were bereft of salmon, said Young,
'owing to pollutions acting in combination with artificial obstructions'. In the Tay district the Ericht and Dight were entirely
ruined while the South Esk below Brechin was 'very much
injured'. In Ayrshire the Irvine 'has been utterly destroyed as a
salmon river by town sewage and other impurities, and the Ayr,
Doon and Garnock have also suffered terribly from pollution of
various kinds'. And so on.

Twenty-five years later Grimble reported that some of the
Scottish streams surveyed by Young had scarcely improved.

Overfishing and poaching

The Scottish journalist Alex Russel sounded the alarm that the
salmon resource was in danger, as Dickens did in England, in
his book *The Salmon* published in 1864. To him the greatest evil
was the excessive number of stake nets, bag nets and other fixed
gear that intercepted the fishes and kept the escapement well
below the level needed for perpetuation of the runs. There was,
of course, no scientific management. 'A sail along almost any
portion of the coast of Scotland . . . will show that the shore is
draped with salmon nets, with very little regard to the neighbour-
hood or distance of a river.' Wherever fixed engines blocked the
migration of fish the river catches usually dropped. On the north-
west coast of Sutherland bag nets were introduced in the 1830s;
in 1839 they caught over 16,000 salmon but in 1850, although
their number doubled, the catch had fallen to 1,300, and soon
after they were abandoned by the proprietor, the Duke of
Sutherland. Similar trends were seen on the Firths of Moray and
Beauly, so that one could only conclude that in the absence of

any kind of regulation or management the stocks were often overfished.

Some statistics are available to prove this contention. On the Tweed a measure of the drop was the decline in rentals from £15,766 in 1807 and £20,000 in 1814 to only £5,358 in 1846. The catch of salmon and grilse fell from an average of 109,000 annually in 1811–1815 to about a third of that level in 1851–1855 and half again at the end of the century. Next to the Tweed the Spey and Tay were probably the most productive Scottish rivers in the nineteenth century. The Duke of Richmond's waters on the Spey produced an average of 57,000 salmon and grilse in the 1850s while the Tay's output fluctuated between 60,000 and 70,000 fish between 1830 and 1846, reaching a peak of over 100,000 in 1842. The Duke of Sutherland's rivers flowing into the Moray Firth and Pentland Firth brought aggregate yearly landings of about 60,000 salmon and grilse between 1864 and 1876. Later figures are not available.

It was not only pollution, weirs and canalization that helped to depopulate the rivers. On some streams and estuaries the maximum amount of floating and fixed gear was employed, often in defiance of the laws, which were poorly enforced if at all. Efficient stake nets were introduced in the early nineteenth century in northern England, notably at the mouth of the Tyne, around Morecambe Bay, at the mouth of the Trent and in the Lune estuary. Putts and putchers, basket-like contraptions that lured the fish into traps, clogged the shores of the Severn estuary – in 1860 there were some 11,000 awaiting the salmon coming home from the sea. Easily erected and removed, they were catching fish without any regard to closed seasons and nothing was done to stop them.

Poachers usually worked with impunity, especially in Scotland where, for example, Sir Walter Scott used to treat his guests at Abbotsford to the nocturnal spectacle of 'burning the waters', vividly described and romanticized in the novel *Guy Mannering*. A. E. Gathorne-Hardy said, 'I hardly know of any sort of poaching which he [Scott] does not describe and countenance, except the serious practice of spearing salmon on horseback.' Tweedside inns resounded with the drinking and singing of poachers who had spent several hours standing in a boat on a cold night spearing the salmon by torchlight. This was regarded as one of the manliest of sports. There are many collections of these songs, of which a good example is Thomas Tod Stoddart's which begins

> A Birr! a whirr! – the salmon's on,
> A noble fish – a thumper!
> Bring up, bring up, the ready gaff,
> And, bending homewards, we shall quaff
> Another glorious bumper!

More salmon, said Stoddart in *The Angler's Companion* (1855), were killed with the leister than the rod on some Scottish rivers. 'At Kirkbank as many fish are sometimes killed in this way in a single night, as would suffice to exercise the ingenuity and encourage the perseverence of twenty honest anglers throughout the season.' (The Tweed Acts passed by Parliament soon outlawed the leister and rendered possession of it liable to prosecution.) Scottish magistrates like Scott might wink at a person who took a salmon for the pot but not at those, of whom there were many, who filched fish for money, though many poachers appear to have made a living at it.

Such, for example, was 'Salmon Job', once a weaver, whose horse-drawn cart was a familiar sight to people living along the road from Perth to Edinburgh. He could supply fresh salmon all year round, usually below the going price. He did not purvey 'black fish' (kelts) but clean salmon and, with his assistants, made a good living. Salmon Job apparently was never caught and continued to ply his trade until the day of his death – he was drowned while working the river Forth, and his body was fished up at Stirling. He left his daughter an estate of some £1,700.

Another famous poacher was 'Fish Tam' who lived in a gypsy colony near Kelso and made frequent trips through the country-side, sometimes as far as Edinburgh, disposing of salmon, kippered he said, according to a secret gypsy formula. His outlets were chiefly inns frequented by carriers and stage-coach drivers. Fish Tam came of a long line of poachers so that he knew all the secrets of the art. In his day he killed thousands of fine Tweed salmon. When he died he left £700 and two small houses, a sizeable estate, to his only child.

England too suffered heavily from poaching. Illegal fishing was not just a sport – the leisterer's recreation – but a profitable and usually safe enterprise because there were never enough guardians to patrol the streams. The Justices of the Peace were disinclined – as are the judges today – to root it out by imposing stiff sentences.

Nineteenth-century legislation

By 1860 it had become apparent that many of Britain's productive rivers had lost a considerable portion of their salmon stocks and some, like the Thames and Mersey, were completely deserted. The age of abundance was giving way to the age of scarcity.

Charles Dickens wrote in his weekly magazine *All the Year Round*, July 20, 1861, 'The salmon are in danger. A few years, a little more over-population, a few more tons of factory poisons, a few fresh poaching devices . . . and the salmon will be gone – he will become extinct.' Parliament must step in 'like a policeman into a riot'. As usual, Dickens was exaggerating but the alarm was real and Parliament had already stepped in by appointing, the previous year, a Royal Commission of Enquiry.

The commission found that the English fisheries had been grossly abused through (1) defective regulation of closed seasons; (2) excessive use of fixed engines; (3) obstruction of free passage of fish; (4) illegal fishing resulting in 'destruction of unseasonable fish, spawning fish, spent fish, young or fry'; (5) lack of an organized system of management of the rivers and fisheries; (6) poisoning of rivers by mine effluents; (7) 'pollution of waters by manufacturers, gas works and other nuisances'; and (8) 'confusion and uncertainty of the law and difficulty of enforcing its penalties against offenders'. So exigent was the situation that Parliament acted promptly and passed the Salmon Fisheries Act of 1861, which codified and modernized all previous legislation dealing with England and Wales. Certain types of commercial gear, such as stationary nets (fixed engines) were made illegal along the coasts, with certain exemptions; all future weirs were required to have a free gap not less than one-tenth the width of the stream; and mill dams could not be used for fishing unless they had approved passes that were in good condition with a constant flow of water to attract migrant fish'. An owner who failed to provide such passes forfeited his right to use the dam for fishing purposes.

The Salmon Fisheries Act of 1865 modernized the regulatory system by setting up Boards of Conservators with jurisdiction over an entire river or group of rivers, the genesis of the present regional water authorities. For the first time a licensing system was instituted for rod fishing as well as commercial fishing in the estuaries. Similar legislation was later provided for Scotland. Although this legislation was well intended it was usually weakly enforced, if at all. Similar legislation was provided for Scotland.

In response to the alarm raised by proprietors and others, Parliament passed the Tweed Acts of 1857 and 1859 which reduced the open season for nets and extended it for rods, lengthened the weekly closed period, outlawed the spear and leister, and banned the stell net from the tidal portion of the rivers and cairn net from the upper portion. This legislation also prohibited the dumping of poisonous substances into the streams, restricted mesh sizes of nets, and attempted to modify or remove obstructions to fish migration caused by dikes or dams. The Tweed was put under the management of Commissioners, a body consisting of all those owners having fishings with an annual value of £30 or a prescribed length of river bank. A similar act for the Tay was passed in 1858, and in 1862 and 1868 came laws covering all Scottish rivers north of the Tweed except the Tay, the first comprehensive revision of Scottish fishery laws in many centuries. Among other things, these Acts created a system of district boards, selected in equal numbers from the upper and lower proprietors on a river, who were responsible for the general policing and overseeing of the fisheries. As a result of these measures the anadromous fisheries in Scotland were probably better protected in the nineteenth century than in England and Wales. Since Scotland was less industrialized this resulted in the retention of a much greater proportion of the original stocks than over the Border.

One of the few real benefits of the 1861 Act was the creation of salmon fishery inspectors for England and Wales. The witty, eccentric Frank Buckland, who held one of the posts from 1867 to 1880, was the ideal man for the position. His primary job was to sell the new laws to river owners and awaken the nation to the need for fishery conservation. He lectured up and down the land, and circulated his message in articles in his magazine *Land and Water*, as well as in the annual reports of the Inspectors of Salmon Fisheries. For the first time the nation learned what had happened to many of the rivers and the fish. For instance, the inspectors found that the Severn was blockaded by seventy-three weirs, the Taw and Torridge by seventy, cutting off some forty miles of spawning grounds, the Welsh Derwent by five, etc. Some of these impoundments had fish passes but others did not and their owners were not required to install them because of the 'grandfather clause' in the 1861 Act.

Buckland humorously depicted the consequences of such blockades. Salmon, he said, could jump 'like arrows out of a bow, as much as nine feet in the air, again and again,' but at some of the weirs he had observed 'not one got over'. One of the owners, the Duke of Northumberland, a kindly man, was planning to provide a fish pass but his plans had not yet been completed. Therefore the inspector pinned up a note at the weir which read

Notice to Salmon and Bull Trout
No road at present over this weir. Go down stream and take the first turn to the right, and you will find good travelling water upstream, and no jumping required. – *F.T.B.*

Buckland wittily summed up the plight of the salmon in *Land and Water*:

Perhaps the most unfortunate thing in the world is the salmon. Everybody and everything, from the otter to the fisherman, persecutes him. He is naturally an inhabitant of the sea. He runs up the rivers, and would almost jump into the pot on the kitchen fire if allowed, but every effort is put forth to keep him at a distance. He gets fat in the sea, though what his food is nobody quite knows. He is in the habit, however, of going up the rivers to his country quarters in the mountains, along with his wife and family. Then almost at the outset, he is caught by a seal lying in wait for him, as in the Tay, for instance. Then comes a net, then a weir, and next a steamer frightens him back; then the refuse from the town forces him to choose between returning and being poisoned. The weirs across rivers are the main cause why our fisheries have fallen off; yet all that is wanted is a fish ladder, a series of steps or boxes extending up over the weir. If the salmon succeeds in leaping the weir, he next meets with an angler, who may however fail to hook him; then on arriving at his proposed destination, he encounters the poacher, who tries to spear him with a trident. Escaping him, the salmon at last reach their breeding place, where Mistress Salmon begins stirring the gravel with her tail, and making a hollow nest lays her eggs . . . The trout then comes to eat the eggs; next a whole swarm of flies and insects; then the water ouzel, who goes to eat the flies, is shot by ourselves, under the idea that the bird is after the eggs, and not after the flies. Other enemies come: the jack, and the otter who follows the little salmon on their way to the sea, where the angler-fish lies in wait for them. The result is that not one egg in ten thousand becomes food for man.

In their report for the year 1869 the Inspectors noted that 'out of 36,000 square miles which ought to be productive of this valuable fish, only one-fourth, or over 9,000 square miles, produces salmon at all'. Not much improvement had occurred since the passage of the new fishery legislation. Each year more gear was employed on some of the best rivers and much of the fishing was illegal. Nor was there any attempt to limit netting licences, so that many streams were fished hard and their stocks were being decimated. Around Morecambe Bay, for example, there were hundreds of stake nets, and at the mouth of the Trent and in the Lune estuary thousands of putts and putchers prevented many of the fish from escaping.

On the Tyne, probably the most productive British salmon river, the nets were working night and day, and in one year,

1872, they took a record 120,000 salmon and grilse. At the mouth of the Tyne, said the Inspector, one could see, as night approached 'hundreds of lights glimmering in every direction from literally hundreds of boats engaged in fishing . . . nets tied together floating along with the tide barred the passage of the harbour in every direction; it was impossible to reach the harbour without steaming through the nets. I found the more distant nets usually anchored in defiance of the law, and the same men constantly fishing with three or even four nets but with one licence.' By the year 1900 the annual catch on the Tyne, suffering from both heavy fishing and pollution, had fallen to 12,000 salmon and by World War II there were very few salmon left.

The Thames fell victim chiefly to pollution from London and to canalization. In Elizabethan times salmon were taken in commercial quantities at Maidenhead, Wandsworth, Fulham, Twickenham, Richmond, Chelsea and London proper. Some of the fish weighed over fifty pounds. The last salmon was said to have been caught in the Thames in 1833. So pervasive was the pollution that few fish could live in London's river. For example, the Reverend Benjamin Armstrong observed in his diary for July 10, 1855:

> Took the children by boat from Vauxhall bridge to show them the great buildings. Fortunately the Queen and Royal Princes drove by. The ride on the water was refreshing except for the stench. What a pity this noble river should be made a common sewer.

However, optimists like Frank Buckland and his friends, ignorant of the habitat requirements of salmonids, especially the need for dissolved oxygen, tried to restock the river by planting salmon ova at Moulsey and Sunbury, but nothing came of this experiment. Only an occasional salmon, having lost its way, strayed into the river on its spawning journey, as one did in 1974 and again in 1975. By the end of the nineteenth century salmon had deserted many of the rivers in the industrial areas of England, Wales and Scotland, or were reduced to token populations.

In recent years the lower Thames has been extensively cleaned up. Most of the species of coarse fish have returned, thanks to an expenditure of over 100 million pounds, and a recent report of the Thames Migratory Fish Committee offers the hope that by 1980 the river will be pure enough to permit 'the successful passage of juvenile and adult salmon and sea trout'.

Hydroelectric development

Hydroelectric development began in Scotland in 1895 primarily to support the manufacture of aluminium. Seven additional plants were built on Scottish rivers before World War II. After the war, with the nationalization of the electric power industry, a number of rivers were harnessed in the Highlands, including the Conon, Ness, Tay, Garry, Tummel and Dee. The dams have created serious barriers to fish migration while the reservoirs have eliminated spawning and rearing grounds. Of the thirty-five fishery districts which in 1963 reported a catch of at least 3,000 salmon, grilse and sea trout, nine have hydroelectric schemes.

In creating the North of Scotland and South of Scotland Electricity Boards, Parliament specified that in undertaking hydroelectric schemes they 'shall have regard to the desirability of avoiding, as far as possible, injury to the fisheries and the stock of fish in any waters'. Among the measures taken to safeguard

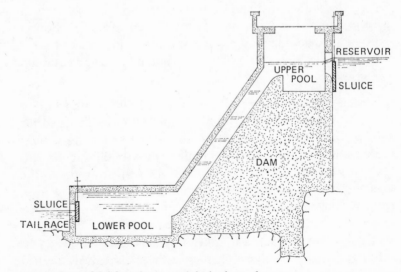

4 *Borland type fish lift used at Scottish hydroelectric dams*

the salmon are ladders at the dams to enable the fish to surmount them, traps to catch the fish for artificial propagation, and hatcheries to produce stock to compensate for losses at the impoundments.

What are the results? Commercial fishermen complain that their catches have been reduced while anglers lament the loss of favourite beats. They point out that landlords like Lord Lovat, who own some 180,000 acres in the Highlands, were amply compensated for damming his river while *they* are much the poorer. Looking at one of his favourite streams in the Garry–Tummel system, Arthur Oglesby spoke for many sportsmen when he said, 'This is a very high price to pay for the doubtful benefits of electricity.'

However, although there have been fish losses the worst fears of opponents of the hydroelectric programme have not been realized. One of the most pressing problems is to safeguard the downstream passage of smolts and kelts. Fish ladders and lifts take them into the reservoirs, but the tiny smolts must go through the turbines in the power houses where the schools may be decimated. Kelts are too large to take this route and have to be passed around the dams by means of grids or screens.

At some hydroelectric projects, like the Galloway in south Scotland, there was at first a falling off in the runs, then a revival. At most of the installations in north Scotland the stocks have been fairly well maintained with help from hatcheries, at least until very recent years when the spread of UDN and netting of British salmon in Greenland waters began to be felt.

Since catch statistics are not published for the various Scottish rivers we cannot say much about the productivity of the different watersheds. Some people argue that there is considerable over-fishing. Bag nets, they point out, are anchored off the coasts near the river mouths seventy to a hundred yards apart, constituting a wall of netting with a leader three to ten yards long. Men come out from time to time to inspect the nets and collect the catches. Fly nets are set between tidal high and low water on sandy shores so that in low water a man can clamber out along the ropes to the head and take the fish. Collections are brought to netting stations, boxed and iced, and sent to markets; many go to Billingsgate in

London. Some of the inlets on the Scottish coasts are so steep that the boxes have to be hoisted up from the beach by winches or carried by sturdy-shanked ponies.

During the open season the nets work day and night except for the forty-two hour weekend closure when the leaders of the bag nets are brought ashore to be dried, checked and mended, while the heads of the fly net are tied up on the poles. On the west coast of Scotland the bag nets are strung out fifty to a hundred yards from the shore on prominent points like Rhu Stoer, Rhu Coigeach, Gailleach Point, Greenstone Point and Ardnamurchan. The number of nets is limited but the right to set them up may be quite lucrative and is zealously guarded by the fishing companies.

Commercial fishing for salmon in Scottish rivers is confined to the coble, a flat-bottomed row boat. The two-man crew moves the coble slowly across the stream, shortening the net as they go, roughly in a semicircle, and finishing at the landing where they are joined by a man with a rope. The ends are then hauled in and the trapped fish, flapping crazily in their endeavour to escape, are removed. If the tide is high and the water turbulent, the fishermen may use a power winch to pull the rope. The net must remain stationary or drift with the tide. The netting season usually begins in February and ends in August.

The introduction of monofilament nylon which is invisible in water has greatly increased the effectiveness of the nets. 'We are now faced,' says the Atlantic Salmon Research Trust's *Newsletter* (January 1975) 'with the actuality of this around the coasts of Scotland, where lengths of monofilament nets operating on the drift net principle but moored to the shore or anchored in comparatively shallow water (known as "hang nets") are being more and more extensively used – apparently with devastating effect.' Unless firm action is taken, 'the whole balanced system of culling our salmon stocks by legalized methods of commercial netting which existed, by and large satisfactorily, for 100 years will be completely thrown out of gear; additionally, it is already known that monofilament injures large numbers of salmon which get entangled but manage finally to escape. Imagination boggles at the scale of damage that may be inflicted on our stocks of salmon through numbers caught or injured, by an explosive expansion of monofilament.' As long ago as 1970 the International Commission for the Northeast Atlantic Fisheries passed a resolution banning monofilament nets throughout its jurisdiction and later the International Commission for the Northwest Atlantic Fisheries followed suit. 'Since Ireland and Canada have implemented these resolutions,' says the Trust, 'it seems pertinent to ask why the United Kingdom has not yet done likewise.'

In 1977 drift netting off the coast of Scotland, mostly illegal, reached crisis proportions.

Twentieth-century legislation

Britain sailed along with ineffective fishery and anti-pollution laws for over sixty years after the revision of the ancient codes in the 1850s and 1860s. In 1923 came the passage of the Salmon and Freshwater Fisheries Act which consolidated all earlier laws and added important new features. Dams or weirs on fish migration routes were now required to have passes or ladders approved by the Minister of Agriculture and Fisheries. It became 'an offence to pollute waters so as to make them harmful to fish', but 'practices in use or employed by prescriptive right' were excepted 'provided that the best practical means within reasonable cost were used to prevent such discharges doing injuries to fisheries' – a fatal weakness in the bill which has never been overcome.

The next milestone in fishery legislation was the River Boards Act of 1948 which placed every river system in England and Wales under a board responsible for the control of fisheries, land drainage and water pollution. Each of the thirty boards was authorized to levy taxes for funds needed to carry out conservation work, thus adding to revenues obtained from fishing licences; to hire adequate protective personnel; to undertake capital improvements. In 1951 came the Rivers Pollution Act which empowered the boards to issue regulations (by-laws) controlling discharges into streams. River boards were subsequently converted into river authorities with broader powers and in 1973 were reorganized and consolidated into regional water authorities.

In general adequate laws protecting inland fisheries and designed to control water pollution are now on the books, but their implementation leaves much to be desired. Omnibus legislation is contained in the Salmon and Freshwater Fisheries Act of 1975 which consolidated the Salmon and Freshwater Fisheries Act of 1923 and other enactments concerning salmon and freshwater fisheries and repealed certain obsolete enactments. Because of the economic crisis in which Britain finds itself, grants by the national government for anti-pollution work have been severely curtailed, hence not much progress can be expected.

The state of the nation's rivers, however, has been closely monitored in recent years by both the press and the government. Thus Anthony Pearson reported in the *Guardian* of July 14, 1969, that 'little notice has been paid to the Rivers Prevention of Pollution Act by those responsible for pollution. Moreover, penalties are ludicrously small, the maximum for conviction being £20, mere pinpricks to large industrial concerns ... It is now more than worthwhile to pay an occasional £20 for the use of a convenient and otherwise free means of waste disposal.' Jeremy Bugler in *Polluting Britain* (1972) concludes that a society obsessed with technological improvements and marked by corporate indifference to the effects of its operations on the environment, needs 'not only new laws, not only new agencies, not only new taxes and technologies, but new attitudes' if the crusade to clean up Britain's rivers is to succeed. In this respect Britain is behind the United States which has an Environmental Protection Act, a federal Department of Environmental Quality, and many state laws and agencies designed to protect the waters and air, and thus, among other things, benefit the fisheries.

The Department of the Environment now makes annual surveys of English and Welsh rivers. Its report for 1972 showed that streams in the industrial and heavily populated areas remain grossly defiled: 59% of the nontidal Trent is polluted, 63% of the Mersey and Weaver, 37% of Hampshire and Lancashire streams, 57% of the waters under the jurisdiction of the Port of London Authority, 40% of Essex rivers, etc. The purest streams are in Lincolnshire, Devon, Cornwall, Wales, including the Wye, and the upper Thames watershed. The Thames, in fact, is beginning to run sweetly again since the authorities closed small, overloaded sewage plants and replaced them with larger and more efficient units and at the same time forced factory owners to channel their pollutants through them. Not many years ago only air-breathing eels could survive in the lower river and gulls replaced the swans and ducks that used to paddle along its waters. Now seventy different species of coarse fish are said to be available to anglers, and gulls are outnumbered by teal, pochard, shelduck, scaup, pintails and tufted ducks.

The Department of the Environment's report *Pollution: Nuisance or Nemesis?* (1972) admits that technology is available to solve most water pollution problems but 'too often we are failing to apply biological treatment techniques which were well known forty years ago. The greatest need is for a more efficient administration and for a system of financial incentives and controls to ensure that the best available technology is used.'

In Scotland too, except on the Tweed and a few other streams, there seems to be a losing fight to reduce pollution. The lower reaches of the Don, for example, have deteriorated alarmingly since 1967, owing to a pollution block which has suffocated thousands of smolts on their way to the sea. When the offending industries, mostly pulp mills, close down for the summer vacation, the water runs crystal clear and a large number of grilse enter the river. After the mills resume operation no more fish come up until October, when the river is clean again.

Pollution has affected the neighbouring Dee, whose toxic waters are attributed mainly to the wash-off of chemicals used by farmers. In the Teith, which flows into the Firth of Forth, the runs are still affected by pollution emanating from Grangemouth and Alloa. Sometimes fishermen haul out of the water salmon that are inedible because of oil contamination. Other 'black spots' are the rivers Ayr and Lugar which receive the slurry from washing plants at the nearby coal pits. Here the efforts of the local Purification Board and the Anglers' Cooperative Association have effected some improvement but much remains to be done. The lower Clyde is still a disgraceful stream; it was more than a half-century ago that a salmon was caught in it and displayed as a curiosity in a Glasgow fish shop. The middle and upper reaches of the river above Bothwell remain clear and support trout.

The Tweed has made a notable comeback. With the passage of effective legislation it is now almost free from pollution, poaching is relatively insignificant, and most of the stream barriers such as the caulds have been removed. As a result, catches have shown an upward trend since the 1930s. However, the Greenland fishery which takes many salmon from British rivers, ultradermal necrosis (UDN) that has killed salmon in many British waters in the past decade, and the upsurge of the grey seal population are making inroads on Tweed stocks.

THE FUTURE OF THE SALMON IN GREAT BRITAIN

England and Wales have lost the great bulk of their salmon wealth, due to the numerous forces we have described. By the end of the nineteenth century all the principal English rivers yielded little more than a half, and even less, of the 1,850,000 salmon and grilse which six rivers, the Tyne, Severn, Tees, Usk, Ribble and Dart, produced annually in the 1870s. Since 1930 catches have seldom exceeded 50,000 salmon and grilse per year, excluding the huge hauls of the nets off the Northumberland coast, mainly fish headed for Scottish rivers.

With so few salmon to share among netters and sportsmen, the latter are demanding a greater portion of the runs and therefore a reduction in netting. In the twentieth century spreading wealth has democratized salmon angling, now the most prestigious form of sport fishing in Europe, and ownership of salmon water is immensely profitable. In 1970 Strutt & Parker, the London firm which arranges sales of salmon rivers, said that the capital value per average salmon caught in a river is between £200 and £300, but in 1977 the Boleside fishings on the Tweed, with an average catch of 234 salmon and grilse, was sold for £155,000 or £660 per fish.

The industrial era has created a need for the kind of recreation offered by fishing, and the prince of game fishes is regarded as the supreme trophy. Merchants, bankers, politicians, diplomats, scholars and others pursue the sport regardless of expense. Books on fishing multiply, hoping to attain some of the popularity of Izaak Walton's *Compleat Angler*. A worthy successor to Walton's

The five species of Pacific salmon found in North American waters, from the top, red or sockeye, chum, pink, silver or coho, and king or chinook. A sixth species, cherry salmon, is found only in Asia.

An Atlantic salmon jumping a fall on its way upstream.

A scale from a sockeye salmon, magnified one hundred times, reveals the fish's biological data. The fine rings in the scale's core record the time the fish spent in fresh water, while the coarser-textured rings surrounding the core records its oceanic life.

The Driva, a fine salmon river in the Norwegian fjord country.

An Atlantic salmon being removed from a stake or weir trap, as used on the River Shannon in Eire.

The River Aulne in Brittany, one of the few French streams still producing salmon.

Salmon fishing in the River Spey in Scotland.

masterpiece is *A Portrait of Salmon Fishing* written and compiled by Geoffrey Nickson and illustrated with original paintings of the great salmon rivers of the United Kingdom; published by Antony Atha Publishers, London. Such books whet the appetite of *aficionados* of *Salmo salar*. Andrew Lang's eulogy of Walton, written at the end of the Victorian era, is perhaps more germane to the nuclear era than it was then:

> Old Izaak, in this angry age of ours,
> This hungry, angry age – how oft of thee
> We dream, and thy tranquility:
> The meads enamelled and the singing showers,
> The shelter of the silvery willow-tree,
> By quiet waters by the river Lea!
> Ah, happy hours, we cry, ah, halcyon hours!

In the halcyon Victorian days anglers travelled to their beats in pony-drawn wagonettes or carts. Few or no rod-caught fish were sold – they were given to friends or dependents – and a gentlemanly code of behaviour prevailed. The size of the bag was only a secondary consideration although many people were determined to set lifetime records, like Robert Pashley who caught 9,800 salmon on the Wye between 1906 and 1951, averaging over two hundred per year. The Wye is now the best salmon angling river in England and Wales, most of the nets having been removed many years ago.

Everywhere in Great Britain the best beats are expensive, especially in Scotland, where one famous beat on the Spey rents for over £1,000 a week. Another on the lower Tay brings £400–500 a week and here the runs seem to be declining. In Scotland there are over 600 hotels catering to salmon and trout fishers and their families, providing the principal boost to economic survival for many communities in the remoter valleys. In England and Wales the rods take one fish for every six landed by the nets while in Scotland (which has far greater stocks) the ratio has been roughly one in eight in the past decade.

Because of the high cost of fishing some anglers sell their catches – the price in 1975 was £1 per pound. 'Nowadays,' says Ian Wood, former editor of *Trout and Salmon*, 'there is too little water, and any stretches that are rented to individuals are very highly priced. This tends to encourage many people who have paid so highly for their privilege to fish hard and sell their fish. Some owners want large bags in order to increase the value of their fishing and therefore permit the use of whatever bait is successful. Tenants want many fish to help pay their rent, thus much of the sport fishing for salmon in Britain is now really commercial.'

In March, 1974, the Association of River Authorities released a report entitled *Taking Stock* which suggests that netting should be reduced in England in order to enhance the seed stock. In fact, this privilege of being permitted to net in public waters, said the Association, is being abused. 'On many rivers, and this is particularly evident in Devon and Lancashire, commercial net licences are held by individuals with full-time employment completely dissociated from fishing. They include hoteliers, brewery and company directors, garage hands, and nurses and the retired. They have little or no interest in conservation and we do not appreciate why they should be allowed to retain such a privilege under the existing net limitation orders. They operate only at the expense of those who are wholly engaged in commercial fishing and to the detriment of other river interests.'

Clearly too much of the small stock of salmon in England and Wales is going to commercial operators, endangering the seed stock as well as depriving anglers of sport. It would be the better part of wisdom to reduce netting, especially drift netting, along the coasts and in some of the estuaries. There are demands that the new regional water authorities should consider buying up commercial fishings, as was done by the proprietors on the Wye in the earlier part of the century. The current climate of opinion, however, is against the expenditure of public funds for conservation programmes that benefit relatively few people. Such a move, says the chairman of one regional water authority, would probably provoke a great deal of public hostility.

Canada offers a prime example of how curtailment of netting benefits anglers and helps to restock the rivers by permitting more fish to reach their spawning grounds. In 1972 the Canadian government came to the conclusion that the Atlantic salmon resource had reached a crisis because too many fish were being taken in the nets around the coasts. This, with the heavy slaughter of Canadian salmon by commercial fishermen in Davis Strait and around the coasts of Greenland, was palpably decreasing the runs in the Maritime provinces as well as in Newfoundland and Labrador. About 40% of the nets were therefore eliminated in 1972 for a period of five years in the province of New Brunswick, along the Quebec coast and the southern tip of Newfoundland. The result was evident in the next few years as some of the runs began to increase notably, to the delight of anglers on the prestigious Restigouche, Miramichi and other streams. The ban was extended in 1977 for one year. 'This,' says Dr Leslie Stewart, one of the best informed salmon experts in England, 'is what we would like to see in England and Wales'.

Greater efforts to curb poaching would also enhance the salmon wealth. As the value of fresh salmon reaches new peaks every year, illegal fishing increases. Fish are snatched by individuals or gangs not only in the rivers but offshore in shoals, landed on deserted beaches and taken in lorries to hotels and inns where they fetch good prices. A veteran poacher who has turned gillie and now helps guard some of the pools he used to loot, describes the modern techniques of this ancient art:

> You spies out the land in the evening before it gets dark. When you go out you use lots of lookouts, spread out well and you have night glasses. If you're going to use a barbed hook you hide it in the instep of your boot – these are trade secrets – and in the dark look along the path just above the ground level and hear better. Those who do not use a hook toss the poison Cymag into the pool, or use explosives . . . One must not take the catch home immediately but hide it and collect it later.

The efficient poacher rarely gets caught, and, if he is, the court often treats him leniently. After sending an offender to jail for nine months a judge in Carlisle remarked, 'It is a repugnant thing to have to deprive a man of his liberty for this type of offence.' There are not enough bailiffs to apprehend poachers, and though the gala sprees enjoyed by Stoddard and Scrope in Scotland over a century ago are no longer tolerated, gangs continue to operate on many rivers throughout the United Kingdom, sometimes in daylight, and have been known to throw anglers in the rivers. In Devonshire sophisticated gangs using several vehicles, inflatable dinghies and walkie-talkies, have proved particularly successful. When caught and fined they seldom pay the fines, a surprisingly effective ploy against which the courts seem powerless.

In the area covered by the North West Water Authority there were 380 successful prosecutions for illegal fishing in 1975, while in Scotland, a much greater area, only about 250 poachers are apprehended each year. According to Peter Liddell (chairman of the North West Water Authority), there is no effective fishery organization in Scotland, no enforcement agency other than private owners' employees or 'very occasionally an apparently unhelpful police force'. All these prosecutions 'do not seem to reduce significantly what amounts to a flourishing industry', says Lieutenant-Colonel Colin Mitchell of the British Field Sports Society.

'It is a tragedy,' adds Liddell, 'that the Conservative government dropped, from sheer inertia, a bill to bring order into Scottish fisheries administration. With the power to levy fishing licence fees they could build up a proper protection and management service – why should I, for instance, be able to fish these splendid rivers without contributing to their maintenance and improvement? Too many lairds still live in the world of the clan and the claymore. Where what was good enough for their fathers is good enough for them; in the day of fast cars, poisons and mobile gangs of netsmen, it isn't, and the sooner they wake up and fight for themselves the better.'

In considering the future of the salmon in the United Kingdom, we must take a hard look at their habitat as well as the industry, both sporting and commercial, that exploits them. It is clear that the stocks in England and Wales have remained more or less at the same low level since World War I. Despite the efforts of various conservation groups, notably the Salmon and Trout Association, the Anglers' Cooperative Association, the Atlantic

Salmon Research Trust and others, relatively little has been done in recent years to enhance the resource, especially south of the Scottish border. The great interest of the medieval English monarchs in the inland fisheries contrasts with the general indifference of the national government in this century. In Parliament there are a few stalwart friends of the salmon both in the House of Commons and the Lords, who from time to time remind their colleagues of this noble heritage, but very little money is appropriated specifically for salmon research or conservation. As the Association of River Authorities states in its report, 'Without adequate finances there can be no progression in fish husbandry or indeed in fishery management or development. We would emphasize that income from licensing cannot provide adequate income compatible with adequate conservation, and it is unlikely that it will be adequate in the foreseeable future.'

In the use of the nation's rivers the fish have a low preference if they interfere with the need of water for domestic or farm supplies, or for manufacturing or power generation. The same is true in the United States, France, Spain and other industrialized countries.

In *Trout and Salmon*, December 1976, Tony George outlines some of the proposed schemes in England and Wales for water abstraction that threaten many of the remaining salmon rivers. To begin with, there are plans for a national water grid, still sketchily drawn, but, he says, 'from what we already know it is unlikely to do many of our salmon fisheries one little bit of good. In Lancashire the North West Water Authority have a £45 million scheme under construction to pump water from the Lune south to the Wyre. From the Wyre the water will flow down to Garstang and then by another pipeline to a treatment works at Caterall ... The scheme will just about put paid to the Lune as a salmon river of any quality.' Further north the same Authority is launching a project for conveying water from the Lake District to serve Manchester. This will affect the Eden whose runs have seriously declined in recent years.

A major water transfer scheme 'of the greatest possible interest to English and Welsh salmon fishers is the projected Wye–Usk aqueduct, to boost the flow of the Usk at the Wye's expense,' intended to supply water for domestic or industrial use before it reaches the estuary at Newport, a project that 'could be very serious' for the Wye, one of the best remaining English salmon rivers.

The Tyne, which is making a bit of a comeback as a salmon producer, is now threatened by the £100 million Kielder dam project to bring Tyne water to the Wear and Tees, designed to benefit the Imperial Chemical Industries and British Steel Corporation industrial complex at the mouth of the Tees. When this scheme is completed the Tees, 'another famous salmon river without a run, is unlikely to benefit at all as far as migratory fish are concerned'.

These are only a few of the projects under consideration that will affect the salmon. There is a grandiose scheme afoot for transporting water from a giant dam in Wales all the way to the Thames. Then there are the estuarial barrages proposed for the Severn, Welsh Dee, Lune and Solway; tidal electricity proposals, etc. 'Who can have any reservations,' says Mr George, 'that, over the next fifty years, the scenario I have outlined will encompass the fate of a number, perhaps many, of our salmon rivers?'

In a nation like Britain which worships the great god Economic Progress and bows down to the Golden Calf called industry, the fishes in the rivers will be sacrificed just like the air and waters which used to be clean and are now horribly polluted wherever certain industries have been allowed to settle. The same is true of the United States, France, Germany and other industry-mad countries. There is no cessation of plans to create more industry on rivers that have a good water supply, build more dams and turn watersheds topsy-turvy. In such societies, what chance have the salmon?

The salmon have fared much better in Scotland than in England primarily because of sparse population and lesser industrialization. Salmon and grilse catches increased from 415,000 per annum in the decade 1955–1964 to 472,000 in 1965–1974; rod catches dropped from 66,000 per annum to 61,000 in the same period.

This is about five times as much as the harvests in England and Wales. Scotland now produces as much or more salmon than any other country with the possible exception of Canada.

The advent of the North Sea oil industry, however, carries portents of danger. As Tony George points out, the east coast of Scotland will 'inevitably become much more industrialized', with the result that water abstraction to feed gargai...uan petrochemical and other industries, and the inevitable pollution, will harm the fisheries that need clean water for survival in the rivers. Oil spills in marine waters will also be harmful.

It is clear that the British people must come to grips with the problem of restoring some of the salmon runs they have lost in the last two centuries or risk the possibility of seeing *Salmo salar* become a vanishing species, as it is in France and Spain. We now have the technical knowledge to manage the fisheries in such a manner as to restore some of their abundance, given a national will and desire to do so with the help of large amounts of public funds.

In the summer of 1977 a crisis was reached in the brazen defiance of authority off the east coast of Scotland. Thousands of salmon were being slaughtered illegally and the British government controlling the Department of Agriculture and Fisheries in Edinburgh and the Scottish Legal Service seemed unable to stop the marauders. Some of the salmon were sold to Danish and other European fishing boats and the rest were landed in English ports such as Berwick. The authorities were bombarded with complaints about illegal drift netting with nylon nets that was not only taking spawning fish but damaging those salmon who escaped the nets and managed to reach the rivers – many of these did not spawn.

At last, in August, the Department of Agriculture and Fisheries went into action and brought the full resource of the Navy, including helicopters, into play, arresting poaching vessels *en masse*. The poachers fought back and sank one patrol boat but the government seemed 'determined to stop this nonsense', said Michael Forsyth-Grant, a former Inspector of Salmon Fisheries for Scotland, 'and there was no relaxation in air and sea surveillance'. (*Atlantic Salmon Journal*, October 1977.)

The impact of heavy offshore netting has been felt in Scottish rivers. 'Some netting stations reported weeks with as few as three fish taken,' said an editorial in *Trout and Salmon* (July 1977). In Aberdeen the wholesale price of salmon jumped to over £3.40 per lb. (over $6.00), and it was reported that on the continent the price was as much as £14 (over $25.00) in places like West Berlin for Scottish salmon caught by Scottish boats and transferred at sea to continental craft.

The editorial warned that 'for the salmon time is running out. It has suffered disease, drought and Greenland netting. Now it has to face even more intensive netting in its own waters. If finally it succumbs to the effects of these accumulated pressures, then so, too, will a whole way of life in Scotland. If both are to be saved, far more drastic action . . . is needed, and needed soon. In five years it could be too late.'

CHAPTER 7

Irish Fisheries

FOR the most part, Ireland is a well watered, verdant land. The mountains, rising to 2,000 feet elevation, are all around the periphery of the island, while the centre is low, wide plain with an undulating terrain.

Ireland has over 600,000 acres of lakes and some 9,000 miles of fish-bearing rivers, many of which are accessible to salmon. The Irish Tourist Board lists over a hundred rivers and lake systems where anglers might try their luck, and the Tourist Board of Ulster adds thirty more in the six counties that form part of the United Kingdom. Eel fisheries are probably more numerous than salmon. Some of the rivers are quite short and drain lakes of various size. The productive Garavogue, for example, only two and a half miles long, is an outlet for Lough Gill, while the five and a half mile Corrib, on which the city of Galway is situated, drains three limestone lakes of which the largest is Lough Corrib, twenty-seven miles long with a maximum breadth of seven miles. There are also many lengthy, full-bodied rivers of which the 190-mile Shannon emanating from the high moors of Culcaigh and reaching its estuary at Limerick City, is the longest in Ireland.

The Shannon is a deep river which passes through three substantial lakes, and is bolstered by the flow of many tributaries such as the Cashen, Maigue, Fergus and Deel, some of which drain a network of lakes. As it spirals across the heart of Ireland the river crosses much historic country, including romantic castles and abbeys burned and plundered by the Vikings a thousand years ago, their grey stone ruins lending a melancholy air to the landscape.

Among the best salmon rivers are the Cork Blackwater, Barrow, Nore and Suir in the southern part of Ireland. The

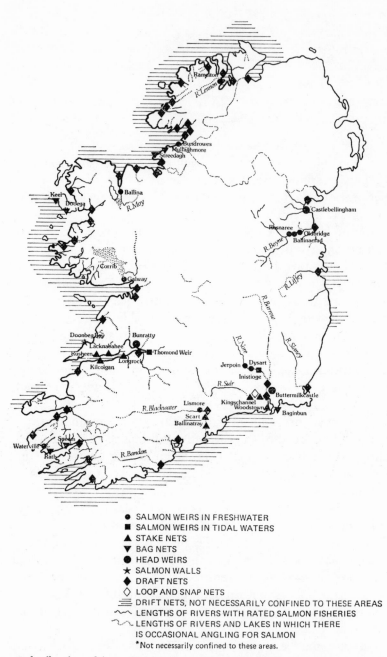

SALMON WEIRS IN FRESHWATER

SALMON WEIRS IN TIDAL WATERS

STAKE NETS

BAG NETS

HEAD WEIRS

SALMON WALLS

DRAFT NETS

LOOP AND SNAP NETS

DRIFT NETS, NOT NECESSARILY CONFINED TO THESE AREAS

LENGTHS OF RIVERS WITH RATED SALMON FISHERIES

LENGTHS OF RIVERS AND LAKES IN WHICH THERE
IS OCCASIONAL ANGLING FOR SALMON
*Not necessarily confined to these areas.

5 Ireland's salmon fisheries (Source: Report of the Inland Fisheries Commission 1975)

Blackwater rises in the wild, rocky uplands of County Kerry, a few miles east of Killarney and the nearby Fairy Lakes, and runs for ninety odd miles to the sea. As Stephen Gwynn said, 'It is a river proper, not the prolongation of a lake system.' The 112-mile Barrow comes out of the Slieve Bloom Mountains of Queen's County, maintains a southerly course, and waters good farming land before it is joined by the Nore, itself a major river, and at Waterford by the Suir, also an important drainage. These 'three sisters' have yielded large quantities of salmon over the centuries.

Among the major salmon rivers in eastern Ireland are the Boyne, Liffey and Slaney. The Boyne flows through County Meath from its south-west corner below Drogheda; the Liffey issues from the Wicklow Mountains only a dozen miles from Dublin and follows a corkscrew course of eighty-two miles to Dublin Bay and its estuary – salmon used to run up as far as Barrymore Eustace. The sixty-mile Slaney, famous for its sea trout as well as salmon, is also a moorland stream, flowing through Counties Carlow and Wexford to Enniscorthy and St George's Channel.

In Northern Ireland, the Foyle, partly in Eire and partly in the United Kingdom, has in recent time overshadowed all other salmon rivers in the British Isles in productivity. Although only twenty-four miles long, it is part of an extensive river system which drains much of County Tyrone and part of southern Donegal and empties into eighteen-mile Lough Foyle after passing the city of Londonderry.

Equally enchanting scenically is the Bann, issuing from the Mourne Mountains, flowing north-east for about twenty-five miles past Coleraine into Lough Neagh, the largest lake in the British Isles. The river runs placidly through the green and neat countryside, oblivious, so to speak, to the bloody civil war now raging in Ulster, its banks a haven for troubled spirits. It is probably better known for its eels than its salmon.

The Erne comes out of County Cavan and runs northward for about sixty miles across the border of Northern Ireland and then turns north-west and widens into upper Lough Erne, continues as a winding river past Enniskillen and through Lough

Erne into Donegal Bay. This is the region made famous by the poet William Butler Yeats.

Other salmon streams of note in Northern Ireland are the Finn, Strule and Roe, flowing into Londonderry Bay. The Main is a tributary of Lough Neagh, draining into the North Channel through the Bann watershed. Among minor salmon streams that flow eastward into the North Channel the Quoille below Belfast is the best known.

There is a considerable range of productivity in these waters. In some an occasional fish enters after a rainfall, while others have consistently large runs and large fish. Grilse (called 'peal' in some parts of Ireland) may constitute a large portion of the runs in some streams, averaging six to eight pounds. Many rivers have fish that have been at sea for two or three years and from these stocks come the Irish contributions to the Greenland fishery. Happily, offshore fishing for salmon around Greenland was phased out in 1976 thanks to an agreement forced upon Denmark (which controls Greenland) by the United States in 1972 and later ratified by the International Commission for North-west Atlantic Fisheries. Inshore salmon fishing in Greenland, limited to about 1100 tons per annum, continues, exploiting the spawning stock of Ireland, Great Britain and Canada.

Irish salmon in history

Ireland has been inhabited for at least 8,000 years. The Danes, who invaded Ireland from the end of the eighth century, were familiar with the salmon for they gave its name to two prominent fishing localities: Leixlip (the word for salmon in old German languages is 'lax' or 'lox') on the River Liffey and the great Lax Weir on the Shannon just above Limerick. With the arrival of the Normans in 1170 we can trace the history of some of the famous Irish fisheries.

In the Middle Ages many Irish fisheries were owned by monastic establishments. One can still see on the River Cong, for example, the fish trap which supplied the monks of Cong Abbey, numbering some 3,000 persons at one time. When a fish was caught a bell rang in the refectory. Like other religious houses, the abbey had tithes of the fishing on distant streams to supplement its own harvests. The priory at Coleraine had the fruits of the fishing on the well-stocked river Bann for one day in the year, and as it fell at the height of the run, June 24, it must have been lucrative.

While the monks usually dined well, the peasants rarely ate fish or dainty meats. In fact, for many of them the potato constituted the basic diet. Fynes Morison, secretary to the viceroy of Ireland in the sixteenth century, found that some of the Irish lords and their retainers hardly fared much better. 'They seldom eat wild fish or fowl,' he said, 'though they have great plenty of both, because they will not take pains in catching them, and so leave all for the English.'

After the Reformation many Irish fisheries came into the hands of English landlords and the fishing was conducted mostly by foreigners. The wealth of the land, like the wealth of the rivers, was chiefly shipped out of the country. In 1689 exports of Irish salmon totalled 900 tons, about half of total landings nowadays. It was said that 'the cargoes of salmon, herring and pilchards and other fish transported into several ports of Spain and Venice' and elsewhere 'would startle the common people', many of whom suffered from malnutrition, at least in the more heavily populated areas.

Most of the salmon were taken with weirs belonging to the monasteries in the Middle Ages and lay proprietors or municipalities. Some of the weirs, designed to work with tidal cycles, were erected as early as the thirteenth century and fished for many centuries. Draft seines or haul nets were used for catching salmon at least as early as the second half of the twelfth century; later bag traps were adopted and in the nineteenth century Scottish fly nets and stake nets were introduced. Spear fishing was a popular method in Galway and elsewhere in the Middle Ages. In the eighteenth century some of the gentry, usually Englishmen, took up the art of angling.

The fisheries aggrandized only the English proprietors. Some Irish people fished for their families or for neighbours and were paid in potatoes. When the potato crop failed, as in the great famine of the 1840s, the fishermen sold or pawned their curraghs (coracles) and nets in order to buy meal. The Irishman, said

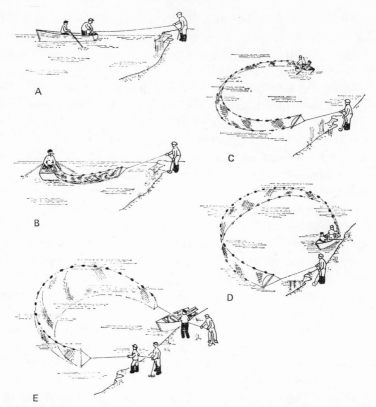

6 *Method of fishing an Irish draft seine or haul net in the river. A. The rope is paid out from the bank; B. part of the net is paid out; C. more net is paid out; D. the circle of the net is completed and the men in the boat take to the bank; E. the net is hauled*

Alexis de Toqueville after his visit to the Emerald Isle in 1835, 'cultivates bountiful crops and takes his harvest to the nearest port and puts it on an English ship; then he goes home and eats potatoes. He rears cattle, sends them to London and never eats meat.' In her book *The Great Hunger* Cecil Woodham-Smith says there was 'scarcely a woman of the peasant class whose culinary art exceeded the boiling of a potato. Bread [was] scarcely ever seen, and an oven unknown'. Not much had changed since the days of Jonathan Swift, dean of St Patrick's Cathedral in Dublin from 1714 to 1744 and author of the blistering satire on the English landlords, *A Modest Proposal.*

The Salmon Fisheries Act of 1863, a counterpart of the 1861 legislation for England and Wales, greatly reduced the number of fixed engines, including fishing weirs, so as to lighten the pressure on Irish salmon stocks. The country was divided into seventeen districts with boards of conservators appointed for each. They had the power to alter closed seasons, issue licences for rods, weirs, cruives, fixed gear, etc. All fixed nets that were not in legal existence in 1862 were declared illegal. Every fishing weir henceforth had to have a free gap. Use of spears, leisters and similar instruments was outlawed, as well as night fishing.

The right to fish appurtenant waters originally went with ownership of the land in Ireland as in Britain. Owners of the manors therefore had the fishing rights, but with the passage of time many of the fisheries were sold separately from the land.

In his book *The Salmon Fisheries* (1877) Archibald Young listed fifty-six major rivers in Ireland, of which the best in his opinion were the Shannon, Erne, Nore, Suir and Barrow, Moy, Ballissodare, Galway, Sligo, Lee, Bush, Bann, Foyle and Cork Blackwater. The Barrow alone yielded over 400 tons in some years; the Moy an average of 32,500 fish annually from 1882 to 1893, and the Lax Weir on the Shannon caught up to 15,000 per annum. Young estimated that the fifty-six rivers produced aggregate catches in the 1870s worth £400,000 yearly, a tremendous sum a century ago.

The first comprehensive survey of the Irish rivers was published by Augustus Grimble early in the twentieth century. He reported that much of the coast was lined with miles of fixed nets, many of them working illegally, without regard to closed periods, under the very eyes of the Coastguard. Some of the estuaries, like the Garavogue in County Sligo, were 'ceaselessly netted by small mesh nets under the pretence of catching small sea fish and flounders, and these nets take myriads of salmon'. The drift nets used in coastal fishing were supplied by London fish companies which, 'under the cloak of helping poverty-stricken Irish fishermen, only gave them a very small percentage of the profits while pocketing the bulk of it themselves'. As these nets took the lion's share of the runs, fewer salmon every season went up the rivers.

'Rivers of twine,' as Grimble called them, were almost everywhere along the coast working day and night when the fish were running. On the Cork Blackwater, mostly owned by the Duke of Devonshire, there were three stake weirs, eighteen draft nets, eighty-nine drift nets, and twenty-seven snap nets in a twenty-mile stretch, or one for every 250 yards. Still, it remained one of the best salmon rivers in Ireland, and as an angling stream had no peer, especially below Fermoy.

In his tour of County Sligo and other parts of Ireland Grimble found evidence of much illegal fishing and poaching on the lakes and their short feeder streams. The bulk of the catches continued to be exported, mainly to London and Liverpool.

Fish vs. dams

After the establishment of the Irish Republic in 1922 the government launched a programme of hydroelectric development designed to raise the nation's standard of living – to ameliorate the drudgery of farm life, light up homes, factories and shops and stimulate manufacturing. The Shannon River scheme, completed in 1927, was the first and remains the largest project undertaken by the government-owned Electricity Supply Board. It was followed by the harnessing of the River Lee above Cork, the Liffey at Leixlip, the Erne at Ballyshannon, and the Clady.

The Shannon project involved the construction of a dam and power station at Ardnacrusha, three and a half miles above Limerick, and a dam at Parteen below Killaloe. Three large lakes in the watershed provide most of the storage capacity. Intensive efforts were made to safeguard the runs by providing fish passes at the dams and opening up new spawning grounds. The Electricity Supply Board purchased all the private fishings above Limerick and 'took statutory responsibility for development of the fisheries, subject to and without prejudice to its primary function of supplying electricity'.

After an initial period of difficulty, during which the fishery could only be maintained at a very low level, for the salmon had to become oriented to radically new environmental conditions, and many died in the attempt, the ESB persuaded licensed netters to reduce their catches. Fingerlings produced at the hatchery at Parteen were planted in the Suck, a tributary which was not affected by the power development. In 1956 a Borland-type fish lift was installed at Ardnacrusha dam. Spawning zones in the watershed were carefully controlled, and by-passes were installed at the dams to protect downstream migrants. All these measures brought significant results.

Despite the ravages of UDN disease and loss of fish in the Greenland fishery, the average run on the Shannon had risen to 45,000 by the 1960s compared to 20,000 in the previous decade. The hatchery at Parteen was producing 200,000 smolts annually by 1970 and was the largest of its kind in the British Isles. Sport fishing was again becoming important in small sections of the Castleconnell water, and in the tributaries.

Less success has been achieved at the other dammed rivers. The ESB reports that stocks in the River Erne are at a dangerously low level. 'This fishing, which had been fully restored following damage by hydroelectric development,' says the Board, 'is being destroyed principally by selfish and thoughtless actions which have no regard to the legitimate interests of the traditional fishermen at the mouth of the river or the anglers upstream on both sides of the border.' On the impounded River Clady the runs have also suffered from widespread illegal fishing.

To compensate for these losses the ESB is investigating the rearing of salmon in sea water, a technique called aquaculture; this would also be a means of increasing its revenues. There is a ready market for salmon bred to pan or adult size in the British Isles.

Condition of the Irish stocks

The bulk of Irish commercial landings are now made by drift-net boats which operate in the open sea off the western and southern coasts (map, page 106). They are up to sixty feet long and carry crews of four to six men, using nets six feet deep suspended from a cork head rope and weighted very lightly or not at all. Every boat, in effect, is working up to 880 yards of net (about half-mile), the legal limit; however, there are also larger boats, defying the limit, using netting up to three miles long. At first the drifters

8

fished only at night, but later it was found that good catches could be made in daylight by intercepting the shoals of salmon heading for home as far as ten miles offshore. In 1974 the drifters took 72% of total landings, compared with 25.5% a decade earlier; bag nets, stake nets, weirs and other gear in the rivers and estuaries took 25%; and rods only 3%.

Ireland has produced almost as much salmon in recent years as Scotland or Canada, and more than Norway. Catches rose substantially from 1961 to 1974 when an all-time high of 4,400,000 pounds were landed. There is, however, much evidence that this record has been attained at the expense of overfishing the stocks.

There are mounting protests, however, against the excessive catches of the drifters. John A. Mulcahy in a letter to the Irish Minister for Agriculture and Fisheries, reprinted in the *Atlantic Salmon Journal* in 1975, expressed horror at the 'wanton destruction of our salmon; the resultant injury being perpetrated on our economy and the callous official disregard being shown to conserve a priceless national asset'. In the Castleton-Bantry area, he pointed out, 'the twenty-five hard core traditional fishermen a few years earlier had increased to 231'. 'Every gillie in Waterville will confirm the tremendous drop in the number of salmon returning to spawn. Surely, if these conditions continue for another three years – when the life cycle of the salmon will have run its full course – there will be no salmon left.'

The relative abundance of salmon in Ireland inspired considerable promotion by the Irish Tourist Board to attract anglers from foreign countries. In the 1960s sport fishermen took an average of 36,000 salmon and grilse annually, or twice as many as in England, thus making an important contribution to the nation's foreign exchange as well as creating jobs for persons catering to anglers in hotels and inns, gillies, and the like. The number of rod licences issued jumped from 5,000 in 1950 to 12,400 in 1974 but in that year anglers caught only 16,000 salmon and grilse. This was a blow to the sport fishing industry which overall contributed more to the economy than the commercial salmon fishermen.

The report of the Inland Fisheries Commission, specially

created to study Ireland's freshwater fisheries, published in July 1975, expressed concern about the excessive landings:

Most of our conservation laws and our existing protection service evolved around salmon fisheries which were located mainly in the rivers and estuaries and which could be supervised without much difficulty or expense. They were not designed to deal with the existing situation where the bulk of the catch is taken at sea and frequently at considerable distance from the coast . . . Salmon fishing in the sea is virtually unsupervised. Regulations regarding nets, and particularly the permitted maximum lengths of drift nets, are ignored on a widespread scale, the weekly close time is often openly infringed and some fishermen fish without licences.

The Commission recommended that 'the rehabilitation of damaged stocks be treated as a matter of high priority. Large scale restocking and development works seem to be necessary, and also appropriate restrictions on fishing in the sea and in the estuaries of affected rivers so as not to lose the benefits of the rehabilitation measures.'

Irish stocks have also been measurably affected by UDN disease which first appeared in 1964 in the Cummeragh River, County Kerry, and spread widely, reaching epidemic proportions in some areas. The scourge is probably due to a virus in the waters, and the secondary infection of fungi that causes discolouration in the fishes can be controlled to some extent by the use of malachite green, thus enabling affected specimens to be spawned artificially and produce healthy offspring. In recent years the disease has begun to taper off somewhat in both Irish and English waters.

The Inland Fisheries Commission report describes conditions in some of the rivers with depleted stocks. On the Liffey, harnessed for hydroelectric power in 1941, the stocks were showing signs of recovery when UDN appeared in 1966. That year the escapement at Leixlip dam was only 655 fish, less than half the average of the previous five years; in 1974 it reached an all-time low of 214.

On the Slaney, noted for its excellent stocks of salmon up to the mid-1960s, the rod catch dropped from about 2,000 yearly in the early 1960s to 300 in 1967 and only 133 in 1973. Catches by draft nets fell from an average of 5,000 in the early 1960s to 2,000 per year since 1971. On the River Lee, harnessed for hydro power in 1957, the average catch declined from over 8,000 annually before the dam was built to sixty-six between 1960 and 1968, but increased to 1,580 in 1969–1973.

An average harvest of 10,000 salmon was recorded on the River Erne before it was dammed. Catches declined rapidly afterwards, only 690 being taken in 1959. Conservation measures, enforced over a relatively long period, succeeded in re-establishing the stocks. UDN appeared in 1967 and subsequent years, wiping out some of the gains, but the real blows have come from severe pressure by drift netting and the use of illegal fixed nets in Donegal Bay.

Rivers flowing into Bantry Bay have also suffered from overfishing, said the Commission; surveys indicated that in three of the main rivers 'fry were found to be virtually absent from the nursery areas' and the number of spawning redds dropped from ninety-nine in 1971–1972 to only six the next year. Investigators found virtually no salmon in these streams in August 1973, April 1974 and March 1975.

An additional difficulty in keeping Ireland's salmon resource at the high levels of former years is the fact that pollution is becoming a serious problem on some rivers. 'Our temperate climate, low population density and comparative lack of industry,' said the Commission, 'may tempt one to assume that pollution could not become a very serious problem for fisheries. This is a dangerous assumption. Serious pollution has occurred. It is increasing in intensity and becoming more widespread with increasing development of industry and intensive farming methods . . . The pollution of lakes, and in particular eutrophication, is now so serious for fisheries that urgent remedial measures are demanded. Estuaries, coastal waters and the high seas have traditionally been regarded as convenient dumping grounds for effluents, and their ability to absorb pollution has been very much over-estimated. This is of particular importance to migratory fish.'

Anti-pollution laws are largely ineffective, concluded the Commission, because they are administered without coordination by agencies, many of which have conflicting interests and objectives. A government survey in 1972 found that 7% of the total length of Ireland's rivers was seriously polluted, 10% was classified as 'doubtful' and the remaining 83% was satisfactory – a far better record than in England and Wales.

In 1970, the Irish Tourist Board invited Peter Liddell, a member of the English Sports Council, to survey the Republic's salmon rivers and recommend improvements in their management. He found many things to criticize. He thought that the seventeen boards of conservators was out of date: 'They have inadequate powers, inadequate resources and inadequate staffs,' and worst of all, are not 'properly backed by the Department of Agriculture and Fisheries'. Poaching was taking an undue toll, and the stiffest penalty, rarely imposed, was £25 compared with £100 in England plus two years' imprisonment and forfeiture of any boat or vehicle used. Liddell concluded that the Irish 'rivers are in decline, and unless legislative and administrative remedial action is taken with the utmost urgency, this decline will continue'.

Foyle River fisheries

The fisheries of the River Foyle system, which includes all the streams flowing into the sea between Malin Head in County Donegal and Downhill, were put under a joint English-Irish Commission in 1952 by the Parliaments of Northern Ireland and the Irish Republic. This system is one of the most productive of salmon in Europe, but in recent years the number successfully reaching upstream spawning beds has been greatly reduced. Spawning counts in the Foyle area dropped from an average of 22,400 in 1965–1966 to only 3,270 in 1974–1975.

In 1973 the Foyle Fisheries Commission invited two Canadian experts, Dr Paul F. Elson and A. L. W. Tuomi to study the fisheries, and their comprehensive report issued in 1975 confirmed what had been suspected: 'The imminent collapse of the Foyle salmon stocks is undoubtedly due to a number of causes, not all of which can be completely identified ... But while habitat alterations, pollution and natural causes are present, the major cause, which fortunately is controllable, is overfishing.'

The report recommends 'a drastic but not complete curtailment of all commercial fishing of Foyle River salmon . . . if present stock levels are to be maintained and future restoration ensured'. In brief, 'it involves settling on an optimal level of economic and social performance'. There is no simple or easy solution to the problem. 'Biologically, stocks need to be restored through a variety of means starting with a massive reduction in exploitation.' The Foyle Commission, says the report, 'has been remarkably successful in most respects [although it has allowed too many fish to be taken by the commercials] and has displayed capabilities which leave no reason to doubt that it can provide management such as will be required both for restoration and the future'.

The time has come for the Irish government to take a hard look at its valuable salmon fisheries, as the Inland Fisheries Commission makes clear, to reorganize the system of management, allocate more funds for conservation and rehabilitation of stocks, and especially to curb offshore netting which threatens to reduce drastically the spawning runs into the rivers. Some steps in that direction have already been taken.

CHAPTER 8

Western Europe

SPAIN AND PORTUGAL

ATLANTIC salmon originally inhabited hundreds of rivers flowing into the Atlantic Ocean from Portugal to northern Scandinavia and into the Arctic and Baltic Sea as well.

The earliest known association of *Salmo salar* with man goes back to the people who lived in the caves of north-western Spain and south-western France in the late Paleolithic Era. Bones of various fishes, including salmon, have been found in these dwellings, usually a vertebrae column, as in the vicinity of the Vézère, a tributary of the Dordogne, indicating that this fish was part of the people's diet. There is a sculpture of a salmonid in low relief on the floor of the Grotte du Poisson near Les Eyzies situated at the confluence of the Beaune and Vézère Rivers, and also on the floor of the cave at Niaux, near Tarascon sur Ariège, in the foothills of the Pyrenees.

North-western Spain is honeycombed with caves where Stone Age men lived. The best known is Altamira near the village of Santillana del Mar, famous for its polychrome animal paintings drawn when the area supported a steppe-tundra biotic community, such as cave bear, mountain goats, deer, wild horses, bison and others. Radio-carbon dating suggests that these paintings were executed 10,000 to 20,000 years ago.

There is a little museum at the entrance to the cave which contains a collection of Stone Age artifacts – stone axes, arrow points, stone awls and a considerable number of shells, some of which contain bits of dried out paints used by the primitive artists, still usable if ground and mixed with oil. In one show case there is a piece of reindeer antler on which the sleek outline of a salmon has been etched.

Below the cave entrance the river Pas, whose fishes nourished Paleolithic man, still flows. Over the centuries its bed has been considerably lowered, and the sea has receded, but a small stock of salmon still comes up every year. In 1975 over 500 were taken from this river.

The north-west portion of the Iberian peninsula is well watered, in contrast to the remainder of this vast area. Most of the rivers emptying into the Atlantic from the Duero, which rises some 490 miles from the sea on the mountain threshold of Aragon, to the Bidasao on the French border, were once populated with salmon. This is a region of ample rainfall, well distributed throughout the year, of deciduous and evergreen forests, and humid types of agriculture. The rivers that issue from the Picos de Europa mountains are swift and cold, and strewn with rocky ledges and cascades. They flow down steep, narrow valleys, past forests of chestnut, oak and poplar, into the *rias* of the Bay of Biscay. Originally there were probably fifty salmon rivers in the peninsula but most of them lost their fishes long ago. In Portugal there is nary a one, though Tirso de Molina, the seventeenth-century author of the original play about Don Juan, *The Trickster of Seville*, tells us that in the Lisbon of his time, situated on the Tagus river:

> Citizens, while they're at table
> Can buy great loads of fish
> And most from their own doors are able
> To catch as many as they wish.
> And from the nets where salmon flounder
> It's scarce a stone's throw to the dish.

In Sweden I met a biologist who had been invited by the Salazar government to investigate the possibility of restoring salmon to some of the Portuguese streams. His conclusion was that it was not feasible.

The salmon rivers in Spain are found in the provinces of Galicia, Asturias, Santander and Guipuzcoa. They are usually relatively short with the exception of the Miño, which flows for 200 miles from the Sierra de Meira to the sea near the Portuguese border. Spanish fisheries nurtured not only the people of the

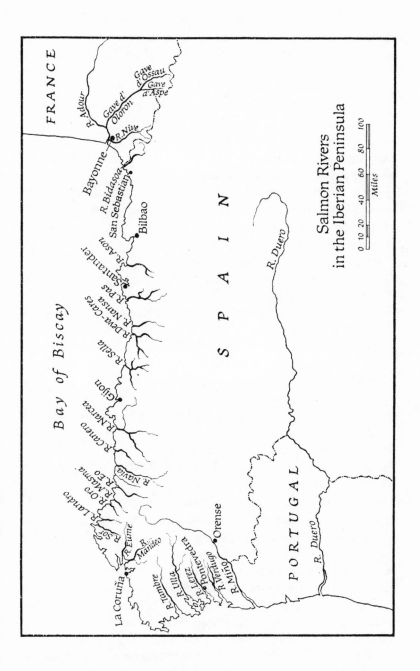

Salmon Rivers
in the Iberian Peninsula

FRANCE

R. Adour
Gave d'Oloron
Gave d'Ossau
Gave d'Aspe
R. Nive
Bayonne
R. Bidasoa
San Sebastián
Bilbao
R. Ason
Santander
R. Pas
R. Nansa
R. Deva-Cares
R. Sella
Gijón
R. Narcea
R. Canero
R. Navia
R. Eo
R. Masma
R. Oro
R. Landro
R. Sor
R. Eume
R. Mandeo
La Coruña
R. Tambre
R. Ulla
R. Lerez
R. Pontevedra
R. Verdugo
R. Miño
Orense
R. Duero

SPAIN

PORTUGAL

R. Duero

Bay of Biscay

0 10 20   40   60   80   100
Miles

Stone Age but the prehistoric Iberians, and later the Celts, Greeks, Phoenicians, and Romans, as well as the Moslems who conquered the peninsula in the Middle Ages. Arched Roman bridges still stand, like the one over the river Sella, where Roman legionnaires angled for salmon, as fishers do today.

In the Middle Ages the streams produced bountiful harvests. As in other European countries, the fishing rights in Christian Spain belonged to the abbeys, nobility and Crown. The best sites were intensively exploited. Weirs, called *postas* or *apostales*, trapped the fish – their remains could still be seen on some streams, like the Pas, in the present century. During the eighteenth century some fishing rights fell into the hands of wealthy merchants and municipalities.

Sañez Requart in his *Historical Dictionary of the National Fishing Arts* (1791–1795) estimated that some 2,000 salmon were caught daily in the province of Asturias alone during the season. 'Considering the quantity and quality of the rest of the rivers in the north of Spain,' concluded Enrique Camino in *La Riqueza Piscicola de los Rios del Norte de España*, 'it is not venturing too much to suppose that . . . no less than 8,000 to 10,000 fish per day were caught at the end of the eighteenth century.' On the basis of sixty days of fishing, the annual harvests were perhaps as much as 600,000 to 900,000 salmon. Income from some of the fisheries was high, judging by the fact that the municipality of San Estaban de Pravia, at the mouth of the Nalón River, obtained some 100,000 reales annually from its fishings in the 1780s. Half a century later this had dwindled to 8,000 reales and now the Nalón is salmonless.

Amid the political and economic upheavals of the nineteenth century the freshwater fisheries deteriorated. Many rivers were blocked by mill dams, the proprietors ignoring the law of 1795 requiring channels to be kept open at all times to permit the fish to reach their spawning grounds. Later came small hydro-electric plants built without fish ladders. Even when they had ladders these were often left dry and useless. In the troubled years before civil war broke out in 1936 some of the streams were looted. Peasants living on the edge of poverty took fish for family use or sold them for needed income. Moreover, the administration of the fisheries during the era of Bourbon rule did not serve conservation ends. Fishing in the estuaries was controlled by the Ministry of Maritime Affairs and in freshwater by the Ministry of Development and Public Works (*Fomento*). Fishing in saltwater began on February 15, which was a month too early, and could be conducted throughout the week, with nets placed too close to each other. Overfishing was the main cause for the depletion of the stocks.

According to the Marquis de Marzales, writing in the 1920s, the river Eo yielded 2,000 salmon at that time, whereas its potential was 50,000; the Sella produced 3,000 or about one-tenth of its capacity; the Narcea barely 1,000 where once 50,000 was taken; and so on. Management of rivers like the Miño which formed the border with Portugal, and the Bidasao with France, created international disputes which were not properly resolved; a series of treaties and commissions failed to establish meaningful regulations and as a result these fruitful waters were overfished and the stocks went downhill, as in other streams.

When the Civil War ended, in 1939, salmon were confined to about twenty rivers. General Francisco Franco, the dictator, a passionate salmon angler, issued a decree on February 20, 1942, banning net fishing for salmon in all rivers, thus turning the resource over to the anglers. Total catches by 1942 had fallen to 2,000 to 3,000 annually.

Since 1942 a modest effort has been made to restore some of the productive rivers, chiefly by restocking, and removal of stream obstructions. However, it is doubtful if these measures have been of great benefit. In a tour of Spanish rivers I found officials complaining about lack of funds and personnel; hatcheries were rather primitive and it was clear that the national government was not ready to back a restoration programme on a substantial scale.

Country folk welcomed the elimination of the nets because now they had greater access to the rivers. They could purchase a licence for a small sum and take legally fish which they used to poach: poaching is severely punished in Spain's tough regime. Thus many of the rod and reel fishermen became professionals and sold their catches, for a hefty salmon would fetch as many pesos in the 1940s and 1950s as a *paisano* could earn in a fortnight.

The rivers were divided into two categories, *cotos* or preserves and free waters. The *cotos* consist of the Narcea and Deva-Cares in Asturias and the Eo in Galicia. To fish them it is necessary to have a permit from the State Tourist Department. Sections of each preserve are divided into beats, each large enough for a day's fishing. On the other rivers the farmers who have riparian rights retain the privilege of obtaining half the fishing licences issued for reserved sections of the streams while the remaining half go to sportsmen. Every salmon caught must be registered with a warden and only those taken in the free zones may be sold. The Guardia Civil one sees everywhere, wearing spruce grey uniforms and tri-cornered patent leather hats, may look like characters in a comic operetta but they carry out their duties very firmly, guarding the rivers as they do the highways and towns.

What has been the result of Spain's experiment in permitting salmon to be caught only with the rod and reel? According to Max Borrell, an international sportsman who is consultant on fishing and hunting to the Tourist Department, the major result has been to convert sport fishing into a professional occupation. 'On a good fishing day in the river Sella,' he says, 'one is likely to see from 300 to 500 professionals fishing with everything. Once upon a time the nets exterminated the salmon; now, unless drastic steps are taken, the runs will be very much depleted by a multitude of hooks. Professionals are only allowed to fish in the best pools for thirty minutes if others are waiting to do so, but I have seen a dozen awaiting their turn.' Meanwhile pressure on the stocks is mounting. The number of national fishing licences jumped from about 10,000 in 1950 to 150,000 in 1966. Many of the rivers that still had much salmon in the pre-Civil War days are now defunct, such as the Eume, Sor, Landro, Jallas, Mandeo, Allones (where twenty-five pounders were frequently caught in the 1930s), Mero, El Puerto, Tambre, Nalón, Saja and Miero.

With the growth of industry pollution is increasing on some rivers and the outbreak of UDN has helped to reduce runs. In the Narcea, for example, one of the most productive of the remaining streams, about 50% of the fish were badly affected by this disease in recent years. Many were found dead on the banks, while others failed to spawn.

Catches have fluctuated greatly since the ban on netting went into effect in 1942. Peaks of 8,000 to 9,000 were reached in some years in the late 1950s followed by sharp drops in the early 1960s, with an upturn in the next five years and a downturn in the 1970s. Owing to the scarcity of reports on the condition of the rivers, and the lack of research, it is difficult to ascertain future prospects. In 1975, 4,615 salmon were registered as legally caught, compared with 2,750 in 1974. According to Max Borrell, one of the best-informed persons on this subject, for every fish registered one or more are taken illegally.

In 1976 catches totalled 3,626; the best rivers were the Narcea, Eo, Cares and Sella. Now that General Franco is dead one wonders if the new government of King Juan Carlos will be equally interested in protecting the salmon. Borrell (who was Franco's fishing companion and mentor) said to me in 1974, 'After a generation or two, *Salmo salar* in Spain will be as dead as the proverbial dodo. I hope I may be proved wrong.'

FRANCE

Salmon were originally found in nearly every river in France emptying into the Atlantic Ocean, from the Bidasoa on the Spanish border to the chalk streams of Normandy and Picardy; they also entered France from the Rhine and its tributaries. Unlike English rivers, many of them are extensive systems with numerous tributaries and lengthy gravelly stretches that used to be ideal for the spawning and rearing of salmonids. Some of these waterways are lacy threads, often swift-running, that move across the landscape with its mosaic of forests, valleys, mountains and plateaux. They wind past fields of wheat, neatly-terraced vineyards and grassy meadows, or dart through pine forests or down narrow defiles. The charm of France, of which the rivers constitute an essential part, is summarized in the phrase *la belle France*. Even with the growth of population, cities, towns and industry, the appellation applies.

Among rivers once famous for their salmon a few may be singled out. The Moselle, a tributary of the Rhine, rises in the

Vosges mountains, forms the boundary with Germany and
Luxembourg, and enters the main river at Coblentz. The 470-
mile Seine drains a large depression occupying much of northern
France, with many tributaries like the Somme and Marne.
Salmon used to ascend to the upper waters of the Seine, before
they were locked out by dams lacking fish ladders.

The fishes were quite abundant in the Loire and its numerous
affluents – perhaps no river in western Europe except the Rhine
was so richly populated with salmon. The Loire cuts a 625-mile
arc across the centre of France from the Cevennes Mountains to
the Bay of Biscay at St Nazaire. This shining waterway with
its gemlike tributaries like the Cher, Vienne, Indre, Loir and
lengthy Allier, flows through the Val d'Orleans, Val de Blois,
Val de Touraine and Val d'Anjou. The middle Loire passes
ancient towns like Orleans (home of Jeanne d'Arc), Tours and
Samur, past grey-stone châteaux, the pride of French Renaissance
architecture, standing on a prominent bluff or spur like Amboise,
Chenanceaux, Blois and the ruin of Chinon. Happily a large
part of the Loire remains much as Victor Hugo described it
over a century ago, 'a tranquil oval sheet that reflects in its
liquid depth a castle with its turrets, woods and springing waters'
where little of the world's hubbub penetrates. However, if you
look for the salmon that once thronged its waters it may be in
vain, for they have deserted nearly all the tributaries except the
Allier.

In the Dordogne Valley Stone Age man was nourished on
the fishes in the nearby rivers, including the salmon. The Garonne
is a larger system than the Dordogne, and used to lure salmon to
the headwaters in the Val d'Aran and as far as the Pyreneean
valley of the Ariège near the border of Spain. The Gironde,
formed by the confluence of the Dordogne and Garonne, flows
through the Medoc wine country; once it too boasted substantial
runs of salmon.

The Adour gushes out of the Pic du Midi in the central
Pyrenees and flows for over 200 miles to Bayonne and the Bay
of Biscay. Some of its affluents are cold mountain streams which
meander through narrow valleys with mouldering stone houses
and little shops and inns where lusty farmers drink wine out of

flagons. Old men and boys fish for salmon and trout from ancient stone bridges. Major tributaries of the Adour are the Gave d'Oloron, the Nive and the Nivelle. Salmon are scarce in these once populous streams.

Normandy and Brittany have numerous short and sometimes swift rivers which once were quite productive. Overshadowing them all is the 820-mile Rhine, an international waterway, the longest and most famous river in western Europe. Originating in the Swiss Alps, the Rhine basin encompasses parts of Switzerland, Austria, Luxembourg, Germany, Belgium, Holland and France. Its terminus is the Hook of Holland in the North Sea. Rhine salmon were once the delight of gourmets, served at banquets of princes and emperors like Bismarck and Kaiser Wilhelm.

French salmon have biological characteristics similar to those in the British Isles. The bulk of the juveniles spend two years in freshwater. The larger adults return to the rivers from November to March and move slowly upstream, while the grilse, called *madeleineux*, usually appear before the main runs. Very few grilse are now found in the Adour or Allier, the only major rivers still harbouring salmon, but they comprise the bulk of the runs in the pastoral Breton and Norman streams. Some idea of where the French salmon feed was obtained when smolts tagged in the Gave d'Oloron, in April 1969, were recovered in Greenland waters in the fall of 1970.

French salmon in history: Age of Plenty

When the Romans colonized Gaul in the age of Julius Caesar they found the inhabitants to be fish-eating people. The most esteemed species were mullet in the east and salmon in the west. Roman gourmets like Lucullus no doubt heard of these fishes and imported them for their feasts. The fourth-century Roman poet Ausonius, a native of Bordeaux, eulogized the salmon among other freshwater fishes in his *Idyll of the Moselle*, the result of a trip on that delightful river.

As in Britain, the freshwater fishes were protected and cherished by the Crown and nobility during the Middle Ages and the fisherman was an important person in his community. In the

town of Oloron Ste-Marie in the Adour basin he is commem-
orated in stone sculpture on the portal of the Romanesque
cathedral, with a salmon on his shoulder.

Statutes designed to protect the fisheries date from the reign
of Charlemagne in the eighth century. A spate of similar laws
followed in succeeding centuries, dealing with the size and type of
nets, meshes, closed seasons and the minimum size of fish that
could be sold in the markets. Until the eleventh century only
fishing for salmon and eels was regulated. The fisheries were
owned by the Crown, feudal nobility, religious establishments
and municipalities. Wealthy people deeded their properties to
religious houses, as for example, Alain, Count of Brittany did
in 1090. Wishing to have the blessings of Heaven, he donated
to the monks of Landevennec the fishery on the river Aulne
which brought 4,500 livres of rent annually. Nearly all the
valuable salmon water in Brittany was held by the Seigneurs or
the Abbeys.

'Owners usually took good care of the rivers in order to
assure an adequate return of the fishes to the spawning grounds,'
says Roger Bachelier, historian of the Loire fishery. Nevertheless
the laws were not always obeyed, as we learn from an edict of
Henri IV, issued in 1597, which declares that 'with an excessive
number of engines, fishermen are depleting the rivers, streams
and ponds. [Therefore] they are forbidden to fish with any gear,
even legal ones, which has not been authorized by our officers.'
Despite the lamentations found in royal decrees, it is believed
that the stocks held up quite well down to the Revolution of 1789.

Georges-Michel Thomas in an article in the Breton magazine
Penn Ar Bed (1968) endorses this view. 'The Seigneurial fisheries
thrived until the Revolution,' he says. 'Not among the least
picturesque of natural phenomena was to watch each January the
return of the fishes hurling themselves at the foaming rapids,
falling back, returning to the assault again and again, until
finally overcoming them with a victorious leap.' In the middle
of the eighteenth century some 4,000 salmon were landed at
Chateaulin annually, and all of Brittany produced 4,500 tons in
good years, over twice as much as are now landed in the United
Kingdom.

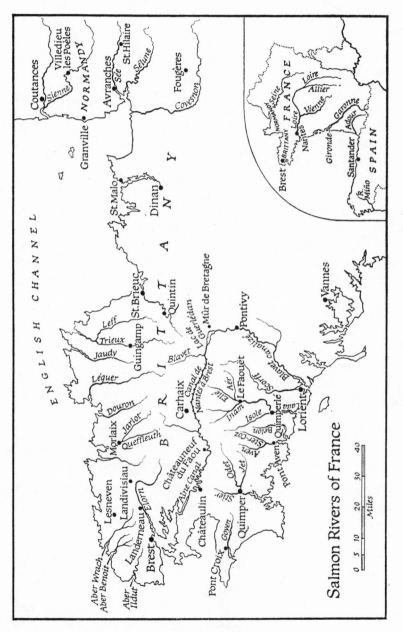

Salmon Rivers of France

0 5 10 20 30 40
Miles

In the happy agricultural age, before the advent of the Industrial Revolution which has played havoc with the environment in every country where it spread, nearly all French rivers ran limpid and pure. The watergates of the mills were closed every night and on Sunday so that the entire flow passed over the channel. When the flow was heavy arrangements were made to permit the simultaneous floating of timber and ascent of the fish.

But by the middle of Louis XIV's reign the fishery laws had become chaotic and contradictory. The Seigneurs added their own regulations to those of the King. From one province to another and one district to the next the laws changed, and there were rivers on which the two banks were not under the same authority. In 1667 Louis XIV's brilliant minister Jean-Baptiste Colbert ended this chaos by abrogating all previous statutes and formulating a new and uniform code. This was not substantially modified, except for the period of the Revolution and Napoleonic rule, until 1829. Unfortunately Colbert, wishing to encourage enlistment in the Navy, granted the enlistees (called *Inscrits Maritimes*) after they had served their term the right to fish with nets in the estuaries and tidal waters of their home rivers, and this right has descended from father to son in perpetuity to this very day. The result has been to make the *Inscrits* difficult to control since they are under the jurisdiction of the Ministry of Maritime Affairs. They often disregard the fishery laws and regulations, and thus have helped to ruin many salmon rivers by overfishing.

Until recent times the French people cherished their freshwater fishes and most of all the salmon. 'The tender flesh of the salmon, oily, sweet, very appetizing and excellent to the taste, is preferable as a delicacy to all other fish,' said Abraham de la Framboisèire, court physician in the sixteenth century. At banquets this fish, in its silvery coat, head and eyes intact, was brought by servants on a pewter platter to the sound of trumpets. Sauces and spices, if available, were handed around and the repast, which might consist of half a dozen courses, was washed down with wine.

Gourmet cooking as we know it in the West is basically the invention of French chefs in the eighteenth and nineteenth centuries. Fish has always been a side dish but some cooks took infinite pains to invent savoury ways of garnishing it. Out of these experiments came such famous dishes as *Salmon à la Royale*, *Salmon à la Chambord*, and *Salmon Impériale*, worthy of standing beside such regional masterpieces as *Sole Normand*, *Pic Anjou*, and *Turbot Franche-Comtois*.

Age of Scarcity

The Age of Abundance passed with the Revolution of 1789. The Legislative Assembly and the Convention at first deprived the nobility who owned the rivers of their fishing rights, thus opening the streams to the people and widespread looting. Under the Consulate, fishing rights on navigable rivers were vested in the state and public fishing was permitted. At the same time riparian owners received the right to fish on non-navigable waters, as the fishery code of 1829 stipulated: 'Proprietors have the right to the soil and bed of the river but not the river itself. The fish become their property only at the moment when they are taken out of the water by legal means.' Nobody was permitted to fish in private waters without authorization. 'The free movement of water and fish must be assured,' said the code but this noble statement was largely ignored.

Rivers were increasingly encroached upon by weirs and mill dams, and some were canalized or polluted. Men of property argued that they had the right to use the waters as they pleased and ignored the conservation laws. For example, a law of 1865 required owners of mill dams to provide fish passes for which the state would reimburse them; but unfortunately it did not apply to existing barriers and there was no stipulation guaranteeing water levels that would keep these structures in operation for the passage of fish. This law, says Bachelier, did little to prevent the eventual lockout of the salmon from many of their ancient haunts. To take but one example, canalization of the Aulne, a Breton river, brought in its train barrages which proved to be serious obstacles to the ascent of the salmon.

In his *Natural History of French Fishes*, published in 1881, Émile Moreau gives an account of the state of the salmon that is very enlightening. They were already rare in the Moselle and quite reduced in the Meuse with its impassable mill dams and in other Rhine tributaries on the French side. They were numerous, in contrast, in streams debouching into the English Channel. There were runs all year in the Loire; they abounded in the Vienne, one of the most important tributaries, but had almost disappeared in the Allier, which was being restocked with fry. Later the Loire salmon suffered heavy losses from the construction of hydroelectric dams without fish ladders. In 1881 the Dordogne and Garonne rivers already had slender stocks while in the Adour basin salmon were still ascending in fair numbers the Nive, Nivelle and some of the *gaves* but not much further. In this river, as in the Loire, they were mercilessly fished by the *Inscrits* in tidal water up to Peyrehorade, as I saw eighty years later when I visited the Adour.

In the past century industrial development and urban growth have all but obliterated the salmon, with the help, of course, of the greedy fishermen. Navigation developments diverted water from salmon rivers and agriculture abstracted much of the flow in many instances. Dams, weirs and flumes blockaded some of the runs – an old familiar tale. In 1944 de Boisset and Vibert in their book *La pêche fluviale en France* estimated that catches had fallen to 6,000–7,000 in Brittany; 5,000–6,000 in the Loire basin; and 10,000–18,000 in the Adour basin.

The Loire is a classic example of the rape of French salmon rivers. A law of December 19, 1853, established a closed season in both salt and freshwater from October 20 to January 31 but this was ignored by the *Inscrits*. Moreover they were permitted to lay their nets as far upstream as Thuare, eleven kilometres above Nantes, where the tidal zone ends. They could get away with anything because they were protected by the Ministry of Marine Affairs, and as Commandant Latour says in *Salmon in Breton Rivers*, 'They had no consideration for regulations governing fishing, knowing full well that nobody would have dared or dreamed of enforcing them.' The fish which passed the breastworks of nets in the estuaries were confronted 200 or 300 metres upstream by a second barrage of twine and so on for a considerable distance. Only a minimum number usually managed to escape, 'and one wonders how that happens,' says Latour.

Conservationists in the national government protested against such overfishing and against usurpation of the rivers by dams without fish ladders. A spokesman for the conservationists warned at a meeting of government officials held at Clermont-Ferrand in the 1920s of the outcome of present trends if steps were not taken to reverse the course of events. 'This important national treasure,' he said, 'will soon become a memory, as in the Seine and Garonne. Why is it necessary that this national wealth should be sacrificed completely to the special interests of certain industries? . . . "This is the cost we pay for progress," it is said. Beautiful progress, in truth, which consists of destroying a collective good which without investment of capital or expense produces benefits for the entire nation, and substituting for it industries which are uncertain, swallow considerable funds and serve but to enrich a small number of individuals.

'To produce kilowatts is doubtless a good thing but it is better in an era of scarcity, and without expense, [to have] food which is as abundant as it is nutritious.'

The meeting had no positive results. The questions asked by friends of *Salmo salar* and the arguments they advanced were the same as those heard in every country where it is or was an important resource, and usually to little or no avail. Hydro-electric dams were built on the Loire, and later nuclear plants as well, and the fishery went steadily downhill. Reliable statistics on fish catches are difficult to find in France because the government, it is alleged, does not wish to invade the privacy of fishermen by asking them to report their catches. The rich harvests of the 1880s and 1890s by the *Inscrits* on the Loire did not last. They are believed to have taken 30,000 salmon in 1893 but only 6,200 in 1901 and 3,100 in 1920. In 1924 they were permitted to fish with drag nets as well as hook nets of any length in all the rivers despite the protests of the Bureau of Waters and Forests which supervised fishing in nontidal streams. By 1960 only 1,500 fish were landed in the entire Loire basin and in 1974 only 500 between Nantes and Bec d'Allier, plus perhaps 100 in the estuary.

In assessing the causes of France's loss poaching must not be ignored. As the fish became scarce and their value increased the temptation to clever poachers was magnified. In *La pêche fluviale en France*, Louis de Boisset and Richard Vibert said, 'Modern poaching is a veritable industry of water pirates and

thieves who, by every means from nets to explosives . . . are
dedicated to extensive devastation of our rivers.' Gangs lurked
behind dams and weirs, bridges and watergates, and wherever
schools of fish were to be found. A person could run up numerous
convictions and small fines and continue to operate successfully.
Henri Boyer, vice-president of the Association of Upper Allier
Anglers, said in 1930 that 'poaching has attained since the war
the status of a national institution. The devastations particularly
affect the waters of angling clubs whose members are powerless
and discouraged by the apathy of the Administration.' Equally
disheartened were wardens and forestry officers (guardians of
the rivers) whom poachers tended to regard as harmless nuisances.

An important factor in the deterioration of the fisheries was
the divided authority of government agencies. The Ministry of
Marine Affairs had jurisdiction of the rivers to the end of tidewater, the Bureau of Waters and Forests of the Ministry of
Agriculture supervised fishing above tidewater, the Bureau of
Bridges and Roads controlled canals, and the Hydraulic Service,
an independent agency, issued licences for hydraulic projects.
Waters and Forests' role was strictly supervisory but it was dedicated to the preservation of the salmon and sought to prevent
other agencies from approving activities which would jeopardize
them. De Boisset and Vibert stated the problem succinctly:

> We would not pretend that all the services charged with
> fishery responsibilities have always had in full degree all the
> desirable technical competence. The reasons are many. They
> stem in large part from . . . lack of comprehension in the seats
> of power of the national interest in the inland fishery. Regu-
> lations were made that were poorly adapted to biological
> conditions, permits for hydraulic projects were too readily
> granted, industrial diversions were tolerated in ignorance of
> the proper methods of attenuating them . . . All true, but we
> should not ignore the patient efforts of certain forest officers
> who fought the evils they saw, efforts which were futile
> because of lack of co-ordination of the services, lack of com-
> prehension of public welfare, and we must say, egoism, anarchy
> and ignorance.

Occasionally Waters and Forests won a victory. Thus it persuaded an interministerial committee in 1929 to set aside seven rivers which were still productive – the Aulne, Ellé, Allier, Adour in part, Gave d'Oloron, Gave de Meulon in part, and the Nive – on which preservation of the salmon should take precedence over industrial uses and licences for hydraulic schemes should no longer be granted. On seven other rivers – the Canche, Sienne, Sée, Sélune, Élorn, Scorff and Gave de Pau – salmon should have equal importance with industry and licences for water uses should be granted only on the basis of an understanding between the Hydraulic Service and Waters and Forests, and with certain restrictions on the height of dams and design of fish passes. Unfortunately this unprecedented agreement merely gave the runs in the sanctuary rivers a little more time before they were overwhelmed by harmful developments.

Interministerial committees met in subsequent years to study proposals for reducing netting and other conservation measures, but with few results. Typical was the attitude of a spokesman for the Ministry of Marine Affairs. When asked to curb the privileges of the *Inscrits*, he said:

> We do not deny that certain new measures are justifiable under the circumstances but would it not be better to make sure at first, by regulations rigorously applied, of the impossibility of polluting streams frequented by salmonids, severely control poaching, impose ladder designs at dams, and finally, if these measures are insufficient demand new restrictions on the rights of fishermen whether they operate in the maritime or freshwater zones?

De Boisset and Vibert's reply is quite pertinent:

> This thesis, of course, rests on a sophism. When we are faced with a grave danger we do not waste time establishing priority of safety measures. We employ all of them simultaneously. If to save the fishery we first attack pollution; then, if this is insufficient, poaching; then, if this is still inadequate, apply restrictions on hydroelectric dams; if, after exhausting all these means, we agree to impose restrictions on fishing in the estuaries

the action would be meaningless because there would no longer be any fish.

When foresters request free movement for the salmon over the dams the electrical engineers reply, 'To what good? First get rid of pollution in the estuaries, the famous biologic blockade which the salmon cannot pierce. When the fish can enter the river, we will talk about dams.' While these academic discussions were being held, the salmon runs continued to decline . . . The fish disappeared from more and more rivers.

A vanishing species

Despite shrinking stocks overfishing continues in France. The eloquent pleas of foresters like Vibert and anglers like René Richard, president of the National Association for the Protection of Salmon Rivers (ANDRS) go unheard. Pierre Phelipot describes the operation of the *Inscrits* in the Breton rivers Laïta and Scorff in *Plaisirs de la Pêche* (summer 1968):

> Six or eight *Inscrits* take 3,000 salmon and grilse annually and almost all the large sea trout in the estuary of the Scorff while 150 anglers take only 400 to 800 . . . I know several of these worthy fellows who profit handsomely from their privileges considering the price of salmon per kilogram. They are quite reticent about their exploits, and listening to them you would think they scarcely eke out a livelihood. However, those who, like us, have taken the trouble to watch them for any length of time, either in the Laïta or the Scorff, can affirm that they make considerable inroads on the salmon runs as they scour the estuary with their nets . . .
>
> One must be blind not to see that net fishing in the estuaries is the principal – I do not say the only – cause for the scarcity of anadromous fish runs in the streams.

In addition to a small run on the Allier, a tributary of the Loire, and in the Adour basin, there are minuscule runs in about fifteen rivers in Brittany and a few in Normandy, of which the most important are the Aulne, Ellé, Elorn and Scorff. According to Yves Harache of the Centre National Pour L'Exploitation des Océans, the Breton catch in 1976 did not exceed 1,000 salmon, 'and a drastic decrease was observed in all the rivers, showing that we are very close to the no-return point'. Possibly another 1,000 fish were landed by netsmen and anglers in the Allier River and the Adour and interior streams. In 1976, owing to the drought, not a single salmon was caught on the Ellé.

Very little is being done to save the species despite the urgings of such organizations as the National Association for the Protection of Salmon Rivers and the Association for the Protection of Salmon and Trout in Brittany and lower Normandy. They pester ministers and issue newsletters and bulletins pointing to the alarming state of the salmon runs but the government remains quite indifferent.

France now imports large quantities of frozen and canned salmon – in 1974 some 3,500 tons worth $916 million came from the United States alone. This is galling to men like Vibert and the late Louis de Boisset who in 1944 exclaimed: 'France, which should be in the front rank of salmon producers, imports annually 20,000 quintals of salmon, of which the greatest portion are mediocre tinned salmon which America distributes in the two hemispheres as proof of its superior civilization.'

For every step forward in fishery conservation France seems to take two backward. When catches on the Allier began to rise at the end of the 1950s, the wheel-type fish traps, laid aside for thirty years, came back on the scene – they had been largely responsible for depletion of this river in the first place. In recent years, as some Breton streams showed improvement, UDN appeared; now the stocks in Brittany are threatened not only by pollution and overfishing but by the upsurge of rainbow trout culture, produced at the rate of 10,000 tons a year. 'These hatcheries,' says Phelipot, 'have the right to dam our small rivers. In many places the greater part of the river is deflected to the hatchery, so salmon and trout cannot run . . . These hatcheries are rudimentary. They do not recirculate the water, so they pollute the streams.' There are other inimical water abstractions, as on the Aulne where a great deal of the flow is needed to supply the submarine base at Ile Longue. Plans for building a modern salmon hatchery and salmon research station on the Nivelle at St Pée are constantly postponed.

In sum, France is the best example in Europe of a nation that has frittered away its salmon wealth as Ernest Schwiebert, a well-known and much-travelled salmon fisher, puts it: 'a text-book case in greed and mismanagement'.

In the summer of 1977 David M. Lank traversed the picturesque Gave d'Oloron which was once a famous salmon stream. Stopping at Oloron Ste-Marie, formerly thronged with anglers, he wrote a fitting requiem to the river and to the salmon in France generally:

> Layer on layer in limestone cave
> The salmon trace, when once they gave
> Cro-Magnon's fare, each year returned.
> Totemic bone of reindeer graved
> Succeeding generations saved,
> Or so thought man, unlearned.
>
> Caesar's legions knew him well,
> Their Scribes and Poets often tell
> Of *Salar*, leaping skyward proud
> In every stream from north to south
> Where gravel clean, above the mouth,
> Was washed by condensed cloud.
>
> From glaciered cirque or forest dew
> The rivulets to rivers grew
> And probed the sea with sweetness clear.
> Unsullied, pure the waters ran
> To nourish earth and service man;
> And salmon spawned with little fear
>
> But now o'er falls and rapids climbed
> To find their gravel redds all slimed
> By progress from the peopled shore.
> Tideward turned, and sped on through
> The sewered river's choking brew
> To die at sea, to spawn no more.
>
> Their days are gone; the rivers sleep.
> No more the Benedictines reap
> A yearly harvest from their mills.

Now leap in stone, on portals arched
Where Rome's triumphant armies marched
Beyond map's end, beyond the rills

Which weep.
No more they leap.

THE IGNOBLE RHINE

Samuel Taylor Coleridge visited Germany with his friend
William Wordsworth in 1798 and upon returning home penned
these lines –

> The River Rhine it is well known
> Doth wash your city of Cologne.
> But tell me, nymphs, what power divine
> Shall henceforth wash the River Rhine?

The poet was probably thinking of the pollution already visible
in Europe's fabled river. Today it is Europe's longest sewer, its
filthy water a danger to aquatic as well as human life.

The 820-mile river originates in the Swiss Alps where in places
it is still pure and invigorating and one may safely drink from it.
As it enters Lake Constance it is thick with mud but emerges
emerald green. At Schaffhausen the river explodes into the
Rheinfall, after which it becomes a fairly swift and sometimes
boisterous stream with numerous tributaries. It then flows for
160 miles across a plain flanked by the Vosges Mountains in the
west and the Black Forest in the east, through German landscapes
rich in knightly lore, cathedral towns and ruins of Roman forts,
passing into less spectacular scenery after entering France. In
the Netherlands the river divides into two arms known as the
Lek and the Waar. At the Hook of Holland it sinks, slimy and
yellow into the North Sea, as if it were tired of life and sought
only annihilation.

The history of the use and abuse of the Rhine mirrors that of
numerous major European rivers. Since the advent of the Industrial Revolution parts of the river have been canalized; sails gave
way to steam and later to diesel engines propelling flotillas of

barges. Numerous factories arose along the banks. Now the bed of the river for much of its navigable length is coated with a thick layer of petroleum sludge and the bacteria count in the estuary is 1,500,000 per cubic centimetre. At times large stretches of the lower Rhine are completely deoxygenated – fishes cannot live there.

Before the industrial age the lengthy river and some of its tributaries were rich in fish life. Salmon fishing was concentrated at the mouth of the Rhine in Holland but there was also considerable netting upstream as far as the Rheinfall and in many of the tributaries. We do not know the size of the original runs in the vast watershed but some catch statistics suggest their abundance. Thus at the bend of the river where the seductive Lorelei is said to have dwelt, fishermen from the villages of St Goar and Goarhausen took as many as 5,000 salmon annually in the nineteenth century. A. D. Barrington, Chief Inspector of Salmon Fisheries for England and Wales, in his report for the year 1886 said that 'the great draft nets at Kralingen [near Rotterdam] dwarf anything seen in England and Wales'. In 1885 they caught 69,500 salmon averaging seventeen pounds each or a total of 1,200,000 pounds, while the nets at Amerstol accounted for 6,500 and at Gorinchen for 6,000, a grand total of 82,000 fish in this area alone.

It is difficult to regulate fishing or maintain a desirable habitat on an international river, especially since before the unification of the German states in 1871 the Rhine was subject to different ruling bodies within Germany itself, in addition to those of the neighbouring countries. The first serious international effort to regulate the fishery was made in 1869 but no convention was signed until 1886; the signatories included the German Empire, the Swiss Confederation and the Netherlands. France abstained. This treaty forbade the placing of stationary nets over halfway across the rivers at low water, set closed seasons in Dutch territory where most of the netting occurred, and established a weekend closure. Both netting and angling were prohibited where the fish were known to spawn, between Mannheim and the Rheinfall, from October 15 to December 31. The contracting parties agreed to restock the river with salmon ova and alevins. An international commission was created to protect the Rhine fishery.

In a paper read at the fourth International Fishery Congress held in Washington, D.C., in September 1908, Dr P. C. Hoek, scientific adviser to the Dutch government, claimed that the convention was working well in Holland waters. The big seines had to cease operations on Sundays and closed a fortnight earlier than before the treaty was signed. 'These changes are quite in accordance with the treaty,' he said. 'Those who fish in the lower parts of the river are to spare a considerable part of the ascending salmon, so that those higher up may profit . . . and also so that part of the fish runs may reach the upper regions, there to spawn. The fishermen of the middle and upper regions, on their part, must also take into consideration the interests of the whole river. They are to spare part of the ascending run for natural propagation.' The number of salmon auctioned at Kralingen dropped from an average of 59,600 in the years 1871–1889 to 38,000 in 1890–1907. In 1907 a total of about 65,000 salmon were caught in the entire river basin and some of the productivity was due to artificial propagation. Worse was to come.

C. L. Deelder and D. E. Van Drummelen described the debacle in a paper read at the seventh annual meeting of the International Union for the Protection of Nature held in Brussels in 1960. In addition to excessive fishing there was a radical alteration of the water regimen in the Rhine. 'Continuous improvement of the navigability of the rivers became a necessity, measures were also taken to ensure a better control of water drainage. At a later phase, hydroelectric plants were constructed in the upper rivers . . . More and more weirs appeared in the upper sections . . . and in most of the tributaries . . . [making] it completely impossible [for migrating fish] to reach their natural spawning grounds.' The salmon runs declined sharply during the turmoil of World War I but improved during the depression that closed many German and French factories. They subsequently fell to very low levels. Ironically World War II provided a temporary respite because the destruction of the great weir near Krembs by Allied bombers facilitated fish migration to the upper waters, resulting in a brief improvement in the runs.

But the rapid growth of industry and increase of power plants on the rivers eventually sealed the doom of the salmon. Deelder and Van Drummelen said, 'Several spawning grounds in the tributaries became so badly polluted that they could no longer serve as such . . . Local pollution in the main river created migration blocks and made the reaches above the affected areas no longer accessible for spawners.' Fewer and fewer salmon appeared at the auctions.

According to Ernest Schwiebert, 'beautiful rivers like the Sieg and Lahn, lined with castles and cathedral towns, no longer hold salmon. The species has vanished from the Moselle, from its mouth at Coblentz throughout Alsace-Lorraine . . . The Saar is also dead with industrial wastes. The Neckar carries the outpourings of the factories surrounding Stuttgart, and holds no salmon from its mouth at Mannheim to its Black Forest origins near the monastery village of Rottwell.' The Main, flowing from the Franconian plateau at Bayreuth through Bamberg and Würzburg to its confluence with the main stem at Mainz, is dead. Its chief affluents like the Pegnitz and Regnitz which meet at Nuremberg, were also salmon producers and are now salmonless. Further upstream hydroelectric projects, as on the Aar and Limmat in Switzerland, blocked fish migration as they do on the Rhine itself between Basel and the Rheinfall.

Some feeble attempts have been made in recent years to clean up parts of the Rhine. But even now some of the towns in Switzerland add their deleterious effluents to the river while potash works in France drop 10,000 tons of salt into it before it reaches Strasbourg; the daily load zooms to 40,000 tons when its flow is dispersed in a series of channels and canals in Holland. Added to this burden are the discharges of petroleum wastes from some 16,000 self-propelled barges that work the river back and forth all the way to Basel.

An International Commission for the Protection of the Rhine Against Pollution was set up in 1963 by all the nations concerned, with the exception of Austria, but it has no power whatsoever, and it is very much hampered by the lack of unanimity. Thus there has been some talk of plans to restore the salmon in German and French parts of the Rhine in recent years, add fish passes to the hydroelectric dams in Switzerland, and restock headwaters with trout and grayling, but nothing has been done. There are now nineteen major nuclear and conventional power plants between the confluence of the River Aar and the Rhine in Switzerland and the German-Dutch border. In an attempt to reduce thermal pollution the German states have required all nuclear plants to have cooling towers and no conventional generating station may heat up the river by more than 3 degrees Centigrade. But France, always intransigent, refuses to abide by these stipulations, and moreover permits potash mines to pollute the streams with enormous deposits of brine, thus seriously reducing the river's capacity to break down sewage and other organic residues. Barges have generally been allowed to empty their tanks with impunity.

However, in December 1970 the West German government finally took action against this abuse of the river. Dr Jurgen Bernhold, head of a Hamburg shipping firm, was found guilty of permitting his barges to dump 20,000 tons of detergents straight into the stream instead of transporting it to Rotterdam as regulations required. He was fined $30,000* and sentenced to a year in jail. The defence claimed that what the firm did was common practice among barge operators.

As we contemplate the destruction of the River Rhine and its once famous salmon, we may recall the words of De Boisset and Vibert: 'Woe to the guardians of the public wealth who, through ignorance or the crime of carelessness, have permitted the property of which they were the keepers to slip through their hands, since they can be sure that God on the Day of Judgment will make them pass on the left side.'

---

* The pound (£) was worth $1.90 at the time of writing.

CHAPTER 9

The Baltic Fisheries

As we move northward on the map of western Europe we may tick off great rivers that were once renowned for their anadromous fishes. Leaving the Low Countries we find that the turbulent North Sea used to feed the Weser and Elbe with a plenitude of salmon before man overfished them and destroyed their habitat. The Weser, flowing northward, rises in the Thuringian forests of East Germany and is formed by the confluence of the Fulda and Werra rivers in Hanover, following a gentle course of 280 miles to Bremerhaven. The Elbe, over twice as long, flows from Czechoslovakia past Dresden and Wittenberg to its estuary at Hamburg. In Germany it is now, like the Rhine, a working river. Several of its numerous tributaries are known to have harboured salmon in the nineteenth century; according to Schwiebert, 'fine spawning runs ascended the Ilmenau, Saale, Mulde and Spree which rise on the Polish border above Berlin'.

The Gudenaa is Denmark's major river, ninety-eight miles long. It rises in East Jutland and flows northward past Silkeborg to Randersfjord. As late as the early twentieth century it supported a sizeable run of *Salmo salar*, now almost extinct in Denmark.

Moving eastward, the rivers draining large parts of Germany and Poland and emptying into the Baltic held substantial salmon populations until recent times. Chief among them were the 680-mile Vistula, Poland's longest river, and the somewhat shorter Oder, both of which rise in the Carpathian Mountains. The Vistula had at least ten tributaries producing salmon, and the Oder probably seven, each of which is a considerable river. Minor Polish rivers also held stocks of these fishes. The Oder is now apparently salmonless while the Vistula supports small runs in one or two of its upper tributaries.

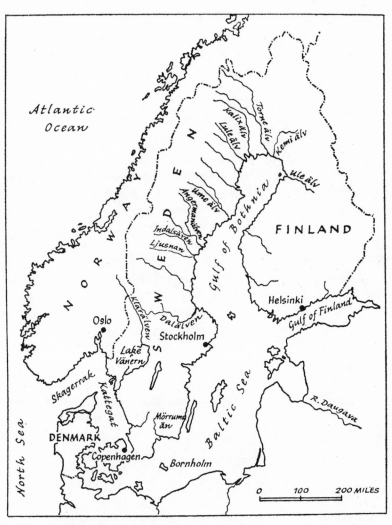

9 *The Baltic area showing major salmon rivers*

A 1975 report on the Baltic salmon by the International Council for the Exploration of the Sea (ICES) lists seventeen rivers in Finland which still hold salmon, some two score in Sweden, and eight major streams in Soviet Russia, draining westward into the sea. According to Dr Arne Lindroth, the Baltic countries, excluding Poland, sent about eight million smolts down to the sea each year at the beginning of the nineteenth century, when a considerable portion of their original stocks had probably already been lost. The ICES estimates that some 4,550,000 smolts are now produced annually in the Baltic countries, of which Sweden contributes 3,215,000, Finland 555,000 and the USSR 780,000; a considerable proportion of these are propagated in hatcheries.

In his study *Salmon in the Baltic Precincts* Gunnar Alm showed that the juveniles usually leave the rivers of Germany and Poland after one year, Denmark and southern Sweden after two years and central and northern Sweden after three years. Northern streams, icebound for several months of the year, are not as rich in food as southern rivers, which permit of a longer breeding season, and thus the fishes take longer to reach the smolt stage, when they are ready to go to sea. Some fishes from the eastern and western Baltic rivers travel together but each returns to its home stream.

They find the Baltic Sea rich in food, and grow rapidly there. They move from the northern rivers southward at a fairly swift pace. Dr Borje Carlin, the late Swedish biologist, reported that smolts released near the mouth of the Indal river in Sweden at the end of May reached the main basin of the Baltic, which is 1,050 miles long, by September and October. After more than a year some of them left their 'green pastures' and started their homeward trek. Many of these grilse, all males, were caught along the Swedish coasts and in their native rivers in July, August and September of the year following smolt migration.

During the second winter the remaining fish of a given year-class are spread throughout the main basin of the southern Baltic and subjected to very intensive fishing by Danish, Polish, Swedish, German and Finnish vessels. In the following spring a considerable proportion of the survivors leave the feeding grounds and return to their native land where they are exposed to a net fishery in the estuaries and rivers.

Some of the fishes stay in the pleasant Baltic waters for three or four winters and upon their return to the rivers may weigh ten to fifteen kilograms. After four winters few members of a given year-class may be found in the sea.

FISH AND POWER, TOO: SWEDEN

Sweden's remaining salmon rivers are in the central and northern part of the country. North-east Sweden is a region of soft and undulating landscapes, covered with forests of spruce, birch and pine. Some of the streams flow past villages of gaily-painted wooden houses, fields where cattle graze and little towns with white wooden churches surmounted by black steeples. In the far north settlements are few and far between, located along the main highway to Haparanda in Finland, on which the motorist is cautioned against moose and elk crossing the road. Railway bridges of astonishing dimensions cross the rivers, on which log rafts are floated to the saw mills.

In winter, snow blankets the north and the ground is frozen. The white-barked, leafless birches are etched against the leaden sky while the pines and spruce form symmetrical patterns of green on the white landscape. Night comes in mid-afternoon but even in daylight the villages and towns seem asleep. Rivers are frozen. Young salmon are hibernating in the deep water, waiting for the spring and the warming sun to call the insect world on which they feed into life.

In the Norrland villages salmon fishing has been an important activity for many centuries, providing subsistence for the farmers and some welcome income. During the Middle Ages the seine was a familiar sight; fish pens, pole traps and float nets were also used. The fishings belonged to the Crown originally but were distributed in time to loyal subjects. They are now owned either by the government or by individuals whose titles are derived from the original grantees or by purchase. Some peasant holdings with fishing rights in the family go back 400 years. The usual arrangement is joint ownership by several families of seines or weirs, with catches divided up according to the number of people in each household.

Rod fishing is limited to four streams on the west coast of Sweden because the salmon are rather unwilling to take the bait in freshwater. Angling is closely regulated with closed seasons set for each river. Commercial fixed or floating gear must shut down one or two days a week.

The Baltic rivers of Sweden offer an enormous potential for power generation, a vital ingredient in the nation's industrial growth which has raised living standards to one of the highest levels in Europe. Since Sweden has only meagre coal deposits, no petroleum or natural gas, flowing water is the prime domestic source of energy. Eighty percent of the hydroelectric potential is found in the Norrland rivers.

Until about World War II the nation's requirements for electric power could be met without significantly intruding upon salmon waters except for the rivers Dal and Ljungen. After the war, the demand for electricity increased rapidly, chiefly for manufacturing, and this brought hydroelectric schemes into other salmon streams. Sweden like other nations in Europe, North America and Asia, was faced with the question of whether it could have fish and power too.

But Sweden has made an enormous and expensive effort to preserve its stock in the face of increasing usurpation of its rivers by hydroelectric projects. No other country in Europe can match its record in salmon conservation.

In the early phases of hydroelectric development the conventional practice was adopted of installing fishways at the dams. It was also customary to plant fry or one-year-old parr in the rivers with favourable nursery grounds to compensate for fish losses. As more power dams were built the pattern became clear: every new project destroyed an additional section of the river until finally all natural production would cease and the nation's salmon stocks would diminish.

Sweden has a unique and exemplary Water Law administered by the Swedish Water Courts which will not approve requests to build hydroelectric plants, either by the State Power Administration or private companies, unless the farmers who own the waters are compensated and the loss of fish is replaced as far as possible by artificial production. In other words, instead of accepting the dictum so frequently heard in many countries that we need kilowatts more than fish, Sweden was determined to have fish and power, too, a challenge that has been successfully met.

At the Bergeforsen dam on the Indal River, one of a network

of thirteen generating plants on this stream stretching from Lake Storsjön to the Gulf of Bothnia, a plaque informs the visitor:

> *The station is built to produce fry and young migratory fish who, before the erection of the power plant, could reproduce freely in the river. Through the river they reached the sea, maintaining rich populations of salmon, sea-trout and river-spawning whitefish. Now, instead, the fry and young are liberated from the rearing station* (below the dam).

The Water Courts stipulate the number of fish to be produced to replace those lost by the impoundment. At Bergeforsen it is 320,000 salmon smolts per annum, 40,000 other smolts, 10 million whitefish fry and 150,000 whitefish fingerlings.

To meet the Courts' stipulations an enormous programme of salmon propagation was started in 1951 'with more hope than actual knowledge about how it would work', said Carlin. 'It could never be a very good business from a fishery point of view since the cost of smolt rearing would be very high anyway. But the Swedish water law says that a power plant must not be built unless everything within reason is done to prevent damage to the fishery and that the losses to the fishery must be taken into consideration in assessing the gains of a project.'

From modest beginnings the hatchery programme has grown to become the largest in Europe. There are now some twenty stations with an annual output of 1,665,000 smolts, or about 30% of the Baltic population. An important factor in the success of the programme has been the development of pelleted food and automated, antiseptic hatcheries as described in Part I, resulting not only in a much higher ratio of survival to the smolt stage than in the wild, but a high rate of adult returns to the point of release. Some of the Swedish hatcheries are hundreds of miles from the rivers where the fish are planted. In addition to the 1,665,000 artificially produced smolts Sweden sends some 1,550,000 wild fish down to the Baltic each year – these come from the rivers Morrüm, Dal, Kalix and Tornio on the Finnish border.

THE DANISH FISHERY

A large majority of Baltic salmon are now caught in the open sea and the remainder in the bays and estuaries of the home rivers. The fish are relentlessly pursued in salt water for eleven months of the year by drift netters and longliners operating from the Danish Island of Bornholm in the southern Baltic, and farther north between the Swedish islands of Öland and Gotland. They are also fished in the eastern Baltic off Memeland down to Brusterort and in the Bay of Danzig. A typical forty-ton Danish cutter setting 1,500 to 2,000 hooks on longlines carries a crew of four. The Danes take more than half of the total Baltic catches.

The Danish fishery has grown rapidly in the past two decades. Before World War II only a few boats fished for salmon. They used drift nets in a zone twenty to twenty-five kilometres from Bornholm, between February and May, and longlines between October and January. Coastal nets were used around the shores of Bornholm. In those days twenty-five to fifty tons were landed annually compared with an average of over 1,100 tons in the 1960s. In 1970 Danish fishermen landed 1,190 tons of salmon, Finnish 450 tons, Swedish 310 tons, German 118 tons, Russian 101 tons, and Polish thirty-eight tons, including fish caught in the rivers, a total of 2,207 tons or 17% of world landings of *Salmo salar*.

Copenhagen, where fishermen land their Baltic and Greenland catches, now vies with London as the major European market-place for Atlantic salmon. About half the volume sold there is smoked for the luxury trade.

RUSSIA'S ATLANTIC SALMON

Russia's Atlantic salmon stocks are quite small compared with its Pacific salmon stocks. Yet the Soviet government endeavours to maintain them, against great difficulties, at maximum levels.

The Baltic rivers hosting these fishes include the two major Lithuanian waterways, the 600-mile Niemen and 215-mile Venta, as well as the Latvian Daugava (also called the West Dvina) which rises in the Valday Hills only a few miles from the sources of the Volga and Dnieper and drops into the Gulf of Riga, 635 miles away. These river systems supplied the Lithuanian and Latvian people with abundant fishes for centuries. Today the West Dvina is one of the few salmon rivers left in the Baltic precincts of the Soviet Union, and its original stocks have been greatly reduced: it sends only 200,000 wild smolts to the sea each year, plus 165,000 produced in hatcheries.

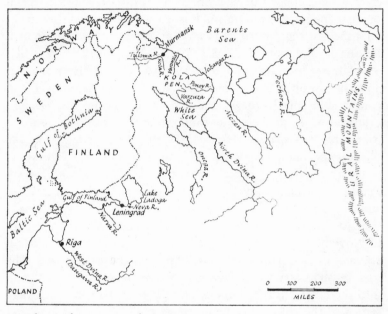

10 *Atlantic salmon rivers in the USSR*

Other Russian salmon rivers draining into the Baltic are the short Neva which issues from Lake Ladoga and flows past Leningrad to the Gulf of Finland; the Salaca, Narva, Luga and Gauya.

The many north-flowing rivers emptying into the Arctic Ocean possess varying amounts of salmon. Some of them drain immense areas and are veined with a large number of tributaries. They include the Onega, 250 miles long; the North Dvina whose main stem is 455 miles and one of its tributaries, the Vychega, 655 miles long; and the 550-mile Mezen, home of the Cossacks. All empty into the White Sea.

Salmon are also found in the Jokanga, Varzuza and Ponoy Rivers of the Kola Peninsula, flowing into the Barents Sea. The longest Atlantic salmon river in the world is the Pechora, which issues from the Ural Mountains and runs into the Barents Sea after an 1,100-mile course; it is a true Arctic river with numerous small tributaries and two large ones, the Usa and Izhma. For the greater part of its length the Pechora is a broad and slow-flowing river which supports navigation. Most of the vegetative cover in the basin consists of tundra and it is sparsely populated. In a paper published in the *Journal de Conseil* of the International Council for the Exploration of the Sea, N. M. Vladimirskaya says that only large salmon reach the upper waters of the Pechora, making a journey of up to a thousand miles, a record for *Salmo salar*, and comparable only to the Pacific salmon that go up the Yukon's headwaters. Moreover, she found that 11% of the fish she examined had spawned twice and 2% thrice, suggesting the phenomenal energy they expended in their upstream journeys.

The easternmost Atlantic salmon river is the Kara (on the Kara Peninsula) which drains the northernmost shoulder of the Urals and forms the boundary between European and Asiatic Russia.

Spawning in the Arctic regions usually occurs from September to November and the eggs take six months to hatch in the frigid climate, or more than twice as long as in the British Isles. The young fish may stay in the rivers up to five years before venturing into the ocean, so that some adults taken in the nets when they return to the rivers may be seven years old, five feet long and weigh up to forty-five kilograms.

The Russians say they do not allow salmon to be fished offshore, either in the Pacific or Atlantic Oceans, and that they can only be taken when they reach their maximum weight and are in prime condition. Fishing is said to be well regulated and catch limits are established. How well these conservation measures are enforced we do not know.

There are fifteen Atlantic salmon hatcheries in operation, both in the Baltic and Arctic drainages. One of the most important is at Murmansk. The hatcheries have an annual production of 1.4 million large parr and one-year smolts. Two additional hatcheries are under construction. The Russians claim they can rear seagoing smolts in eight months, compared with two years in Sweden, through the use of special feeds that speed up growth.

The status of Russia's Atlantic salmon stocks is difficult to ascertain. Kazimierz and Rutkowicz in their book *The Barents Sea* claim that the Russians harvested an average of 1,800 metric tons in this area annually in the period 1920 to 1929. Data published by the International Council for the Exploration of the Sea show that total Russian catches of Atlantic salmon in the years 1964–1973 averaged only 700 tons.

Under the Czarist regime, before the industrialization of Soviet Russia, salmon were quite abundant in the vast areas drained by the rivers we have listed. It must have formed a staple of the peasant diet as well as of townspeople. This is suggested by the fact that poor Jewish immigrants from eastern Europe to the United States brought their taste for mild-cure salmon, which they call 'lox', with them, and it has become a universal delicacy in Jewish communities.

The industrialization of Russia has no doubt resulted in the ruin of salmon rivers as in other countries. For example, Russian engineers are engaged in an ambitious scheme affecting the Pechora River. They have exploded a nuclear device with the force of 45,000 pounds of TNT near Berezovka in order to build a canal to divert water from the northward-flowing Pechora into the Kolva River in the Urals. In a dramatic reversal of flow the Pechora water will wind up in the Caspian Sea, which has been shrinking for half a century, thus ruining one of the best remaining Atlantic salmon stocks in Russia.

FINLAND'S SALMON

Finland is a heavily forested land dissected by thousands of rivers and lakes. Almost the entire country lies north of latitude 60 degrees north, stretching from the Gulf of Finland to well within the Arctic Circle. Some of the rivers flow into the Baltic Sea and others into the Arctic. About 70% of the country is covered with trees – pine, Scots fir, Norway spruce and birch mixed with aspen predominate. Since most of these species are excellent pulping trees, paper, pulp and other forest products are the leading exports. Their processing requires considerable amounts of water and electricity; hence many rivers have been dammed and the anadromous fishes sacrificed. In the conflict of fish versus power, the Finns have usually opted for kilowatts.

The Kemi River which flows for 300 miles through the Lapland fells and tundra to the Gulf of Bothnia, a region inhabited by relatively few human beings but large numbers of reindeer, lynx and elk, has the largest power potential of any Finnish stream. The Kaekemi weir at the mouth of the river was fished for several hundred years, providing the farmers with food and extra income. The Kemi was destroyed as a salmon river by dams before and after World War II – there are now thirteen hydro-electric installations on this waterway. South of the Kemi flows the much shorter Oulü River over a series of waterfalls from Lake Oulü to the Gulf of Bothnia. Before hydroelectric plants were built salmon used to ascend to Lake Oulujarvi and its feeder streams and spawned both in the lake and river. There are few salmon left in the Oulü.

A similar fate befell the two great rivers of southern Finland, the Kymi and Kokenmaeki. As far back as 1948 the biologist T. H. Jarvi wrote, 'These streams completely lost their original conditions and simultaneously their importance as salmon rivers. Dams now block the ascent of salmon and consequently have done away with feeding areas for parr. Several fishing stations where my material was formerly collected have had to cease operations.'

There are still salmon in Arctic Lapland, especially in tributaries of the mighty Tana which forms the border with Norway. Other Norwegian salmon ascend into Finland above the town of Kirkenes near the Russian border, in the headwaters of the Neiden river.

In 1966 Seppo Hurme published a survey of Finland's salmon and trout rivers at the behest of the International Council for the Exploration of the Sea. He divided the forty-seven streams into four classes on the basis of their 'nature, usage, care and conservation'. Six large rivers were placed in Class I; twenty medium-sized streams in Class II; seventeen small rivers in Class III; and four uncertain ones in Class IV. He found that 'natural salmon and trout stocks have now died in fifteen rivers due to cultural effects. This includes four large and six medium-sized rivers, so that the loss of salmon and trout is notably large.' The remaining thirty-two rivers had salmonid populations of varying size but it was clear that 'the greater part of the resource has been destroyed due to damming of rivers, pollution, regulation of flow for drainage and flood control, drying up of swamps and bogs, timber floating, silting of river mouths, overfishing at river mouths, and catches of small salmon in the Baltic which reduced the seed stock.'

Hurme has proposed an ambitious programme for repopulating the rivers by means of large-scale artificial production – the fishes would be released, as in Sweden, below the lowermost dams and the runs cropped as they return to the mouths of the river, thus supplying the Baltic fishery as well. He estimated that the six large rivers could support plantings of about 3,500,000 smolts per year and all the other suitable streams an additional 1,100,000, or about as much as the potential of all Baltic rivers on the Swedish side. So far only one hatchery has been built, at Monata, with a capacity of 120,000 smolts, as a result of the Finnish Water Law which imposes an obligation on dam builders to compensate for losses of natural runs.

Hurme is also investigating the possibility of rehabilitating some of the small salmon and trout rivers in the area from Hango to Turku that have been ruined by dams and pollution, especially from pulp mills. However, a letter from Hurme of January 13, 1975, says that the Finnish government is in no mood to rehabilitate the salmonid fisheries: 'The state machinery works very slowly in handling such matters. There are only some plans on paper, the concrete results lie ahead in the future.'

The increasing pollution of the Baltic Sea does not bode well for its fisheries, especially sensitive species like salmon. Two hundred rivers pour their filth along 12,000 miles of coastline into what used to be sea-green and crystal-clear waters. The 70,000 ships sailing the sea annually, including 3,000 tankers carrying petroleum products, burden the Baltic with their refuse. In some areas, especially in deeper water, the oxygen concentration is zero and almost no forms of aquatic life can be supported.

DDT washing off farmland is destroying marine fauna; blue algae blooms generated from organic wastes are spreading; broad slicks of oil lie on the beaches. In short, first aid measures are urgently needed if the Baltic is not to become a dying body of water. International conventions are in the making but getting agreement among nations on environmental problems is a very slow process.

CHAPTER 10

Norway and Iceland

NORWAY'S SALMON

THE coastline of Norway is about 1,200 miles long, deeply indented by numerous fjords of incredible beauty and protected by offshore islands and strings of skerries. Mountains and fjords mould the landscape and the ocean washes the shores with the warm current of the Gulf Stream, enticing hordes of anadromous fishes – salmon and sea trout – into the rivers and returning them in an endless cycle. Glaciers cover many of the escarpments from Stavanger in the south to the Lyngen Alps in the north. Some of the fjords, like Sognefjord, run inland for a hundred miles into the towering mountains and are up to two and a half miles wide and two-thirds of a mile deep. Many salmon rivers empty into this fjord, of which some are long like the fabled Laerdal. Others are like the Aurland, which springs full blown from Lake Vassbygd, makes a swift course of only four miles yet has an abundance of fish in good years.

Many Norwegian rivers issue from snow-clad mountains or glaciers, like the Gaula in the south which runs for fifty miles over a hard and rocky terrain that gives the stream its crystalline clarity. Numerous waterfalls have been laddered in Norway to enable the salmon to surmount them, the cold water crashing down in a milky foam that spends itself on the way to the sea. The rivers are dotted with quiet pools where the fish can be taken by rods amid idyllic settings; hence Norway is one of the world's leading salmon angling countries.

Some of the best rivers are relatively short and often furious. They are concentrated in the central and northern counties, especially Finnmark, which borders the Arctic Ocean. I have seen creeks in Norway so narrow a tall man could step across yet

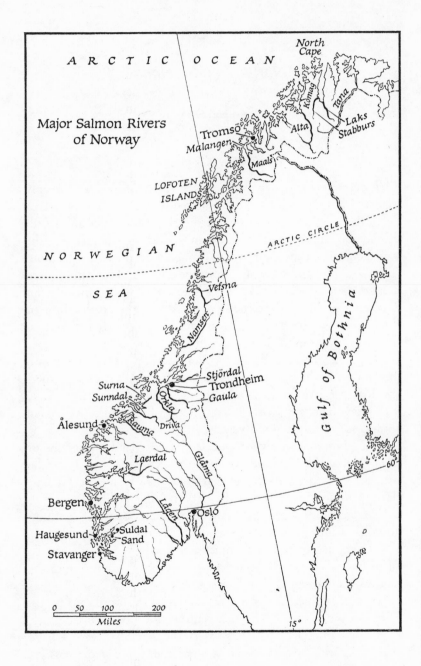

ARCTIC OCEAN

North
Cape

Major Salmon Rivers
of Norway

Tromsö
Malangen

Komag

Tana

Alta

Laks
Stabburs

Maals

LOFOTEN
ISLANDS

ARCTIC CIRCLE

NORWEGIAN

Vefsna

SEA

Namsen

Surna
Sunndal

Stjördal
Trondheim
Gaula

Orkla

Ålesund

Rauma

Driva

Gulf of Bothnia

Laerdal

Glåma

Bergen

Lågen

Oslo

Haugesund
Stavanger

Suldal
Sand

60°

0   50   100   200
Miles

15°

they teemed with spawning salmon. About 200 rivers and their tributaries attract regular runs of these fishes.

In the cold waters of the north juvenile salmon mature slowly. In the Trøndelag district most of the parr remain in freshwater for three or four years and occasional specimens for five years. They also tend to stay longer in the ocean than those emanating from the southern areas because feed is less abundant. Norway is famous for its hefty salmon. The world's record for a rod-caught Atlantic fish weighing seventy-nine pounds came from the Tana River, while the Arøy yielded the largest fly-caught salmon, sixty-eight and a half pounds.

Norwegian salmon in history

The association of man with salmon in Scandinavia dates at least from the Neolithic Age. Inhabitants of sub-Arctic areas showed their appreciation of the animals that sustained them by carving their images on rocks, as the cave dwellers did in France and Spain. A number of primitive fishing implements made of antler have been discovered in ancient fishing sites around Varangerfjord. The nomadic Lapps of the far north used osier traps to catch fish at the mouths of the rivers and sometimes fashioned crude seines. In southern Scandinavia, especially Denmark, where the Neolithic people lived on the banks of rivers or margins of lakes, excavations show they fished on a considerable scale.

In the Middle Ages fish was one of the most important foods and hence the runs were well protected. The earliest fishing legislation dates from about 900; it laid down the principle that 'the salmon shall go from the beach to the mountains, if it wishes to go'. 'This means that no man should be allowed to close the river and take all the fish for himself,' says the biologist Magnus Berg. So valuable were these fishes that when King Haakon I in 950 decided to fix the boundaries between the maritime and interior provinces, he set the line of demarcation at the farthest limit of salmon migration into the interior. Taxes on herring and salmon catches became one of the principal sources of Crown revenues in the Middle Ages.

But, as in other countries, 'as the centuries passed and

population increased many rivers were closed by traps or other gear, or by dams, and in some of them, especially in south-east Norway, the salmon almost disappeared'.

The first comprehensive salmon law was passed in 1848. At that date it was probably the best in Europe: but it took a long time to become effective.

In a country with very little arable land the fisheries were highly prized by landowners as a source of food. In the summer and fall men, women and children worked together to harvest the runs and prepare the fish for storage during the winter. The custom was to divide the catches among the participants in equal shares. The most common gear was the bag net; the first contraption of this kind was set up at the mouth of the Haa River at Jaederen in the 1820s; by 1875 there were 200 in operation. From then on they increased rapidly until a peak of 9,000 was reached in 1903. In the past century salmon fishing has tended to move from the river and fjords out to the sea. In 1977 about 85% of the total harvest was landed in saltwater and 15% in the rivers.

Sport fishing

The idea of fishing for sport was unknown in Norway until after the Napoleonic wars, when Englishmen ventured into the country with their rods. The unlettered farmers, astonished at the visitors' willingness to pay for the privilege of fishing their waters, welcomed them with a warmth that contrasted with their native taciturnity. Among the first to try the Norwegian streams were William Belton and Sir Hyde Parker, 8th Baronet. They fished several rivers from 1829 to 1840 and sent back jubilant reports to their friends. In 1837 Belton landed 1,172 pounds of salmon from the Namsen river in Trøndelag. His book, *Two Summers in Norway*, published in 1840, spread the news of marvellous sport but warned 'the tourist of common activity and hardihood (and no others have any business to penetrate into Norway) he will have to buy his own cariole, the carriage of the country, take with him his own harness and be his own charioteer.' A trip to Norway was then an arduous adventure, 'demanding not only time and money but the readiness and zest to rough it'. In the nineteenth century many wealthy Britons did.

A host of titled and untitled sportsmen followed Belton and Parker to the fjord rivers, purchased leases and spent their summers there. The natives called the streams they leased 'Lords Rivers', as they still do. Such were the Namsen, Stjørdal, Driva, Alta, Rauma and many others.

Among the aristocrats who fished these streams in the nineteenth century were the Dukes of Marlborough, Roxburgh and Westminster, Lord William Beresford, the Earl of Leicester, Lord Arbuthnot, and others. They used hickory rods as long as twenty-four feet, traditional English tackle, and brought provisions not obtainable in that 'barbarian country,' as Sir Humphry Davy called it. The visitors really lived like lords. They built sturdy lodges and stocked them with comfortable furniture, books, gaming tables, and choice food and drinks. Some of them brought their wives, who were equally ardent anglers. John Dean Caton in *A Summer in Norway* describes the arrival of an American family on a fishing expedition at Kristiansand in the 1870s. It took a lighter to carry all their baggage and supplies, 'among which were many baskets of champagne, with a great abundance of provisions of nearly all kinds which good living suggests . . . Off they went, with the good wishes of their friends left behind, with a journey of thirty to forty miles before them to reach the river they rented.'

British fishermen left a tradition of courtesy and gentility behind them and some fantastic angling records. They loved the rivers and the country and treated the gillies and other natives who worked for them with great consideration. A collection of letters written to the gillie Nils Renå by his English employers reveals the deep affection Englishmen had for the rivers and people associated with the sport. Captain Harry L. Townshend wrote to the old man in 1918:

I have been thinking a great deal lately about Renaa. Poor Lord Estcourt and myself always made a note in red ink that the fish never arrived at Renaa until June 14th. I hope you will have a good season and plenty of water and fish . . .

I have not heard Norway very much talked about, and I

think it will be some time longer before things are the same. All the old lot of fishermen who were mostly country gentlemen are so heavily taxed now that they have no money left for the pleasures and for sport. It is the munitions makers and those who have profiteered during the war who have got all the money now, and they don't know anything about sport and what it means . . .

Since the sun never quite sets in the far north during the summer, men fished all night as well as during the day, hiring gillies in shifts. Thus the Duke of Roxburgh caught thirty-nine salmon and grilse in one night on the Alta in 1860 and the Duke of Westminster seventy-five years later landed thirty-six salmon weighing 792 pounds, in one night on the same stream. Major Charles Wingfield, who held the lease on the Stjørdal from 1859 to 1893, recorded catches, with his friends, of 2,214 grilse weighing 10,955 pounds and 4,135 salmon totalling 64,552 pounds in that period, or an average of 187 fish weighing 2,220 pounds per year.

As two world wars and socialist governments in Europe reduced the ranks of royalty and aristocracy, and taxed their wealth, many of the lords' rivers were leased to industrialists, bankers, and newspapers; they were used to promote business by travel agencies, airlines, shipping firms and the like.

The Laerdal, flowing into Sognefjord, has probably hosted more bluebloods – kings, princes, titled personages of many lands – than any angling stream in the world. Its source lies in the high Fillefjell country, a region of mountains and glaciers about 150 miles above Oslo. It drops fifty miles through a spectacular valley of forests, farmsteads and waterfalls. There are salmon in sixteen miles of the river between Ulvisfossen and the village of Laerdalsoyri at the mouth. A waterfall above the village forms a picturesque backdrop for the Lindstrom hotel, where the nobs stay.

The Laerdal was discovered in 1854 by the British painter James Randall, who spent a summer there. He leased the river for thirty years and his portfolios of the landscape, published in England, attracted wide attention to Norway's scenic splendours. John Chatworth Masters, master of the Quorn in Victoria's reign, held the lease after Randall, followed by Edward Portman and his brother Lord Henry Portman. In the summer of 1868 the Portman party caught some 660 salmon, weighing over 5,000 pounds.

The Mals, 250 miles above the Arctic Circle, is probably the most spectacular of Norwegian rivers for it contains the renowned Malangsfoss pool lying below the Malang waterfall. Here the river churns through 500 yards of broken boulders and mossy ledges before dropping seventy-five feet into the whirligig. The thundering falls block the entire spawning run and hold it up for almost a month. Thousands of silvery-pink fish lie waiting until the water level drops and permits them to move up the ladder to reach their spawning grounds in the tributaries. The pool itself has been likened to a 'water-filled stadium 300 yards in diameter, shaped like a gargantuan bottle with the waterfall in the narrow throat'. There is room for two or three boats at the edge of the pool where record catches have been made. A beat could be rented in 1974 for $1,380 a week per rod.

The Namsen lies in an idyllic and secluded part of southern Norway, rushing through a deep and often rocky valley. From his boat the fisherman may see elk pause in the forest clearing.

In 1975 catches on the twenty most productive rivers, including small amounts of sea trout and char, were as follows (in kilograms):

Tana	184,327	Komag	7,074
Alta	33,109	Neiden	6,798
Lågen	19,817	Mals	6,163
Namsen	17,611	Laks & Porsanger	5,622
Gaula	16,536	Stordal	5,046
Ørsta	14,503	Etne	4,991
Laerdal	10,308	Gaula	4,492
Driva	10,203	Søndre Vartal	4,442
Stjørdal	8,698	Repparfjord	4,432
Vefsna	8,200		

The future of the Norwegian fishery

Norway has been one of the top producers of Atlantic salmon

in the twentieth century, husbanding and building up the resource and, until very recent years, keeping overfishing in check. The most important gear is still the bag net, a self-fishing device commonly set in the estuaries and along the coast, which traps the fish as they seek their home rivers.

After World War II the Norwegian government made an investigation of the status of the freshwater fisheries and as a result inaugurated a salmon enhancement programme financed partly by a tax on catches and anglers' fees. Many hatcheries were built (in 1973 there were forty-two stations which produced 4,360,000 salmon fry); fishways were erected over difficult cascades and waterfalls; and some 600 miles of new spawning grounds were opened up. Harvests increased considerably in the ensuing years.

In 1966 a drift-net fishery beyond territorial limits arose which threatened to make serious inroads on the stocks. These modern drifters are large, gasoline-powered vessels; their nets are shot as they steam slowly downwind, then the engines are stopped and they swing around to face upwind. They not only catch mature fish but many immatures as well. Besides decimating the breeding stock, the offshore monofilament gillnet fishery injures even the fish that escape. Many die and others are prevented from spawning when they finally reach home waters.

The fishery began with ten boats which caught about eighty tons of salmon in 1966 and increased to fifty-one vessels and 918 tons in 1969, including forty Danish, some Norwegian and a few German, Swedish and Faroese boats. That year the alarmed Norwegian government, seeing homewater catches decline, proclaimed a ban on drift-net fishing inside a basic line drawn between the outermost skerries and the coast. Norwegian fishermen are permitted to take salmon inside this line but not beyond it – in 1973 they landed some 250 tons. Mainly as a result of the ban (which does not affect foreign vessels) Norwegian salmon landings rose from 1,288 tons in 1970, the lowest in twenty years, to 1806 tons in 1973. River catches that year were double those of 1969. The year 1974 was equally good.

In 1975, however, a new threat arose with an upsurge of netting by small, private boat-owners living along Norway's coast and using monofilament nets similar to those employed by professional drifters outside territorial waters. According to R. J. Brooks, writing in *Salmon and Trout* (December 1975), these fishermen 'have absolutely no restrictions, they pay no licence fees, and they make no returns of catches, for either statistical or tax purposes. By using many thirty to forty–metre nets joined together they can completely bar the entrance to any fjord with nets effectively two kilometres long.' So far the Norwegian government has failed to crack down on them, and the result has been a decrease in salmon landings in many prolific rivers such as the Laerdal and Arøy, to the dismay of anglers in these dearly rented waters.

'To make matters worse,' says Brooks, 'the plunderers do not confine their activities to the area where there are no restrictions, i.e. between the inshore boundary of four nautical miles from the coast and the international boundary of twelve nautical miles, but operate also, quite unlawfully, within the inshore limits.' The boats are equipped with walkie-talkies to warn each other of police in the vicinity, in which case they quickly pull in their drift nets and begin to fish with permissible tackle. Many have electronic equipment to locate salmon shoals; 'clearly the present supervising force is quite unable to cope with the problem, and entirely new laws are needed to halt the destruction'.

A communication from Mr Brooks, who lives in Denmark and watches the Norwegian fishery closely, dated September 26, 1977, says: 'New regulations for drift netting were finally introduced in the spring of 1977 but again the Minister refused to follow the advice of his experts and permitted a far greater length of nets per boat than recommended.

'Politics and vote catching was clearly more important than the survival of salmon, as not only did the Minister allow too many nets but, half way through the season, actually gave way to pressure . . . by increasing the permitted net length still further. Laughably enough, even this did not satisfy the drift netters for they openly defied the government by continuing to fish with as many nets as they wished until the government would agree to pay them full compensation to stop.

'There the matter stood all through the 1977 season with the obvious result that Norwegian fjords and rivers had their worst season ever and it is now doubtful if any hatcheries will contain salmon roe this winter let alone the spawning beds in the rivers themselves.'

There are additional threats to the salmon runs. Increased demand for hydroelectricity indicates that more rivers may soon be dammed. For example, the government plans to build a dam on the upper Gaula and also a generating plant to tap the great waterfall, where there is now an ancient fish ladder. In southeastern Norway some stocks are menaced by atmospheric pollution drifting from Britain and the continent. According to Brynjulf Ottar, head of the Norwegian Institute for Air Research, quoted in the *Guardian* of January 8, 1970, southern Norway's forests and fisheries could eventually be destroyed unless steps are taken internationally to curb air pollution. His warning seems, so far, to have gone unheeded.

What does the future hold for Norway's salmon? In the past the Norwegian people have shown that, unlike the French, Spanish and English, they cherish this unique resource, and hence one can assume they will curb excessive netting. As Brooks says, 'Nowhere in the [Atlantic salmon] world are the possibilities so great. Norway's clear, unpolluted and sparkling rivers are ideal for salmon and sea-trout culture. The snow-covered mountains are ideal reservoirs to provide perfect water conditions for fishing from the beginning to the end of the seasons. Anglers can enjoy perfect weather conditions in brilliant sunshine without the anxiety of a possible water shortage. Such a combination applies in no other salmon producing country.'

ICELAND'S SALMON

Iceland is an island jutting against the Arctic Circle in the northeast Atlantic Ocean. About a fourth larger than Ireland, it supports only 210,000 people. Ice-cold waters wash the northeast coast but the rest of the country is warmed by the Gulf Stream; here the climate is humid and temperate with rare periods of frost. In fact, a large part of Iceland has a climate like that of northern Scotland. The scenery is marked by glaciation and vulcanism. One-eighth of Iceland is under ice and one glacier, the Vatna Jøkull, is 3,000 feet thick, the largest in Europe. The interior is for the most part a striking plateau of volcanic rock.

The country is richly endowed with rivers and lakes. Except in the desert region the streams are rapid and large, fed by heavy precipitation and by melting glaciers in summer. A majority of the inhabitants live in the south-west around the capital Reykjavik. Except for birches here and there and mountain ash which seldom attain more than thirty feet in height, the landscape is treeless. Along the coastal plain there is a vast grassland and alongside the glaciers are green meadows covered in summer with wildflowers and supporting populations of sheep, cattle and horses.

Salmon frequent about seventy rivers and penetrate inland up to sixty miles, rarely more. Most of them are in the western half of the country: the most productive is the Ellidaá which flows in the outskirts of the capital. In the Arnessysla district there is the Ölfuss-Hvita complex, while in the Borgarfjördur valley there is another Hvita River system, with Grimsa, Thvera and Nordura as the most important tributaries. Towards the north of the capital there is Laxa i Kjos, while in the north-west there are the Midfjardara, Vididalsa, Vatnsdalsa, Laxa and Blanda Rivers. The best and largest salmon stream in the north-east is the Laxa which flows near the town of Husavik.

Iceland has been inhabited since the ninth century by people of Scandinavian origin who still use a language that is close to the Germanic tongues of the Middle Ages from which English is mainly derived. That salmon were plentiful originally is evident from historical records. Terkel M. Terkelsen, writing in *Salmon and Trout* (May, 1965), quotes from a history of the Grimsa valley: 'In the autumn the fjord is sometimes so tightly packed with salmon that the traveller cannot force the horse across.' The Ellidaá is said to have been so populous fifty years ago, according to Major-General R. N. Stewart, that a single party of fishermen caught over 2,000 salmon in one season.

The mainstay of the Icelandic diet is fish, and fisheries are the basis of the economy. After World War II, when overfishing was diagnosed in some rivers, salmon was declared a 'freshwater fish' and netting in the estuaries was forbidden. Only three glacial streams may now be netted and this is done with fixed nets on the banks. There is no fishing for salmon in the sea, and all rivers are open to angling, which is closely regulated. Natural stocks are bolstered by eight artificial rearing stations; they are of small capacity, producing 30,000 to 40,000 smolts per year. Annual salmon landings are around 200 metric tons.

Icelandic salmon tend to have a long juvenile life in the frigid rivers, waiting up to six years before venturing out to sea, where they spend an average of two years. Their migratory routes are generally unknown although a few have turned up in the nets of Greenland fishermen. The full-grown adults are rather small, weighing from four to twelve pounds, and larger specimen are rare – very few have been recorded weighing as much as forty pounds.

Despite its small resource, and small-sized fish, Iceland has become a popular haunt of foreign anglers who pay large sums for their sport. As in Norway, the British introduced the sport. 'When I first visited the country in 1912,' said Major-General R. N. Stewart, 'no Icelander that I heard of fished for sport, except a few boys. This was due to the fact that few of them had any leisure, partly to the consideration that fish was food and the less time spent in securing food, the more time there was for attending to more urgent problems. When the farmers learned they could derive considerable income from foreigners who wished to lease their streams they welcomed them.'

Iceland is one of the few countries in Europe where the natural environment is still universally pristine. It has been 'little damaged by hydroelectric developments or pollution,' says Thor Gudjonsson, Director of the Institute of Freshwater Fisheries. 'Thus, the rivers are producing Atlantic salmon to their full capacity, and fishing is successfully restricted to prevent overfishing.'

Rod fishing is booming and the price of beats rises continually. Fishing associations whose members own the rights now control the rivers and rent them to clubs, travel agencies and others. The number of rods in each stream is determined by the Directorate of Freshwater Fisheries and is kept within reasonable limits in order to ensure good sport. Angling is permitted between 7 am and 10 pm in summer with a mid-day break of two or three hours. As in other European countries, there are no bag limits and the angler is permitted to retain his catch. Rod fishermen take an estimated 30,000 salmon yearly, considerably more than in England and Wales. The most fruitful river is the Ellidaá.

Nearly all the salmon rivers are controlled by farmers who own the adjoining land. They band together to control a stretch of the river, decide how many rods can be accommodated, and reap the profits. On one of the most frequented rivers, the Laxa i Kjos, for example, there are about fifteen miles of fishable water limited to ten rods at a time. One man fishes a beat in the morning and another in the afternoon and evening. An agent usually handles arrangements with anglers or tourist agencies who book foreign visitors.

To keep up the level of the stocks the owners watch the runs and plant parr or smolts for restocking when necessary. Poaching is minimal because in a closed society like that of Iceland there is a social stigma attached to this practice. As Ernest Schwiebert, who has fished in Iceland, says, 'If an Icelander is caught poaching a lenient judge doesn't merely fine him part of a night's profit – he is unceremoniously slapped in the pokey, and no excuses are accepted . . . His fellow townsmen brand him as a poacher and turn their backs when he passes.' Nevertheless a poor man can gain access to a river by joining a club at very small cost and fish an uncommitted beat, first obtaining permission from the owner.

CHAPTER II

The American Debacle

THE Old Norse saga of Eric the Red describes the adventures of Leif Ericsson who, around the year 955, founded the first colony in North America, which he called Vinland. The site may have been on the Newfoundland coast or Cape Cod, but wherever it was salmon abounded in nearby waters. The saga says: 'We found that there were quite a few salmon in the river, especially in the autumn, and sometimes we even caught one with our hands. The fishermen also from time to time made excellent catches of salmon out at sea and the fishes were, on the average, larger than their relatives that we knew from Greenland.'

Historical perspective

Long before the Greenlanders came to America the Indians had made good use of the salmon in the coastal rivers, from Long Island Sound and possibly the Hudson and Susquehanna River drainage, to Ungava Bay in Canada. They had excellent hunting and fishing gear, including toggle harpoon heads made of stone and leisters with finely carved bone barbs for taking large fish.

Salmon wandered far inland in Labrador and Quebec and up the St Lawrence into numerous feeder streams. For the most part the rivers flowed through one of the world's richest forest belts, covering the undulating valleys, mountains and hills, the margins of lakes and other waterways. The predominantly coniferous forest stretched from Newfoundland to New York state and sent an arm along the main body of the Appalachian Mountains.

Of the numerous rivers which harboured *Salmo salar* in New England the Connecticut was the longest and perhaps the richest. It originates in lakes near the Canadian border, forms the

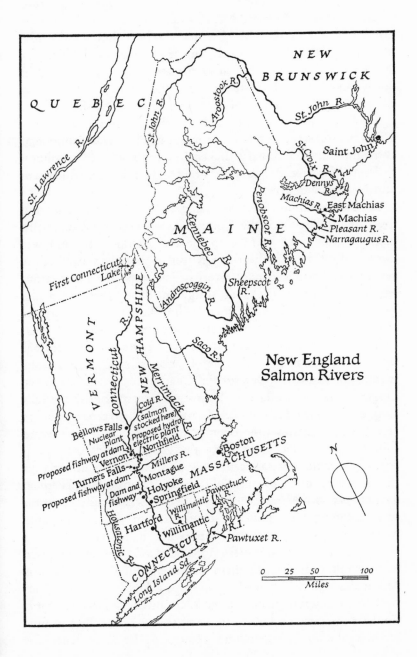

New England
Salmon Rivers

boundary between New Hampshire and Vermont, and runs southward through central Massachusetts and Connecticut to the sea at Old Saybrook. The Merrimack, which rises in the White Mountains, flows southward through New Hampshire for seventy-eight miles, drops into Massachusetts and then runs north-eastward for thirty-five miles to the ocean. Salmon used to come up the Connecticut as far as Colebrook, New Hampshire, a distance of 300 miles and on the Merrimack all the way to the Pemigewasset River, one of its sources in New Hampshire, and even into the subtributary, Baker River. Rhode Island salmon rivers included the Paweatuck, Wood and Pawtucket which runs into Narragansett Bay.

The richest salmon river in Maine was the Penobscot, about a third of the length of the Connecticut. Samuel de Champlain sailed up this river in 1604 to the end of tidewater and was impressed by the wealth of fish as well as its clear waters. Altogether Maine had a score of rivers which supported anadromous fish like salmon, shad, and sturgeon. Salmon ascended the Penobscot to Grand Falls near Millinocket, the Kennebec to above Caratunk Falls, and the Androscoggin to Rumford Falls. There were small landlocked salmon called *Ouananiche* in several lakes in Maine, and populations of larger salmon in numerous streams feeding Lakes Ontario and Champlain.

The Indians had ancient fishing stations at many of the falls such as Amoskeag Falls on the Merrimack, where the river drops eighty feet in half a mile over granite ledges, and at Bellows Falls on the Connecticut where the flow descends over steep rocks into a roaring cataract. They also built weirs at strategic places to take their annual supply of fish. Thoreau in *A Week on the Concord and Merrimack Rivers* describes the vestiges of an ancient Indian weir near the confluence of the two streams where salmon, eel, sturgeon, lamprey and bass were caught in Colonial times. At Amoskeag Falls, Colonial gentlemen came to take salmon, spearing them or taking them with fly nets stretched across the channel, or in traps called 'pots'. The fishes were so abundant in many streams that sometimes, as in Hartford, Connecticut, when a housewife went to the fishmonger to buy mackerel she had to take salmon as a tie-in sale.

Families in the Connecticut valley salted salmon in casks. In Hartford they fetched a penny a pound in the eighteenth century, rising to two or three pence at the time of the American Revolution. Salmon and shad were taken together in sweep nets worked from the wharves, or in scoop nets in the deep basin at the foot of South Hadley Falls. As many as 3,700 salmon were caught in a single drift at Old Saybrook's South Cove. Peters in his *History of Connecticut*, published in 1783, reported that 'from the number of seines employed to catch the fish passing up the locks one might be led to suppose that the whole [run] must be stopped, yet in six months' time they return to the sea in such multitudes of young ones as to fill the Connecticut River for many days, and no finite being can stop them.'

Like the Connecticut, the Merrimack was rich in salmon, shad, lamprey, eel, striped bass and sturgeon, all desirable food fishes. They were taken by the colonists with nets, scoops, spears and snares, much the same gear used by the Indians. A report prepared by the first Fish Commissioners of Massachusetts in 1866, mentions a Mr Barron of Woodstock, New Hampshire, aged seventy-eight, who remembered that the salmon used to come up the river in his youth in such vast numbers that 'it was then the habit for each family that lived near the stream to lay in some four barrels of salted salmon which would be equal to one hundred fish'. Another old man, Mr Charles Ramsay of Amesbury, then ninety-one, who began to fish in 1789, said 'it was customary to get, with a ninety-yard seine, from sixty to one hundred salmon a day in the lower river.'

Depopulation of the rivers

As settlement spread in New England and industries began to usurp the streams the anadromous fishes that spawned in freshwater faced increasing difficulties. Already at the end of the Colonial period the runs were diminishing in some rivers due to the custom of blockading them to provide a water supply for a local mill or settlement. Some communities like Machias, Maine, passed laws requiring fish by-passes at impoundments but sometimes they were ignored and if there were such facilities they often proved ineffective. Many fell into disrepair and were abandoned but they continued to obstruct or hinder fish migration at time of low water.

The demise of the southern New England salmon rivers occurred in the nineteenth century with the rise of cotton weaving and spinning industries along with other manufactures requiring the use of considerable amounts of water. In 1798 a corporation known as the Upper Locks and Canals Company built a sixteen-foot dam across the Connecticut River above Holyoke, Massachusetts. The salmon congregated below the dam for a number of years, vainly trying to reach their spawning grounds, then disappeared. Later other dams arose downstream to block fish passage, so that by 1814 Dr Samuel Latham Mitchill in *The Fishes of New York* reported that New York City could no longer obtain its salmon from the Connecticut. Shad, formerly taken as far as Bellows Falls, Vermont, were stopped by a dam at Montague. Instead of salmon and shad to which the people of the Connecticut Valley had been accustomed, the river offered bass. It is not known when the last salmon was taken in the river, but in 1872, when a solitary specimen strayed into a fisherman's net at Old Saybrook, nobody could identify it!

By 1840 there were 1,200 textile mills in the United States, of which two-thirds were in New England. The Connecticut and Merrimack were the primary sources of water power. The dams conveying this power to the mills were built with the knowledge that they would disrupt the natural flow and harm the fisheries. But the prevailing attitude was that industry was more important than the fish, an attitude that still prevails in the United States and other countries. Brown's dam, built in 1820, sealed off the spawning grounds in the Pemigewasset River, but the salmon continued to come up the Merrimack in smaller numbers. In 1847 Francis C. Lowell, inventor of the American power loom, built an imposing mill at Lawrence which effectively barred upstream migration, and within a dozen years the salmon were extinct.

As the Industrial Revolution spread few people seemed concerned about the decline of the freshwater fishes. Industrialists like the Lowells and Lawrences became quite wealthy and their names acquired a special sanctity. They provided jobs for many people, gave large sums to charity, founded educational institutes and endowed chairs at Harvard, were pillars of society and of the churches. They followed, consciously or not, the Old Testament dictum that 'man hath dominion over the fishes of the sea and over the fowl of the air, and over every living thing that creepeth upon the earth'. It did not bother them, apparently, that like their compeers in Lancashire, they were helping to exterminate the salmon and other valuable fishes. They ignored laws requiring the provision of fish passes at their dams, arguing they could not afford the expense. Even as I write a New England power company is fighting a federal order that it must install a fish ladder at its Turners Falls dam on the Connecticut, pleading it cannot afford the expense.

A few people complained about the depopulation of the rivers in the days of Lawrence and Lowell. One of them was the iconoclastic philosopher of Concord, Henry David Thoreau. In *A Week on the Concord and Merrimack Rivers*, describing a journey taken in 1839, he said the river 'comes murmuring to itself by the base of stately and retired mountains, through moist primitive woods whose juices it receives where the bear still drinks it, and the cabins of settlers are far between, and there are few to cross its streams.' In the lower reaches where 'salmon, shad and alewives were formerly abundant . . . and taken in weirs by Indians, who taught this method to the whites, by whom they were used as food and manure, until the dam and afterward the canal at Billerica, and the factories at Lowell, put an end to this migration hitherward; though it is thought that a few more enterprising shad may still occasionally be seen in this part of the river.'

Musing on this phenomenon, Thoreau remarked, 'Perchance after a thousand years, if the fishes will be patient, and pass their summers elsewhere, meanwhile nature will have levelled the dam and afterward the canal at Billerica, and the Lowell factories, and the Grass-ground [Concord] River run clear again, to be explored by new migratory shoals.' Today the Merrimack is one of America's most polluted streams. Senator Frank Moss in *The Water Crisis* (1967) says, 'Were the philosopher of Walden to look upon today's Merrimack he would likely weep for the river and the children of this nation's tomorrow. If the Merrimack of today represents the future of American water courses, the time may yet come when nature will indeed have levelled the dams, the factories and the towns of America. Its long history of pollution makes the famed river an instructive example of how this water sickness spreads.' Nevertheless efforts, probably foolhardy, are being made to restore the salmon to the Merrimack.

Maine's 31,000 square miles were almost entirely covered with majestic forests except for occasional meadows where wild grass flourished, and were watered by many river systems – the Piscataquis, Saco, Presumpscot, Mousam, Androscoggin, Medomack, Kennebec, St George, Orange, Penobscot, Union, Narraguagus, Machias, St Croix, St John (the border with Canada), and Dennys, all rich in fishlife and usually harbouring salmon.

'It is wonderful how well watered this country is,' says Thoreau in *The Maine Woods*, an account of a ramble he took when Maine was the leading lumbering state in the union. The princely white pine, choicest of woods, often attained a height of 150 feet and occasionally 250 feet, growing straight as a candle, universally in demand for everything from matches to masts. Mixed with white pine were the shorter but valuable Norway or red pine, red spruce, pitch pine, sometimes hemlock, tamarack, and such hardwoods as birch, beech, ash, maple and oak, that lit up the forests in autumn with their prismatic colours. Rivers and running brooks wound in and out of the woods, sometimes feeding numerous lakes.

Deer, elk, caribou, moose and bear as well as smaller furbearers roamed the forests, finding plenty of food and shelter. But as Thoreau sensed, earth's beauty is transient where man thrusts his axe. 'The aim of the lumberman,' he said, is 'to drive the forest all out of the country, from every solitary beaver swamp and mountain-side, as soon as possible,' leaving behind scarred, ugly landscapes, logjams, muddied streams, and stream beds full of debris and sawdust. The lumber barons grew rich and founded potent dynasties but the forests, watersheds and fishlife were greatly impoverished.

By 1870 there were only seven Maine rivers left that had substantial quantities of salmon – the Androscoggin, Kennebec,

Sheepscot, Dennys, Penobscot, Machias and St Croix. Occasionally they appeared in a half-dozen others but in all the rest, said
Charles G. Atkins, Maine Commissioner of Fisheries, 'the ancient
brood of salmon was long ago extinguished and the rare specimens
occasionally observed must be regarded as strays . . . or as early
returning members of the new brood established by artificial
culture in several rivers'.

Atkins tersely described the causes of this catastrophe: 'The
fishermen's nets and spears and pounds would hardly have
sufficed to extinguish the brood of salmon in a single river.
Commonly these two classes of destructive agents cooperated.
The dams held the fish in check while the fishermen caught them
out. In some rivers the dams alone would have sufficed to exterminate them.'

In navigable waters the riparian proprietors owned the banks
of the streams from high to low water mark. This title carried
the right to erect 'fixtures for fishing or other purposes, or even
to make a net fast to the shores or bottom within the hundred-rod
limit'. In non-navigable rivers the riparian owner held the land
under the water to the middle of the stream, and had the exclusive
right to this stretch. The public right extended only to the use
of boats and flotation of timber.

Using these rights, proprietors blockaded the streams at will,
even though there were in Maine, according to Atkins, over
400 fishery laws passed by the legislature between 1820 and 1880,
of which 160 related to anadromous species. All aimed 'first,
at the harmonizing of conflicting interests; second, preservation
of the supply of fish; and third, the prevention of fraud in the
sale of fish products'. The courts repeatedly upheld the principle
that the right of 'every owner of a mill or dam built under the
condition that a sufficient passageway be allowed for the fish,
and the limitation being for the public benefit, is not extinguished
by any neglect to compel compliance.' Relatively heavy penalties
were specified for breaches of these laws, some of which went
back as far as 1741. In the nineteenth century the county commissioners and later the Maine Fisheries Commission were empowered to enforce the laws, ordering fishways to be built or
repairs to them made and also to keep water flowing so the fish

could get over them. However, little was done to enforce the statutes and the Maine salmon rivers went out of production one by one.

On the Penobscot, said Atkins, 'the works of man interfered less with the migration of salmon than in any other large river south of the St John'. Here dams were probably less important in the loss of the runs than overfishing and deterioration of habitat.

In Penobscot Bay fishing was carried on with weirs, drift nets and pound nets which were eleven to twelve feet deep and eighteen to twenty fathoms long, supported by wooden floats, so that they rose and fell with the tide and were held in place by anchors planted at the end of long 'warps'. In 1870 there were 160 such weirs in operation; in 1872 the catch amounted to 15,000 salmon and in the next couple of decades the runs held up fairly well but then declined swiftly despite planting of stock from the hatchery at East Orland, the first in the United States, built in 1872. Weirs were not declared illegal until 1947 when there were scarcely any salmon left in the river. That year only forty were taken by the nets; sport fishing in Bangor Pool was at an end. Overfishing, poaching, pollution by pulp mills and insufficient stocking, added to excess fishing, ruined the best salmon producer in Maine.

When I visited the lower Penobscot in 1969 there was no trace of the booms and sawmills around Bangor, Veazie, Old Town and Orono which Thoreau saw. No merchant ships were at the docks. Masses of sawdust were still lying at the bottom of the river and sometimes were found in suspension in fishermen's nets. The river flowed in lonely splendour, deserted alike by the salmon and by men, for the waters were too polluted for swimming. A few years earlier *Salmo salar* had been declared an endangered species by the Secretary of the Interior.

It is worth glancing at the Androscoggin River to see how the Americans, carried away like the English or the Japanese by the worship of industrial progress, abused their rivers and drove out the fishes which earlier generations protected. The Androscoggin drops 1,250 feet in its course of 120 miles from its source in northern Maine around Umbagog Lake close to the New Hampshire border, twisting in and out of that state and Maine until it meets the Kennebec River in Merrymeeting Bay. Famous for its birds and fish, the river abounded in salmon and trout – its gravelly bottom and its tributaries were especially suitable to spawning salmon which came by the thousands, easily leaping the lower falls. Here the Indians and later the white men speared and netted the fish. At Rumford, Maine a higher falls stopped fish migration.

The falls brought about the ruin of the river. Forests and abundant water supplies were the wealth of an area poor in other natural resources. Dams multiplied as textile mills and pulp mills arose where water flow could be harnessed. There are now thirty-two dams on the main river, and the falls are all but obliterated. Like the salmon, the shad can no longer surmount these obstacles. The last salmon was said to have been taken at Lewiston falls in 1815 and a few were seen downstream at Brunswick as late as 1844.

In 1840 there were 250 saw mills on the lower Penobscot, then the chief lumbering centre in the United States. When Thoreau visited the river in 1857 he saw the river choked with logs, timber rafts, booms and sawmill debris. More damaging pollution came to the Penobscot and other Maine rivers with the advent of the pulp mills later in the century, exploiting the second growth of white pine and other species suitable for the purpose. This industry dumped cooking liquors into the rivers as well as chips and bark dust to the point where they exceeded the capacity of the water to absorb the loads, thus making life ever more hazardous for migrating fishes.

Because of pollution, impassable dams or weirs, and excessive fishing, the Maine rivers went out of production one by one. By 1940 there were few salmon left in the streams of the state. In the late 1950s *Salmo salar* was declared an endangered species by the Secretary of the Interior.

Lake Ontario and Lake Champlain

In 1654 the Jesuit Fathers LeMoyne and LeMercier on their mission to the Onondaga Indians were surprised to see canoes filled with salmon coming down the Oswego River which empties into Lake Ontario. There was such an abundance of

these fishes in the fifty streams feeding the lake, as far west as
the River Don in Canada and the Genessee in the United States,
that they could be killed with paddles. The runs passed Oswego,
New York, easternmost port on Lake Ontario, in such numbers
that they were pitch-forked by the wagonload. They were taken
with gillnets at the mouth of the Oswego River. The Salmon
river in New York had good fishing as late as the 1830s and was
still productive in the 1870s. On the Genessee the fish passed
the city of Rochester and migrated almost to Niagara Falls to
spawn.

These salmon spent their juvenile years in the feeder streams
and used the lake for feeding, as sea-run fish use the ocean, and
returned to the rivers to spawn. They attained sizes comparable
to oceangoing Atlantic salmon.

On the Canadian side of Lake Ontario the fishes ceased to
appear in the streams from Toronto westward by the 1860s but
were still found in the eastward rivers, partly due to the pioneer
fish culturist Samuel Wilmot through whose property flowed
Wilmot Creek, one of the best Lake Ontario feeders. Wilmot
built the Newcastle salmon hatchery, which in 1876 incubated
1½ million eggs, and planted the fry in the streams and the lake
itself. At that time adult salmon still ran up most of the Canadian
rivers from Belleville westward to the Credit River 'but not in
nearly the numbers that once favoured the sticks, nets and spears
of the Indians and white men alike,' says Hugh McCrimmon in
his paper, 'The Beginning of Salmon Culture in Canada'. The
Newcastle hatchery also furnished eggs to fish culturists in New
England who attempted to arrest the decline of the salmon in
some of their rivers.

There was some increase in abundance as a result of Wilmot's
activities. He was appointed Superintendent of Fish Culture in
Canada in 1876 in recognition of his pioneer work, a post he held
until 1895. But the inevitable extinction of the Lake Ontario
runs nevertheless occurred. By 1883 it was possible to collect
only 84,000 eggs compared with 1½ million seven years earlier.
The last adult salmon was observed in Wilmot Creek in 1896.
The causes for their disappearance, according to Wilmot, were:
(1) 'murder on the fishing grounds' – that is, unrestrained trapnet

fishing along the lake shores and at the mouths of the rivers (there was apparently no government regulation or controls on either side of the border), and (2) settlement and land clearance that stripped the vegetative cover and, with poor farming practices, induced erosion and siltation of streams.

Now the state of New York is restocking Lake Ontario with Atlantic salmon and also Pacific species.

Lake Champlain is much smaller than any of the Great Lakes. It separates the Adirondack and Green Mountains and is connected with the St Lawrence River and the sea through the Richelieu River. Lake Champlain salmon made their appearance in history in the report of Samuel de Champlain, who marked on his chart a point near the present village of Champlain, New York, where an Indian fishery existed on the Big Chazy river. There were so many salmon in the streams that Benedict Arnold, commander of the Continental Army in this region in the War of Independence (and later a traitor) reported that one William Gilliland, a settler in Willsborough, New York, 'complimented the American army with 1,500 salmon in one year'. At least a dozen streams harboured Lake Champlain salmon, believed to be a seagoing variety making their way to the Atlantic Ocean via the Richelieu and St Lawrence Rivers. No biological studies seem to have been made of them. Only two stuffed specimen are known to exist.

By 1842, when Daniel P. Thompson published his *History of Vermont*, the anadromous fishes had become fairly rare in Lake Champlain. Thirty years later M. C. Edmunds, Fish Commissioner of Vermont, could find no trace of them in some of their well-known haunts like Otter Creek on the west side of the lake, or the Winooski, Missisquoi, Saranac, Salmon, Big or Little Chazy Rivers. The last run in the Ausable River was said to have occurred in 1838. Yet tales of their abundance floated around upper New York state as late as the 1870s.

Winslow C. Watson, historian of Essex County in upstate New York, said that the reasons for their extinction were as follows:

The secluded haunts they loved have been invaded; dams have impeded their wonted routes, the filth of occupied streams disturbed their cleanly habits, and the clangor of steamboats and machinery has excited their fears. Each of these causes is assigned as a circumstance that has deprived the country of an important article of food and a choice luxury.

Restoring the New England rivers

Salmon rivers are difficult to restore even when considerable sums and scientific know-how are available. Yet, 'in a land where fishing and hunting is accepted as a God-given right,' says Alfred L. Meister, biologist with Maine Atlantic Sea-Run Salmon Commission, 'it was inevitable that a public clamour would arise for Atlantic salmon fishing.' Flyfishers longed to challenge the wily fish in Bangor Pool, or on the St Croix, Dennys, Aroostook and other streams where once this was a popular sport. In 1947 they managed to persuade the Maine legislature to create the Atlantic Sea-Run Salmon Commission and provide a small appropriation, supplemented by contributions from private industry, to study the feasibility of bringing *Salmo salar* back to rivers that still had migration and spawning potentials. It was determined that eight streams should be chosen for restoration: Penobscot, Dennys, Sheepscot, Machias and East Machias, Narragaugus, Pleasant and Aroostook. Fish for restocking would be obtained from the East Orland hatchery. Work began in 1954 to remove obstructions, build fish passes, water control facilities, and the like.

After 1966 federal funds became available to the states on a matching basis from the Anadromous Fisheries Act and the Accelerated Public Works Act, thus enabling the restoration programme to be stepped up in Maine and extended to the Connecticut, Merrimack and other rivers. Nevertheless the programme has had hard going. The Penobscot, the major object of restoration in Maine, was in a parlous state, said Alfred Meister, 'victimized by a citizenry unwilling to accept responsibility for waste treatment as an essential of civilized progress'. 'Polluters dragged their feet,' said David O. Locke, a member of the Atlantic Sea-Run Salmon Commission, 'saying it would do no good if there were obstacles the fish could not pass. Owners of dams without fishways took the position that fishways would be of no avail if the unclear condition of the rivers continued. No one wanted to be first.' It took years to persuade the Maine legislature to classify the Penobscot as a Class C river, meaning it must be rendered suitable for fish life, but the deadline for meeting this goal was set far ahead. It was hoped to establish a run of 1,200 to 3,000 fish, which would provide a harvest of 180 to 750 annually for anglers. This was a modest goal considering that a century earlier some 15,000 salmon were taken annually in the river and Penobscot Bay. No commercial fishing is permitted, although Maine salmon are caught in Greenland and also by Canadian netsmen before they reach home waters.

The Maine restoration programme has not lived up to expectations with the one exception of the Penobscot. In 1975, 933 salmon were taken in the trap nets at the mouth of this river for spawning and seventy-three were caught by anglers. The run was being sustained by planting juveniles reared in two Maine hatcheries until such time as there would be enough wild fish to keep it going without artificial propagation, probably still years away. On seven other Maine rivers, open only to sport fishing, catches were less in 1975 and 1976 than in 1959, before massive amounts of federal and state funds were invested in restoration work, as shown in the following table:

River	Catches in 1959	Catches in 1975	Catches in 1976
Narraguagus	167	113	33
Machias	135	51	25
Dennys	132	40	20
Pleasant	67	8	0
East Machias	NA	30	25
Sheepscot	NA	11	15
Union	NA	81	30*
Incidental	–	20	–
Total	501	354	148

* 219 salmon were taken in the research trap at the dam in Ellsworth.

While the Maine programme is faltering, except for the Penobscot, the Connecticut restoration attempt, launched in 1967 by
the four states through which the river passes, seems to be a
failure. Much of the main stem is blockaded by impassable dams,
and pollution is rampant. 'When one crosses the Connecticut
on the bridge at Lebanon, New Hampshire,' said the late Philip
K. Crowe, 'one can see the ruin of a great river: oily-looking
water, and at times the faint, rank smell of fermenting sewage.'
In the Hartford-Springfield area downstream, fish returning to
their spawning grounds have to cope with the poisons of industrial wastes and in other places with hydroelectric dams without
fish passes.

It was hoped to create a run of 40,000 salmon and two million
shad on the Connecticut. The shad have returned in reasonably
satisfactory numbers because they do not migrate very far
upstream, but the salmon have not. Some 600,000 salmon smolts
and pre-smolts have been released in the watershed in recent
years, and the first return of adults was expected in the spring
of 1974. Anticipating this event, an angling season was announced
with considerable fanfare by the state of Connecticut, and $3,400
in awards were offered to anglers or others who turned in adult
salmon found in the river dead or alive. Only one dead fish,
thirty inches long, was discovered in 1974, on the bank at
Middleton, Connecticut. The finder received $25.00. This was
the first specimen of an adult *Salmo salar* seen in the river in a
century. One hesitates to calculate how much money it had cost
to bring it back from the ocean. Since 1974, several salmon
have been taken in the Connecticut and a gene pool has been
established but the dream of seeing hundreds of fish come into
the river – let alone thousands – remains a dream even though
two big Atlantic salmon hatcheries are being built, with taxpayers' money, to produce about a million smolts annually to
supply the river.

The Merrimack programme has only recently started. According to the International Atlantic Salmon Foundation in its report
for 1976, thanks to 'an extensive cleanup programme, water
quality has improved dramatically, leading to the return of
anadromous species such as the American shad and the river

herring, and making Atlantic salmon restoration possible.' About 100,000 inch-long juveniles were liberated in the tributary Mad River in 1975 and 1976, the first plantings of Atlantics in nearly a century. These releases plus the stocking of smolts in the spring of 1977 should result in 40,000 smolts leaving the Merrimack system in that year, to return as adults in 1979. However, as on the Connecticut, efficient fishways and fish collection facilities must be provided at the dams at Lawrence and Lowell, the famous barriers that helped to exterminate the runs in the first place. The private companies owning these dams have refused to expend their funds, hence state and federal agencies will have to make the investment. The chances of successful salmon restoration on the Merrimack, dammed and polluted by private industry, will probably be as difficult as on the Connecticut but the programme will go on, at the taxpayers' expense.

Pacific Salmon in New England

As hopes for the large-scale return of Atlantic salmon to New England began to wane, federal and state agencies began looking for a substitute. They hit on the idea of introducing the most versatile of Pacific species, coho, into suitable rivers.

Massachusetts and New Hampshire became actively involved in the programme, financed by the federal government with state matching funds. Considerable opposition to introducing an exotic species where *Salmo salar* was indigenous was quickly generated by organizations like the International Atlantic Salmon Foundation and its affiliates and the Restoration of Atlantic Salmon Association (RASA). They felt that Atlantic salmon should be given priority and coho introduction delayed until a complete and accurate assessment of possible damage to runs of *Salmo salar* could be made.

The Massachusetts programme offers a promise of success. Forty-five adults were recaptured in 1975 at the base of the dam in North River and about a dozen were taken by fishermen elsewhere. Some 14,000 eggs from these fish were fertilized for rearing in a state hatchery. Fifteen thousand smolts were released in North River in the spring of 1975, and 50,000 in the spring of 1976, a portion of which were expected to return as adults in the fall of 1977, thus promising the establishment of a sport fishery. The Massachusetts Division of Marine Fisheries plans to build a coho hatchery at the nuclear power plant at Plymouth using waste heat to heat the water supply, thus making it possible to rear smolts in half the normal time. The eventual release of up to one million juveniles annually is envisaged, producing a possible marine sport catch of 50,000 salmon per year. Funding of the $6 million hatchery, with $265,000 annual operating costs, will be mainly by the federal government.

The New Hampshire coho programme has been less successful. Coho catches in Great Bay amounted to 159 in 1970, 423 in 1971, and 1,018 in 1972 but dropped to 504 in 1973 and only 171 in 1975. The state Fish and Game Commission voted in 1976 to terminate the programme and withdraw support from the state subsidized coho hatchery nearing completion at Milford. The Commission claimed that the programme, which started in 1967, cost the state more than $300,000, and that only about 3,000 fish had been caught by anglers. 'They never gave the programme a chance,' said Richard Seamans, chief of the New Hampshire Fish and Game Department's Fisheries Division. 'Just when it was on the verge of success, they cancelled it.' Also cancelled was the Atlantic salmon restoration programme in New Hampshire.

The National Marine Fisheries Service, however, is planning to launch a unique and more ambitious scheme to naturalize Pacific salmon in New England waters, based on the experimental work of Dr Timothy Joyner and his associates in Puget Sound. Coho will be reared in hatcheries in New England to smolt size, then transported in late spring or early summer to saltwater stations where they will be held for additional growth before being released in the bays and sounds of southern New England. It is assumed they will wander at will in the ocean and, when mature, return to the tidal areas of release. There they will be available to sport fishermen, as in the Great Lakes. It is anticipated that some fish will move into rivers near the saltwater rearing stations and there they will be trapped and the spawn taken to an appropriate hatchery to begin the cycle over again.

'With such a system,' says Dr Joyner, 'a recreational fishery for Pacific salmon could be generated along the New England coast without the need for many large hatcheries or extensive natural spawning.'

The plan has aroused fears among advocates of Atlantic salmon restoration, such as Richard Buck, chairman of RASA, that 'coho salmon stocked in rivers neighbouring Atlantic salmon rivers will, on their return, wander from their point of stocking. Of cohos previously stocked in the Lamprey and Exeter Rivers in New Hampshire, 15% of those caught by sport fishermen in 1972 were taken in the Merrimack River.' Buck also argues that anglers fishing for coho from boats would take Atlantics returning to their home rivers. And, with large concentrations of coho along the shores and in the mouths of rivers, there would be a clamour from commercial fishermen that they too should have access to it.

The National Marine Fisheries Service replies that if coho become competitive with Atlantics, production and stocking of this species will be curtailed or stopped. At this writing Dr Joyner's ingenious scheme has not yet been launched, and will probably remain in limbo a long time.

CHAPTER 12

Canada's Atlantic Salmon

The fabulous resource

THE Atlantic salmon have fared much better in Canada than in the United States, owing to the slower pace of settlement and industrialization and their ubiquitous environmental horrors. Much of the pristine wilderness remains in eastern Canada although the Canadians have begun to develop the mineral wealth of the subarctic region on a massive scale as in the $13 billion James Bay scheme that threatens all wildlife, as well as the landscape.

The range of *Salmo salar* is from about latitude 45 to 60 degrees north and as far westward as the central part of Ungava Bay and possibly beyond into Hudson Bay. There are many hundreds of rivers in the provinces of Quebec, New Brunswick, Nova Scotia and Newfoundland-Labrador where salmon are found. Accounts of the original salmon cornucopia in these waters, gleaned from the documents of old settlers and explorers, represent them as probably equal to that of British Columbia.

'There are almost incredible tales of the hordes of sleek salmon which filled the rivers,' says Dr Wilfred Carter, executive director of the International Atlantic Salmon Foundation. 'We are told of streams choked so thickly with ascending salmon that one could almost literally walk from shore to shore on their backs.' They were pitchforked by the cartloads and used for fertilizer as well as food, consumed at home and shipped in great volume by schooner to Britain in Colonial times.

Salmo salar thrives in Canada in a variety of climates and habitats. There are considerable runs of fish in the Newfoundland rivers and along its shores. South of Newfoundland are the shallow seas, or banks, sunken remnants of the northern Appalachian

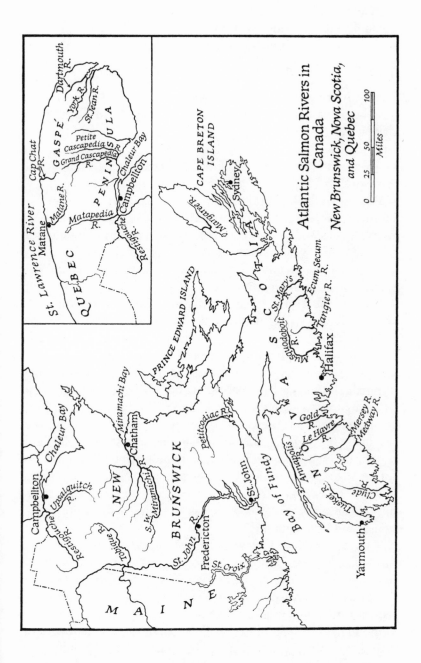

Atlantic Salmon Rivers in
Canada
*New Brunswick, Nova Scotia,
and Quebec*

highlands and the Atlantic coastal plain, which in a remote geological era extended past Nova Scotia and Newfoundland. In these waters the immense shoals of cod shed their eggs; their larvae feed on the plankton and their fry on the tiny crustaceans. As the cod grow to maturity they follow their food supply, mainly herring, capelin and squid. In their wake come the far less abundant anadromous fishes, salmon, shad and others from their feeding grounds, in the case of the salmon the cold Greenland waters. They head for their spawning rivers through the Gulf of St Lawrence or along the coasts of Labrador and Newfoundland, Nova Scotia, New Brunswick, or Maine.

Because of the plentiful fish, the Grand Banks attract enormous numbers of sea birds. There are kittiwakes, terns, razorbills, murres, gulls and puffins constantly wheeling and plunging into the often icy waters, filling the air with their mewings and squawkings, sometimes bewilderingly to the trawler men searching for fish through the fog.

Quebec, the largest of the eastern provinces, has over a hundred salmon rivers. The Canadian Shield occupies much of the area north of the St Lawrence River, while the Appalachian Mountains extend through the area south of the St Lawrence. Southern Quebec has a warm and humid climate in summer, while much of northern Quebec has a very short but pleasant summer. Many of them flow through a plateau wall to the St Lawrence and most of them, from the Ontario border to the Strait of Belle Isle, originally supported good runs of salmon. In contrast to the bleak tundra of Newfoundland, Quebec is mountainous and heavily forested; forests drop down at times to the water's edge, in the Gulf of St Lawrence; there is considerable farm land, and numerous villages dot the landscape with their trim, white frame houses and little churches.

The topography of New Brunswick generally resembles that of Maine, especially in the eastern part. Some of the world's highest tides occur in the Bay of Fundy which anadromous fishes must traverse to reach their home rivers. Agriculture, forestry and fisheries are the mainstays of the province's economy. The major salmon rivers include the 450-mile St John, one of the longest in eastern Canada, which empties into the Bay of Fundy. The

Miramichi which drops into Miramichi Bay, and the Restigouche
which flows into Chaleur Bay are also important for their salmon
runs.

Nova Scotia is the smallest of the eastern provinces, a picturesque peninsula of 21,100 miles (compared with 28,000 square
miles for New Brunswick, 524,000 square miles for Quebec,
and 153,000 square miles for Newfoundland-Labrador). With
many excellent harbours and numerous rivers, Nova Scotia
became a major fishing centre during the Colonial period, when
it was the gateway to British North America from the homeland.
The earliest settlers found the rivers so full of salmon and other
fishes that they established town sites like Liverpool and Medway
near the mouths of the streams to take advantage of the fishery.

Exploitation of the salmon

As early as 1708 George Skeffington obtained a twenty-one-year
monopoly on the fisheries at Freshwater Bay, Rugged Harbor
and Gander Bay in Newfoundland. At the outbreak of the
Seven Years War in 1756 about 51,000 tierces of salmon and
other fishes were being shipped annually to Europe, but this high
level could not be maintained. During and after the American
Revolution the fishing industry of the Maritime colonies expanded
rapidly, with cod as a mainstay but herring, mackerel and salmon
were also fished heavily and sent to England and the West Indies.
John Cartwright, brother of Edmund Cartwright, inventor of
the power loom, was the first to organize the salmon trade in
Labrador and was said to have made a fortune.

In the nineteenth century the Quebec and Newfoundland runs
were exploited, at times mercilessly, by the Hudson's Bay
Company and others. In its lust for profits the Company overfished the rivers as it overkilled the populations of beaver, otter,
marten and other furbearers.

Many of the rivers draining into the St Lawrence, an 800-mile
waterway flowing from the eastern end of Lake Ontario to the
Gulf of St Lawrence, were among the first to be depleted of their
anadromous fishes. Richard Nettle in his *Salmon Fisheries of the
St Lawrence*, published in 1857, described the assault on the
principal streams from Anse au Sablon westward to the Saguenay,

including the island of Anticosti, whose inlets, bays and creeks 'swarmed with large quantities of salmon'. Here an afternoon tide would sweep 500 to 600 fish into the Hudson's Bay Company nets. 'Not content with netting and spearing in the bay, [they] ascend the rivers and fish by day and by night, not only during the fishing seasons but also spearing the fish on their spawning beds,' said Nettle.

Nettle found that the rivers and estuaries were poorly protected throughout the colony. American schooners with armed crews used to anchor in the Bay of Seven Islands and set their nets in the Moisie River in defiance of the Hudson's Bay people. Americans also gaffed large numbers of salmon in the Bersimis River. Almost everywhere there was perceptible overfishing and illegal netting, and on many streams mill dams were hindering fish migration. For example, on the Escoumains a mill dam usurped the right of way 'and that splendid and valuable stream (which yielded its proprietors £6,000–8,000 per annum) was utterly destroyed'.

The lower Saguenay River flows through a broad fjord-like channel and hence 'as a nursery for the salmon few rivers can equal it'. Logjams damaged many of the tributaries but some were still populated with salmon. The Murray used to be called the Salmon River because of its rich stock. A mill dam was erected that blocked the stream and drove out the salmon. Eventually this structure was demolished and the fish began to return. 'Now the poachers are active night after night,' using the spear which had lately been outlawed.

The Jacques Cartier River on the south shore of the St Lawrence used to have excellent runs as far as Dery's Bridge, a dozen miles from the mouth, until Louis Dery, the leasee, began to fish them mercilessly in the narrow gorge at the bottom of a waterfall. 'Once the salmon were counted by the thousands; a few years ago by the hundreds; and now they can scarcely be numbered by the dozen.' Only when a new proprietor purchased the fishing rights and ended netting at the pool were large numbers of fish able to reach the upper waters.

Nettle told much the same story about all the south shore rivers he studied, and concluded that if they were protected

A fish pass at the Parteen hatchery in Eire, showing ponds and a feeder pipe.

The Bergeforsen salmon hatchery on the River Indal in Sweden, built as a requirement to compensate for the loss of wild fish. It can produce over 300,000 smolts annually.

Fishermen using trap nets at Chaleur Bay in eastern Canada, a profitable fishery that was halted to enable more spawners to return to the rivers.

Casting for Atlantic salmon in the Miramichi River, New Brunswick, one of the most productive in eastern Canada.

A fish wheel used to capture spawners for artificial propagation on a Japanese 'salmon culture river'.

Freshly caught salmon at a cannery at Steveston, once the greatest canning centre in British Columbia.

The John Day dam on the Columbia River forms a reservoir 77 miles long. This view shows the northern shore, fish ladder in the foreground, the spillways and power-house. The dam was built to produce electric power and facilitate navigation but with other high dams on the Columbia has helped to substantially reduce the once fabulous salmon runs.

during the spawning season and if fishways were provided at the dams and rapids, this district 'would soon become a mine of wealth and a source of great profit to both fishermen and purchasers'.

In the Gaspé Peninsula and Bonaventure regions, said Nettle, there were salmon rivers 'richer than the diamond mines of the East'. The Restigouche used to yield daily hauls of 2,000–3,000 fish but the catches had lately fallen to about one-tenth that number while the annual export of 2,000 barrels of salmon from Campbellton to Britain and the United States had dwindled to 300. This loss was due to excessive spearing and netting on the spawning grounds by the Indians 'who are driven to this nefarious practice by the white man who purchases the fish'. Salmon were still relatively abundant in the Gaspé rivers but lack of protection and impassable obstructions were helping to depopulate them.

Many of the superb salmon fisheries above Quebec City were decimated in Colonial times, particularly those draining the Laurentian Mountains. Fifty years after Nettle published his book, E. D. T. Chambers in *Game Fishes of Quebec* reported that there were few salmon rivers left west of the Saugenay River. Roughly similar conditions prevailed in some of the other eastern provinces. Like the Americans, the Canadians used their fishery resources prodigally but as their original stocks were much larger, considerable numbers have survived.

Sport fishing

Sport fishing became a popular recreation in the nineteenth century in both Canada and the United States as increasing wealth enabled many people to pursue the salmon in the wilderness rivers. Genio Scott in *Fishing in American Waters*, published in 1875, succinctly described the pleasures of the sport:

> To spend a summer month on one of the great rivers which empty into the Gulf of St Lawrence is to rest the mind by the most absolute exclusion from the world. When I essayed the ascent of one of the great rivers . . . north of the island of Anticosti, the world was tranquil. For a month I admired the grandeur of the mountains, the majesty of the broad and rapid

river, the elegant play of salmon, and the dexterity of the seals; and at night the brilliancy of the northern horizon and gorgeousness of the lunar bow enraptured me.

In Scott's day relatively few American anglers could enjoy the delights of dancing a fly on salmon rivers in Canada because they were difficult of access and costs were high. For example, to reach the Miramichi one had to go by way of St John, there take a boat for Fredericton, where one bought provisions, and thence by stage coach to Boiestown. Here a guide and canoe men were engaged for the duration of one's stay on the river.

Some of the rivers were owned by the Crown and others by individual proprietors. Fishing was incomparable: the water was usually so clear the fish could be seen quite plainly and one could play a fly at their very noses. The stillness and solitude were a tonic to the nerves. 'If the birds sing high above the shrubbery and stunted trees,' said Thad Norris in *The American Angler's Guide* (1864), 'they are not heard by the fisher down in the deep ravine through which the river flows; but a voice of ordinary pitch, a thump of the canoe, or the splash of a salmon when it falls, after leaping above the water, is heard a long distance off, and the sound is prolonged and reflected from almost perpendicular rock that walls in the stream on either side. Thus you frequently know when another angler, though he is not visible, has a fish on.'

Moisie, Restigouche and Miramichi were names that thrilled anglers. The Moisie was owned in part by the Moisie Salmon Club, formed in 1925, by a small group of American millionaires. Here, before the white men came the Montagnais Indians used to spear as many as 900 fish by torchlight in one evening. In the 1890s those who fished the Restigouche (or its tributaries like the Upsalquitch) which forms the boundary between Quebec and New Brunswick, took the train from Montreal to Matapedia and sometimes embarked on a yacht, pulled by horses, on which was mounted a cottage. The driver sat in the middle and steered the animals through the shallow water. On the afterdeck there was a cow to provide fresh milk; the interior had sleeping rooms, a kitchen and saloon. A couple of canoes tied to the barge were used for fishing. Dr Henry Van Dyke described a fishing expedition on such a yacht in *Little Rivers* (1903):

As soon as one learns to regard the horse yacht as a sort of moving house, it appears admirable. There is no dust or smoke, no rumble of wheels, or shriek of whistles. You are gliding along steadily through an evergreen world; skirting the silent hills; passing from one side of the river to the other when the horses have to swim the current to find a good foothold on the bank . . . You may sleep, or read, or write in your cabin, or sit upon the floating piazza in an arm-chair and smoke the pipe of peace, while the cool breeze blows in your face and the musical waves go singing down to the sea . . . The canoes are waiting and in the early morning, when the white fog is lifting from the river, the fishing begins. Often it is a struggle between man and fish, the salmon jumping and trying to eject the fly from its mouth, the angler reeling him in, until he is exhausted. Fishing is over by eleven o'clock and the day's work is done.

This is angling in paradise. A Restigouche Salmon Club was formed by American tycoons to control the best pools in the river. In the wealth and corporate prominence of its members it was the peer of the Moisie Salmon Club.

Nowadays good highways and airlines have made the salmon rivers of eastern Canada accessible from every part of the continent. Even the Koksoak and George River systems flowing into Ungava Bay are accessible by hardy anglers. There are salmon in streams below Goose Bay in Labrador like the Sandhill and the Eagle; and farther north, the cold waters of the Adlatok, Fraser and Koraluk have been opened up to intrepid fly fishermen chasing *Salmo salar*. Most of the Canadian Atlantic salmon rivers are privately owned, but each year more are being opened to the public at a moderate cost for a daily permit. *The Atlantic Salmon Journal*, January 1976, lists all the fishable salmon rivers in the province of Quebec and their status.

Deteriorating environments
Canadian stocks continued to diminish in the first half of the

twentieth century, and concern for the future led to the formation in 1949 of a Federal-Provincial Coordinating Committee on Atlantic Salmon, which promoted conservation programmes including hatchery propagation, fish passage facilities and expanded research by both the federal and provincial governments.

In 1951 the late Scottish expert, J. W. M. Menzies, was invited by the Atlantic Salmon Association of Canada to make a comprehensive study of the resource. He concluded that there had been a great decline in the stocks during the previous two decades. Quebec had not lost as much as New Brunswick and Nova Scotia 'because of better protection and possibly the more remote situation of most of the north shore rivers'. From his long experience Menzies offered recommendations for reversing the trend; the most important dealt with reducing the toll of commercial fishermen operating from the shore or in coastal waters; increasing and strengthening the warden service on the rivers, which was then based on a political patronage system; and stiffening the penalties for poaching. He also recommended that fish passes be built wherever needed, a code of regulations for operating power facilities at dams be drawn up, and a comprehensive research programme pursued. In due course most of these suggestions were adopted in one way or another except that dealing with the poaching menace, which perhaps is greater now than it was a quarter of a century ago.

Meantime, as population swelled in eastern Canada, industries multiplied, agriculture boomed, mineral and forest wealth was increasingly tapped, and many rivers deteriorated. They were polluted by untreated sewage, discharges from mines, smelters and factories, farm runoff and aerial spraying of forests with DDT and other toxic pesticides.

Numerous examples may be cited. At Buchans on the island of Newfoundland, where some 360,000 tons of ore producing lead, copper and zinc concentrates were processed annually, 260,000 tons of wastes were dumped into Buchans Creek which flows into Red Indian Lake and thence to Exploits River, an excellent salmon stream. Studies showed that below the point where the material entered the creek no life existed, lethal deposits were found on the lake bottom, while on the lower river dissolved zinc and copper concentrates were present in sufficient amounts to harm migratory fish.

In 1965 two large newsprint mills at Corner Brook, Newfoundland on the west coast and Grand Falls on the Exploits River were polluting prime salmon water so that at low flows the oxygen content, reduced by algae blooms generated by waste liquor, was killing many fish.

'In New Brunswick we've had some sharp lessons in what pollution can do to our salmon,' Dr Paul F. Elson, formerly of the Fisheries Research Board of Canada, told the Kiwanis Club of Lancaster, New Brunswick in August, 1969. 'In the 1950s we inadvertently killed over 90% of the baby salmon in much of the salmon nursery areas of the St John and Miramichi systems . . . It was a side effect of our effort to protect our valuable forests from the ravages of spruce budworm. While many young salmon were killed outright, others escaped with a sublethal dose which killed them when they met the added stress of winter cold . . . DDT stays around in the stream environment for a long time after actual application. We have identified some of its breakdown products in young salmon spawned in a sprayed stream more than ten years after the last spraying.'

Elson described other effects from industrialism and forestry on fish populations. Creosoting of power poles, for example, produces a deadly effluent in very diluted solutions that sometimes finds its way into the streams and stays a long time. 'If fish don't get killed it can give them an unpalatable oily taste.' A common form of pollution in tidal waters is oil spills from shore-based plants and shipping, accidental or deliberate. 'Gasoline and diesel oils can kill rainbow trout (a close relative of the salmon) in dilutions well under fifty parts per million, if they contain certain common additives and are well mixed in the water. Mixing occurs readily in running water, while tides and waves provide ready mixing in estuaries and seas.'

Elson added that Atlantic salmon are not only worth saving for the food and sport they provide but are 'one of the best indicators that we are doing good housekeeping in our waters'. A stream that cannot support salmon is easily recognized as one which is badly polluted.

Impact of hydroelectric dams

The most important salmon producing watershed to be affected by hydroelectric developments in eastern Canada is the St John system. There were already six small dams on the main stem and its tributaries before the huge Mactaquac project was built in 1968–1972, eleven miles above Fredericton. The scheme supplies electricity to farms, factories, and homes throughout New Brunswick.

At the dams on the Aroostook and Tobique Rivers, conventional fish ladders were installed and at Beechwood Dam on the main stem there was an ingenious fish hoist. At Mactaquac elaborate facilities are used to collect the fish in a holding pond where the salmon are separated from other species and then released in the reservoir so that they become available to anglers. A large hatchery was built just below the dam to produce smolts for planting in the river as compensation for losses of wild stock.

Before Mactaquac was built the St John runs had shown signs of decline. The Tobique sport catch, for example, dropped from about 2,200 in 1951 to only sixty-five in 1957, believed to be caused partly by the construction of Beechwood dam and partly by the spraying of surrounding forests with DDT. After spraying was stopped the salmon population increased but the sport catch did not, forcing many guides and outfitters out of business. After Mactaquac was completed catches of salmon and grilse on the St John fell drastically, from an average of 19,000 in the years 1964–1968 to an average of 5,500 in 1970–1973. A comeback was staged in the next two years when over 12,000 were taken annually, of which a great portion were hatchery fish.

Effects of Greenland fishery

The decline of Canadian salmon runs was perceptibly accelerated, as in the British Isles, by the upsurge of the Greenland fishery. In the period 1969–1971, for example, when catches around the coast of Greenland and in Davis Strait averaged 2,260 tons per year, or about 17–20% of the world catch of *Salmo salar*, it was estimated by an international team of scientists that Canada supplied over half the total. For the most part these fish would have returned to their natal rivers to provide harvests for sportsmen and commercials and seed stock as well. Bertrand Tetrault and Wilfred Carter studied the fate of some 20,000 smolts tagged in 1968 in Quebec. They postulated that, of the fish who survived to enter the commercial fishery, 27% were taken by the inshore and 29% by the offshore Greenland nets, 32% by the netsmen operating along the Newfoundland coast, 9% by the Quebec commercial fishery, and 3% by anglers.

If these figures show the typical fate of Canadian smolts feeding in waters around Greenland this may well account, at least in part, for the sharp fall-off of adult salmon (excluding grilse) in home waters between 1969 and 1971. These years were disastrous for both commercial and sport fishermen and pressures mounted on government officials to curtail the number of netting licences.

In 1971 the newly-formed North American Atlantic Salmon Council, embracing many of the leading conservation groups on the continent, declared that 'within North America . . . there has been an unfortunate tardiness in recognizing that some of the ills afflicting the salmon are rooted in outdated concepts of what constitutes progressive management. Another inimical factor is the exploitation privileges inherited from an era when the abundance of salmon may have justified an obvious luxury.' The Council urged that in addition to working for an international agreement that would curtail the Greenland fishrey – accomplished in 1972 – the Canadian government should reduce commercial fishing and 'also step up the rehabilitation of the Atlantic salmon habitat through government assistance'. The Ottawa government and the province of Quebec responded to the plea. Greenland salmon netting ceased in 1976 but inshore nets continue to take about 1,100 tons annually, chiefly Canadian and British fish.

In April, 1972, Jack Davis, Minister of the Environment, announced an immediate ban on commercial salmon fishing for at least five years with floating nets in the St John and Miramichi estuaries, on inshore fishing throughout the New Brunswick coast, and on floating nets off Port-aux-Basques in Newfoundland. On May 26, 1972, the province of Quebec proclaimed total prohibition of commercial salmon fishing in the Gaspé Peninsula. Excluded from these restrictions were the Newfoundland and Labrador inshore fishery, the inshore fishery on the north shore of the St Lawrence to the eastern limit of the province of Quebec, and the entire province of Nova Scotia. The ban eliminated about 40% of the entire commercial fishery, involving 900 fishermen who were compensated for lost income. The official reason for excluding Newfoundland and Labrador fisheries, which take up to 80% of Canadian landings in some years, was that they had not been seriously affected by the Greenland fishing. 'In the light of available catch data,' commented Wilfred Carter, 'these reasons leave us somewhat skeptical and unconvinced.'

Results from the 1972 actions were rather quick in coming as, in the following years, more fish returned to the rivers. The year 1973 was generally better for anglers than 1971 or 1972 and since then the catches have continued to increase in all provinces except Newfoundland-Labrador. Rod catches in 1975 and 1976, in numbers of fish, were as follows in 1976:

	1975	1976
Quebec	15,507	15,344
New Brunswick	27,593	43,169
Nova Scotia	3,560	7,309
Newfoundland-Labrador	38,925	42,073
Total	85,585	107,085

Typical of the beneficial results from the ban are the Restigouche, which produced a record catch of 5,790 salmon and grilse in 1974 and 4,770 in 1976, and the Miramichi with almost 33,000 in 1974 and 25,540 in 1976. Phasing out of the Greenland offshore fishing may have been an important factor. And, despite the elimination of 40% of the gear, commercial landings have been well sustained, making Canada one of the leading producers of *Salmo salar* in the world. In 1975 2,044 metric tons were harvested, roughly one-sixth of world catches.

'Could there be any better indication,' says the Atlantic Salmon Association, 'of the wisdom and initial success of the ban? Can there be stronger argument for maintaining the ban in effect?

Fisheries authorities should be gratified by the improvement in salmon runs, and equally cautious about relaxing the conservation measures in effect until there has been a prolonged period of recovery. One New Brunswick Fish and Wildlife biologist estimates that the Restigouche (alone) could support 250,000 salmon. There is obviously a long way to go before the nets are allowed back.' In 1977, the ban, due to expire, was extended for one year. At the same time the Province of Newfoundland announced that in order to help protect rivers which are experiencing drastic declines in the number of fish returning to spawning grounds due to overfishing, special restrictions will be introduced on both recreational and commercial salmon fishing in 1978.

Poaching

One of the eternal problems in managing salmon rivers, poaching, has been heightened in Canada by the revival of some of the runs. Poaching is a lucrative business and encourages professionals, some of whom are netsmen who lost their licences in 1972 and are obtaining compensation from the government.

Hardest hit are rivers that cater to the recreational industry. A three-day conference on illegal Atlantic salmon fishing was held in Montreal in February, 1974, bringing together seventy experts who explored nearly every phase of the commercial and sport fishing industries. However, by the end of 1975 little progress seemed to have been made. The International Atlantic Salmon Foundation reported that '1975 may be distinguished as one of the worst illegal fishing years on record. Perhaps not for the number of convictions recorded, but it will certainly be remembered for the audacity of some of the incidents and the inability of protection services to cope with the problem.' A few examples of horrendous offences are given. 'At the mouth of the York and St John Rivers snagging was the favourite pursuit of a gang of poachers operating in broad daylight, in total defiance of provincial wardens and the Quebec Provincial Police . . . Incidents of threats and intimidation involving wardens and their families were widespread and numerous.' On the estuary of the Restigouche Indians flout the law, take salmon in commercial nets and sell them openly. This is a no man's land where neither New Brunswick nor Quebec claims jurisdiction.

'It's time for us to decide,' says the IASF, 'if we want to keep Atlantic salmon or if we don't really give a damn . . . We don't need a rash of new regulations to save the salmon from destruction by bandits and hoodlums; laws are already on the books to cope with the situation. All that's required is for the various protection agencies to take well prepared cases to court, and then for the courts to support the enforcement people by applying the law, instead of regarding salmon poaching as simple misdemeanour to be treated with indulgence – as it used to be in Scotland in Sir Walter Scott's day.

Provincial and federal governments in Canada are spending large sums on Atlantic salmon programmes, although they are small compared with what is being spent on Pacific salmon enhancement in British Columbia. Capital expenditures from 1945 to 1973 in Newfoundland, the Maritimes and Quebec totalled $5.6 million with operating costs of $1.2 million. The nine hatcheries accounted for 54% of the total investment and 70% of the operating costs, not including Mactaquac. The remaining 46% of the capital investment has been devoted chiefly to establishing fish in barren areas upstream from natural or man-made obstructions. This is a slow process as it takes ten to twenty years for *Salmo salar* to colonize newly accessible territory.

On the whole, in the light of its sad history, Canada is doing relatively well by its remaining Atlantic salmon treasure trove.

L'Envoi

The plight of the Atlantic salmon gets worse every year. While there are bright spots in the picture as we survey its range in Europe and North America, the dark spots increase. Where not many years ago stocks were increasing in Ireland, Scotland and Norway, these countries have allowed success to generate over-fishing, and overfishing, especially in the ocean, reduces the number of fish that manage to return home and spawn. Other countries have permitted their runs to wither away, as in France and Spain, and seemingly no longer care if the resource disappears, although sportsmen in France, at least, continue to agitate for conservation programmes which only governments can properly finance. Overall catches of Atlantic salmon are now probably at an all time low.

When an anadromous fishery dwindles it is extremely hard to bring it back. I have heard biologists say, 'Give us enough money and we will guarantee more fish.' Nature and biology, however, may defeat the biologists and fish culturists who, armed with extensive funds, build hatcheries, breed smolts, send hundreds of thousands of them to sea every year, and wait patiently (or impatiently) for them to return as adults to the rivers. Not many return, for reasons not always identifiable. Some of them do not survive in the ocean; others probably grow to maturity and begin their homeward journey but are caught in the nets at sea or those strung out along the coasts. The Connecticut River is a prime example of the failure of the concept that if enough money is invested in a restoration programme, and some work is done to clean up a fouled river and remove some obstacles to migration, a substantial run of salmon will result.

To save the salmon we must, I think, reorient our thinking. We must see that the riverine habitat remains pure and un-blockaded. Because of their marvellous instinct that directs them back to their home stream, usually unerringly, the best way to harvest the salmon is to take them, fat with the spoils of the sea, as they return to freshwater. Here the catches can be monitored and the escapements adjusted to the maintenance of a perpetual crop.

'Commercial netting of Atlantic salmon at locations other than at the mouths of rivers or in the rivers themselves is unscientific and contrary to sound principles of management,' says Richard A. Buck, one of the most stalwart fighters in the crusade to save the Atlantic salmon, in a letter to Romeo Leblanc, Canadian Minister of Fisheries. 'Salmon feeding in the ocean or on migration are inextricably intermingled. They come from different spawning streams, different river systems, different hemispheres. No man, and no type of fishing gear known to man, no method of control, can sort them out.'

A drift net fishery such as became rampant in Irish, Scottish, Norwegian and some Canadian waters, 'takes indiscriminately from perhaps the very river runs needing special protection, and results in absolutely no rational or effective means of conserving basic stocks or ensuring adequate escapements for spawning.'

The surest way to conserve what is left of the salmon populations is to phase out commercial netting in all countries except at the mouths of rivers or in the rivers themselves, 'under a programme encompassing the relocation of nets, where possible, and always with adequate reimbursement to those fishermen adversely affected economically,' says Buck. This was done in Canada.

In sum, the ultimate answer to the question, 'How can we have more salmon?' is to clean up the rivers, remove blockades to their migration to the spawning grounds, and eliminate inshore and offshore netting. However, implementation of such a programme is extremely difficult and very costly. The money to clean up the rivers must come usually from government sources; the removal of blockades by building fish passes at dams or weirs is the responsibility of private industry which uses the water and is generally loath to invest in what will not enhance its profits – an idea inherited from the age of *laissez faire* that was responsible for much of the disaster which has befallen the salmon. Politics may prevent taking measures to halt netting that is decimating the runs. Thus Michael Forsyth-Grant, who says he is 'not a supporter of any of the parties represented in London's Palace of Westminster,' accuses the British government of failing to take stern measures to suppress illegal drift netting off the Scottish coast because of 'a last desperate attempt to retain the inshore white fisherman's vote'. (*Atlantic Salmon Journal*, October 1977.) Similar accusations are made against the Norwegian Minister who refused to crack down on widespread drift netting in inshore waters.

Whatever the causes and reasons for *Salmo salar's* plight, a crisis exists in most of the countries that still retain relatively large stocks. Even the Russians, who do not fish for salmon in the sea, are unhappy because their fish are taken in huge numbers by Danish and other fishermen in the Baltic. The crisis can be eased only by international action, resulting in a treaty with teeth in it, that gives salmon a guarantee of safety while it wanders over the globe and attempts to return to its natal stream to complete its life cycle. In short, while we have the biological and technical knowledge to sustain the species at much higher levels than at the present time, it is ultimately – as with nearly all bio-ecological problems – up to the politicians to make the right decisions that will bring much needed results. Time is running out for *Salmo salar.*

Part Three

THE PACIFIC SALMON

CHAPTER 13

California and Oregon

WHEN the aborigines began to populate North America, thousands of rivers flowing into the Pacific Ocean from Kotzebue Sound to Monterey Bay harboured regular runs of salmon and sometimes steelhead trout (a Pacific relative of *Salmo salar*) as well. Chinook were found from the Yukon River to Monterey Bay and were especially prolific in the Columbia and Sacramento River watersheds; coho proliferated in many watersheds from Norton Sound to Monterey Bay; sockeye inhabited watersheds containing lakes from the Bristol Bay area, and even farther north, to southern British Columbia and Washington state and were prominent in the upper Columbia River though scarce below Puget Sound. Pinks were probably the most abundant species in both Asia and North America, where they occurred from northern Alaska to the Klamath River in California, as well as in the Mackenzie, which empties into the Arctic Ocean. Chums inhabited rivers from Bering Strait to San Francisco Bay but were relatively scarce south of Puget Sound. Steelhead trout was a denizen of countless rivers from Alaska to northern California, attaining special prominence in the Columbia River watershed of 260,000 square miles.

The diminutive and highly edible kokanee, a landlocked variety of sockeye, dwelt in lakes whose outlets to the sea had been blocked by land upheavals. It was found in what is now Alaska, Yukon Territory, British Columbia, Washington, Oregon and Idaho, sometimes attaining a weight of nine pounds.

Chinook and chum tend to roam farther inland than other Pacific species. Some chinook ploughed their way up the Yukon River for over a thousand miles, as they did on the Columbia before Grand Coulee Dam blocked off their Canadian spawning grounds, and sockeye went equally far.

CALIFORNIA'S BOUNTY

It was in California that North American Pacific salmon were first fished on a large scale. Only chinook (called 'king') and coho are native to California, along with steelhead trout. Originally the 380-mile Sacramento River and 300-mile San Joaquin, which join and empty into San Francisco Bay, were among the richest chinook rivers in North America. Steelhead inhabit the Sacramento and some of its tributaries but are most abundant in numerous north coast rivers.

The Sacramento-San Joaquin Rivers fertilize the great central valley which lies between the coast range on the west and the Sierra Nevada on the east. They are the lifeblood of California, making possible agricultural production on a large scale in a semiarid climate and also providing water supplies for industries, cities and other communities.

Before the rivers were dammed and diverted from their natural courses, the fishes proliferated in numerous tributaries of these two great rivers, as in the McCloud, Feather, American and Yuba systems of the Sacramento, and the Mokelumne, Stanislaus, Tuolumne and Merced of the San Joaquin. The two rivers merge in a vast swampy area, now largely drained and cultivated and studded with densely-packed communities, forming a confusion of channels from which they turn westward, passing Suisan Bay, Carquinez Strait and San Pablo Bay through the Golden Gate to the sea.

The chinook usually migrate to the sea as fry, but in rivers that are cool all summer they may remain until they reach fingerling size. Through the wisdom of nature they generally return from the sea to the warmer rivers when there is cool water for spawning, below 58 degrees Fahrenheit. There is also a unique winter run of chinook who reach the upper Sacramento around Christmas and do not spawn until May or June, when other streams would be too warm for them.

Juvenile coho spend about a year in the river so they cannot survive in streams that dry up and become too warm in summer. Steelhead trout are found in large numbers in such coastal rivers as the Trinity, Smith, Klamath, Redwood Creek, Mad, Eel,

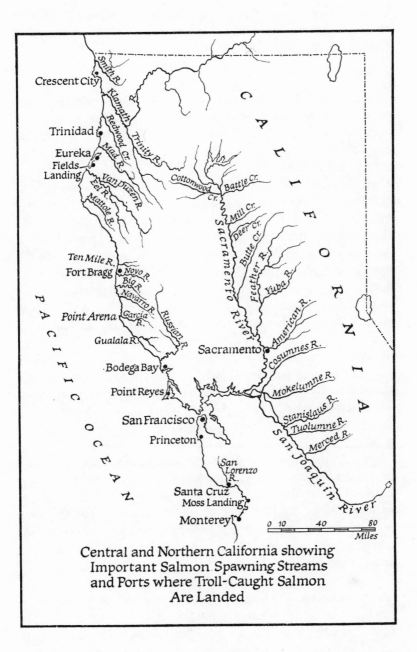

Central and Northern California showing
Important Salmon Spawning Streams
and Ports where Troll-Caught Salmon
Are Landed

Russian, Napa, **Carmel** and Big Sur. Their numbers have been reduced in the inland streams where water developments have altered or manipulated the flows.

Commercial fishing

Commercial fishing for salmon began in California about the time of the gold rush of 1849, when gill nets and seines were operating in both the Sacramento and San Joaquin Rivers and especially in Suisan and San Pablo Bays. Johann Sutter, owner of a ranch on the American River where gold was first found in 1848, was engaged in commercial salmon fishing among other activities. The stampede to the gold fields stimulated the fishing industry and led to the creation of a canning industry. In 1864 the brothers Hume and their partner Andrew Hapgood, all of whom came from Maine, set up the first salmon cannery in the world, on a scow moored at the foot of K Street in the city of Sacramento. With their crude machinery they produced 4,000 cases of forty-eight one-pound cans that year, but half of them were unsaleable. In 1867 the firm moved to the Columbia River where they set up their machinery at Eagle Cliff on the north bank, a place that has vanished. Eventually the canned salmon of Hapgood, Hume and Company found their way into the markets of England, Australia and South America, from canneries in Alaska as well as in Oregon and Washington. Americans themselves were slow in acquiring a taste for the product.

By 1883 there were twenty-one canneries in California, mostly on the Sacramento River, with San Francisco as the marketing centre. Here fishing boats were outfitted and the labour force, mainly Chinese coolies, was recruited, not only for the local industry but for Oregon and Washington. San Francisco was succeeded by Seattle when California's salmon runs declined and the industry petered out.

A peak of 200,000 cases, with a catch of 12 million pounds, was produced in California in 1882, but in the next decade the catch fell to about 6 million pounds and in 1891, when only three canneries were left, to 2 million pounds. Salmon canning ceased in 1919 although landings picked up with the advent of power boats which fished offshore with hook and line (trolling), while gillnetters worked the rivers. In addition to excessive fishing, destruction of habitat affected the stocks in the nineteenth century to some extent, mainly owing to hydraulic gold mining which did not end until 1891.

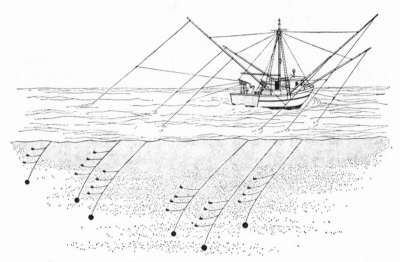

15 *Trolling*

The situation was succinctly described by Livingstone Stone of the US Bureau of Fisheries, who built the first salmon hatchery on the Pacific coast, in an address to the American Fisheries Society in 1892:

> Not only is every contrivance employed that human ingenuity can devise to destroy the salmon of our west coast rivers, but more surely destructive, more fatal than all is the slow but inexorable march of these destroying agencies of human progress, before which the salmon must surely disappear as did the buffalo of the plains and the Indian of California. The helpless salmon's life is gripped between these two forces – the murderous greed of the fishermen and the white man's advancing civilization – and what hope is there for the salmon in the end?

As the remaining chapters of this book will show, these remarks were prophetic, and apply not only to the Pacific salmon in the United States but in other countries as well.

Habitat destruction

The fate of California's anadromous fishes mirrors the state's use and misuse of its natural resources generally. In the past fifty years California, endowed with an abundance of fertile soils, immense forests and grasslands, mountain ranges and deserts, has been invaded by millions of people from all ends of the country, seeking a better life in a pleasant climate, free of abysmally cold winters and blessed with a great deal of sunshine. With them has come agricultural and industrial development, and upsurging towns and cities that paved over bucolic landscapes, destroyed orchards and farms, soiled rivers and usurped water needed by aquatic life. Cyclopean highways now ribbon the densely populated coastal regions, and the whole is a kind of nightmarish landscape dominated by megalopolises, one stretching from Sacramento to almost Monterey Bay, and the other from Los Angeles almost to San Diego. In the process, much of the wildlife has been destroyed and salmon and other freshwater fishes driven from their immemorial haunts.

The advent of irrigation agriculture had a significant effect on the freshwater fisheries. Before 1890, grain, which can be grown in dry farming areas, was the major crop in the Central Valley. After 1890 private developers built irrigation works which permitted large ranches, many laid out by Spanish proprietors before California became an American state, to be broken up into smaller units. Farming was destined to be greatly diversified: fruit, vineyards, alfalfa and vegetable crops were found to be adaptable to the soils and climate if water became available during the growing season. Later came rice, cotton, sugar beets and cattle raising.

After the passage of the federal Reclamation Act in 1902 large reclamation projects were launched, requiring large, multi-purpose dams. By 1929 there were eleven dams in the San Joaquin system and thirty-five in the Sacramento which directly or indirectly affected salmon migration and cut off about 80% of the spawning grounds in this part of California. Public and private agencies paid little or no attention to the needs of the fish in planning these obstructions, many of which were built without fish ladders: even when there were ladders they sometimes proved to be useless. At diversion dams ladders might be effective at first but the gravelly river bottoms below them were scoured away through the years and the fish could no longer dig their redds. Many juvenile salmon were lured into unscreened concrete ditches (which brought water to the farms and orchards) and died in them.

For example, Folsom Dam on the American River, 340 feet high, was impassable since no feasible method of getting fish over such an obstruction could be devised. Where fish-passage facilities were provided, considerable numbers of juveniles were lost going through the swiftly-revolving turbines in the powerhouse or over the spillways. On the plus side was the fact that the great overflow basins, which used to flood the Sacramento for miles during the winter rainy season and trapped and killed many fish, were being reduced by drainage in the 1920s and bypasses were built around the marshes to facilitate fish migration.

Drainage of polluted water from the rice fields into the rivers was also inimical to fish life.

As agriculture and settlement spread throughout the Central Valley there was a steady diminution of habitat suitable for migratory fish. In 1929 the California Fish and Game Department estimated that only 510 linear miles of the original 6,000 miles of spawning grounds remained to the salmon in the Sacramento-San Joaquin watershed.

Central Valley Project

In the 1930s California entered a new era with the launching of the Central Valley Project by the federal Bureau of Reclamation, an extremely complicated network of canals, dams and other works designed to bring water from the Sacramento Valley, where it is abundant, southward to the irrigable lands of the semiarid San Joaquin Valley. The key structures are Shasta Dam, north of Redding, which stabilizes the flow of the Sacramento River and Friant Dam in the south which cuts off the flow of the San Joaquin and diverts it southward instead of northward. At the Tracy pumping plant the Sacramento is lifted into the San Joaquin and is channelled by means of canals southward through the valley. Thus the dams and canals store and move river water, diverting it to where it is needed. The system is mainly responsible for the phenomenal growth of towns and cities as well as agricultural and industrial developments which boosted the state's population from 5.7 million in 1930 to about 22 million in 1975. Little attention was paid by the planners of the Central Valley and other water development projects to the needs of the fishes.

Nobody knows how many salmon were killed by the Chinese maze of structures in the Central Valley Project which is still unfinished. In 1964 the ecologist Raymond Dasmann wrote: 'Today dams stand on most of the major rivers draining into the Central Valley, and are proposed or under construction on all the others. Two major operations under way include the Feather River project being carried forward by the state, and the San Luis project of the federal government. The state project will pen up the largest remaining free river in the Sierra Nevada, and transfer Feather River water southward. The San Luis project will make possible the transfer of water from the Feather and other northern rivers southward, along the west side of the San Joaquin valley, to irrigate lands across the way and ultimately to supply the needs of southern California communities as far south as San Diego.'

Nor was this all. Both the Bureau of Reclamation and US Corps of Engineers had their eyes on the still untrammelled north coast rivers which they wished to dam.

To compensate at least in part for the losses of wild runs, there are now six hatcheries producing king salmon and three artificial spawning channels to accommodate this species. In the years 1968–1971 the Central Valley hatcheries produced an average of 14 million fingerlings (smolts) and in 1972 it was estimated that they contributed about 100,000 fish to the catch, of which 65,000 were taken by commercial fishermen and 35,000 by sportsmen.

In May 1972 the California Department of Fish and Game

installed the world's largest fish screen along the upper Sacramento River to halt the annual loss of 10 to 20 million young king salmon who perished in irrigation ditches. Costing $2,600,000 it has already paid for itself in terms of the number of fish saved, adding, it is estimated, 120,000 adult salmon to the commercial catch per year and probably as much as 45,000 salmon and steelhead trout to sport-fishing yields.

The balance sheet

Prodded by sportsmen, charter boat operators who take parties on salmon fishing trips, and commercial fishermen who were alarmed over the withering stocks, the California state legislature in 1970 passed a resolution which ordered the Fish and Game Department to appoint a Citizens Advisory Committee to investigate the status of the anadromous fishes. Its findings appeared in March 1971 in a report entitled 'An Environmental Tragedy' which bluntly declared that 'man unfortunately in his headlong rush to develop California and provide goods and services, has paid little heed to environmental quality and the uniqueness and irreplaceability of the salmon and steelhead resources. These resources are now seriously threatened and once lost, may be gone forever. Only resolute action will prevent such a disaster . . . Analysis of the Department of Fish and Game records on the status of the salmon and steelhead populations provides startling evidence of declining trends headed towards ultimate disaster. The lowest point in salmon catches in the state occurred in 1939 when 2.7 million pounds were landed compared with 13 million in 1919, 1945 and 1946. There were eighteen consecutive years, from 1926 to 1943, when the commercial catch never reached 7 million pounds. The 1950s saw some improvement, but the Sacramento River runs went steadily downhill after an upsurge in the 1940s and in 1957 the river was closed to commercial fishing.'

In the decade 1964–1973 commercial landings averaged about 8 million pounds but a fairly large proportion were coho and chinook of Oregon and Washington origin.

The committee found that in north coast streams steelhead runs dropped from an average of 290,000 in 1940–1949 to

100,000 in 1960–1969, an 80% loss; silver (coho) runs fell from 147,000 to 47,000 or 65%; and king salmon runs from 255,000 to 91,000. Heavier losses occurred in the Sacramento and San Joaquin watersheds. The committee attributed these disasters to extensive habitat damage, especially loss of spawning grounds due to logging, mining, road construction, gravel extraction from river beds, grazing practices, pollution and most of all damming of rivers without fish ladders. Only 300 miles of spawning grounds were left in the Central Valley.

The Committee said that an 'all out effort is now needed to correct past damage and restore the potential of these spawning streams, to prevent damage from future developments, and to expand salmon and steelhead programmes for priority protection and enhancement work.' Time was indeed running out.

Citizen protests, sparked by the Committee of Two Million dedicated to the preservation of the wild rivers, pushed the Behr Bill through the legislature in 1972. It created a scenic river sanctuary system that included the Eel, Klamath, Trinity and Smith Rivers and the north fork of the American. Dam building is prohibited on the Eel for twelve years and on the others indefinitely.

The Citizens Advisory Committee issued a second report on May 15, 1972, entitled 'A Conservation Opportunity'. It affirmed that 'the history of fish and wildlife resources in the country leads to one universal principle. Attempts to maintain the status quo result in gradual attrition and eventual loss of the resource. Federal and state mitigation policies have been a failure and are no longer acceptable to meet society's needs . . . Those responsible for management of the resource, for its harvest and for the environmental changes that threaten it must cooperate in a positive effort not only to protect, but to *maximize* the salmon and steelhead fishery.' The committee outlined a basic plan by which federal and state agencies could cooperate to prevent future fish losses and recoup some of the lost ground by restocking streams, protect and improve water quality and flows, and 'maintain and enforce scientifically sound and equitable regulations on catch – the final product'.

The future of California's salmon

While the commercial and sport fishing industry still flourishes in California, it is now confined to offshore areas and a large portion of the catches comprise Oregon and Washington salmon. In the decade 1964–1973 an average of 9 million pounds were caught by Californians, including 6.6 million pounds of chinook and 2.4 million of coho. In addition, sportsmen caught an average of 150,000 salmon each year in the period 1962–1971 and 250,000 in 1972. The number of spawning salmon counted on the redds in 1975 totalled only 6,800 in the vast San Joaquin watershed and 183,000 in the Sacramento system, a serious drop from the 314,000 in 1973. That year the sport fishery was the poorest in a decade, reflecting decreasing runs in California and adjacent states.

Thanks to the activities of the citizens committees, federal and state bureaux involved with water projects seem to be assuming a more enlightened attitude towards the freshwater fisheries. For example, a 1972 report of the Bureau of Reclamation affirms that 'now fish and wildlife agencies, both state and federal, are consulted concerning the effect of proposed developments on anadromous fishery resources and have more authority than at any time during more than a century of abuse to compel specific measures be taken to protect remaining migration runs.'

Stronger efforts are being made to protect the fishes passing the intricate installations on the rivers like the pumping station at Orland where over 10 million downstream migrants were lost one year, and around the irrigation canals that honeycomb the Central Valley. More spawning channels are being built to replace lost breeding areas and dams are being constructed to catch debris flowing from abandoned copper and zinc mines; some of these areas are being drained to keep deleterious acids out of the Sacramento River. One senses a rising awareness in California of the value of its piscatorial riches and this presages, hopefully, a better day for the salmon and other wild creatures.

OREGON FISHERIES

The Columbia River drains an area of 260,000 square miles in

British Columbia, Washington, Oregon, Idaho, Montana, Nevada and Wyoming. Originating as a rivulet near Lake Windermere which nestles in the great trench between the Selkirk and Rocky Mountains in British Columbia, the river flows north for 150 miles and then reverses itself, leaving the trench and turning southward, entering the United States near the northwest corner of Washington state. There it forms another big bend and heads south-west for the Pacific Ocean. In its course of 1,270 miles, of which about 500 are in Canada, the Columbia passes through Rocky Mountain trenches and valleys, long semiarid stretches, and areas of heavy rainfall and dense evergreen forests west of the Cascade Mountains, pouring more water into the sea than any river system in North America except the St Lawrence, Mississippi and Mackenzie. Between the headwaters and the sea the Columbia drops 2,400 feet, thus creating the largest hydroelectric potential of any river in the United States, the bulk of which has now been developed, to the great detriment of the anadromous fishes.

The Snake River, largest of the tributaries, is itself over a thousand miles long, rising in the Continental Divide in Grand Teton National Park, and flowing southward through Wyoming, west across Idaho and then north to form the border with Oregon and Washington before turning west to meet the Columbia. It too traverses a variety of landscapes, many spectacular. In Idaho it crosses arid plateaux, and as it curves northward flows through Hell's Canyon, the deepest gorge in North America, now a scenic sanctuary. Then it veers west and the terrain flattens out, the land becomes suitable, with the help of irrigation, for growing abundant crops of sugar beets, potatoes and wheat.

Salmon and the Columbia River are synonymous. Originally there were more chinook, coho (here called silvers or silversides) and steelhead trout than in any other river system in North America, in addition to large populations of sockeye (here called bluebacks) and chum, as well as a small run of pinks. The fish spawned wherever suitable gravel could be found, in creeks, lakes, brooks and even rivulets, and the supply seemed inexhaustible.

There were spring, summer and fall chinook runs; summer and winter steelhead runs; coho came mostly in late summer and fall; sockeye in spring and summer. Before the advent of irrigation agriculture and hydroelectric dams the fish usually passed easily to the spawning grounds. Some of them ascended the river for a thousand miles into Canada and hundreds of miles up the Snake. Their oceanic wanderings are also quite extensive. Some chinook head southwards towards California after leaving the river while others go northward as far as the Queen Charlotte Islands and a few have been tracked all the way to Adak Island in the Aleutians. Usually chinook stay in the ocean two or three years, and coho about one and a half years.

Indian subsistence fishery

Along the Columbia from the Dalles to the sea lived a group of Indians called Chinook, divided into several bands, to whom the abundant salmon were the mainstay of their diet. We know a great deal about them from the diaries and reports of early explorers like Captains Meriwether Lewis and William Clark who led an expedition across the continent in the years 1804–1806, David Douglas the Scottish plant hunter who scoured the Pacific Northwest in the 1820s, and many others. Lewis and Clark saw Indians fishing for salmon in over a hundred places and in one day's journey passed twenty-nine lodges below the Snake where they were catching fish. Outside nearly every hut hung stacks of fish drying in the sun on scaffolds or being smoked on hot stones. Farther downstream the red men were seen pounding the dried fish between stones and putting the pulverized products, called pemmican, into 'a species of basket neatly made of grass and rushes better than 2 feet long and one foot in diameter . . . lined with the skin of salmon stretched and dried for the purpose.' Pemmican, 'sound and sweet', would keep for years and great quantities were bartered with white or native visitors.

The Indian population in the Columbia basin was fairly numerous. Craig and Hacker in their study, *The History and Development of the Fisheries of the Columbia River*, estimated it at about 50,000 in the early nineteenth century. If every man, woman and child consumed at least one pound of salmon per day, the catch totalled 18 million pounds annually, or much less than is now taken from the river. The Indians were expert fishermen and taught the white men not only how to fish but how to fashion their nets and other gear.

To visualize the aboriginal fishery we may betake ourselves to Celilo Falls where the pellucid river, flowing between low sagebrush hills, dropped into a long, narrow and deep chasm. Here the water course was broken into narrow channels by protruding rocks and rugged waterfalls, all of which provided ideal if slippery fishing spots. Here during the salmon runs was a vast concentration of red men and their families, a place of noisy activity.

Every able-bodied male had to be a skilled fisherman, since without an adequate supply of fish the tribe would starve. They used a variety of gear. Standing on the slippery rocks or on precarious wooden platforms to which they were roped, they caught the salmon with dipnets or speared them in the narrow channels as they leaped up from the water in a desperate attempt to climb the falls, or as they fell back from the promontories. To land a heavy fish from a narrow perch with a dipnet was no mean feat, and occasionally a fisherman slid into the water and disappeared. Sometimes a man was lowered in a basket down the sheer side of a cliff where he would wait until a big fish jumped up which he could spear or haul in with his net.

Away from the falls and cascades the aborigines planted weirs across the channels, usually in a slough or at the mouth of a river. Lewis and Clark drew sketches of these contraptions which consisted of branches of trees supported by willow stakes to which wicker baskets were attached. Fishing from dugout canoes was also common, using hook and line with a stone sinker; herring or smelt served as bait. The main gear, however, consisted of seines or gillnets made from wild hemp, wild flax or grass, and placed where the river bottom was fairly smooth and the slope of the bank gentle. One end of the net was kept on shore and the other was taken out in a canoe and circled around the area where the fish were believed to pass.

Fishing stands were a family inheritance, passed down from

father to son. One man took his place on the rocks and caught all his family could clean and dry in a day and then another replaced him. Ten or more people might fish from one stand in the course of twenty-four hours. Fishing would start at three or four in the morning when the salmon began to move, every day of the week as long as the run continued.

When the Indians were moved by the American government from their ancestral lands in the middle of the nineteenth century, they were guaranteed in the treaties perpetual access to their 'usual and accustomed fishing places'. This concession was destined to create endless difficulties, which, in recent years, have hindered proper management of the fisheries.

The commercial fishery

In 1823 the Hudson's Bay Company, primarily engaged in the fur business, began to salt salmon for export at Fort George at the mouth of the Columbia River. Thus began the commercial exploitation of the rich salmon trove. Later the company moved its headquarters to Fort Langley near the mouth of the Fraser. When the Oregon boundary treaty was negotiated with Great Britain in 1846, confining the Company to Canada, large quantities of salmon were being shipped from the Columbia to the east coast, South America and the Sandwich Islands (Hawaii). By then the Oregon country was filling up with settlers and before long the Indians were moved to reservations.

The first cannery appeared on the Columbia in 1867; the industry grew rapidly and in 1883 there were some fifty on both banks of the river, producing 630,000 cases, from a catch of 43 million pounds. This was an historic peak, reached again only a few times in later years.

With ample supplies of fish, a relatively small investment, and a cheap labour force consisting mainly of Chinese coolies, salmon canning was a profitable enterprise for many operators. Others could not stand the competition, and failed.

At the height of the fishery, from 1870 to the end of World War I, armadas of gillnetters and seiners worked the river, and after the turn of the century trollers operated offshore. There was an ineradicable belief that the salmon, like the omnipresent forests, were inexhaustible. It was impossible to imagine they could ever diminish. Yet there was scarcely any regulation of the fishery, and fishermen spread their nets, wheels and traps without much restraint in the rivers and estuaries, usually ignoring whatever laws were on the books. The Oregon Board of Fish Commissioners reported as early as 1889 that 'nets and traps (are) extended nearly, and in some instances entirely across the stream, thus virtually preventing all the salmon from reaching their spawning grounds.' Oregon's coastal rivers were similarly depleted by excessive fishing and were closed to commercial fishing in 1956 except for chum fishing in Tillamook Bay. Now only sport fishing with hook and line is permitted on these streams.

In the 1930s the most productive gear such as wheels and traps was outlawed by the Oregon and Washington legislatures and commercial as well as sport fishing began to be closely regulated. Catches held up after 1890 only because other species than chinook, upon which the canning industry had relied for two decades, were taken. Nevertheless in 1917 John N. Cobb of the US Bureau of Fisheries declared in his annual report, 'Man is undoubtedly the greatest menace to the perpetuation of the great salmon fisheries of the Pacific Coast. When the enormous numbers of fishermen engaged and the immense quantity of gear employed is considered, one sometimes wonders how any of the fish, in certain streams at least, escape.'

Twenty years later, just before the advent of the dam building era which was to have disastrous consequences for the resource, Willis H. Rich, director of research for the Oregon Fish Commission, warned that 'such regulation and restrictions as have been imposed upon the Columbia River salmon fisheries apparently have very little effect insofar as they may act to reduce the intensity of fishing and provide a greater escapement'.

Fish vs. dams

Until the 1930s the economy of the Pacific Northwest depended mainly on forestry, fishing and agriculture. Industrialization was minimal. Rivers usually ran clear and sweet. Cascades and waterfalls which salmon could not negotiate were sometimes laddered.

Many low and impassable dams had already been built to store water for irrigation.

The Army Corps of Engineers surveyed the extensive watershed south of the Canadian border, as did the Bureau of Reclamation. Each published exclusive plans for harnessing the free-flowing waters. The Corps' '308 Report' of 1932 proposed ten high multipurpose dams to create a navigation channel from the ocean to Lewiston, Idaho, controlling the frequent and heavy floods, and generating huge amounts of electricity. The first dam in this plan (later extended to twelve projects), Bonneville, 145 miles from the sea, was started in 1933 by President Roosevelt as a public works project. The Bureau of Reclamation's much larger Grand Coulee Dam on the upper Columbia was begun about the same time, also as a public works project to provide jobs for the unemployed. With a capacity of 2 million kilowatts, Grand Coulee was then the world's largest dam, backing up water for 150 miles into Canada and destroying 1,100 linear miles of salmon spawning grounds. No fish could be passed over this 350-foot impoundment.

At Bonneville Dam no fish-passage facilities were at first contemplated by the Corps of Engineers. When this oversight was brought to the attention of the Chief of the Corps, he said, 'We don't intend to play nursemaid to the fish!' Had his view prevailed the entire salmon and steelhead population that spawned above the dam would have been wiped out. Protests from the fishing industry and conservationists forced the Corps to change its mind and a team of biologists and engineers was selected to design some means of getting fish over this seventy-foot hurdle.

Hopes were pinned on pool-type fish ladders similar to those found on some Atlantic salmon streams in Europe, down which powerful jets of water acted as an attraction current. There were ladders at the face of the dam on both banks of the river and on Bradford Island, as well as elevators to lift the fish in case the ladders failed. The fingerlings were expected to go over the spillway if their migration coincided with periods of high water, otherwise they had to pass through the revolving turbines in the powerhouse. Since little was known about the size of juvenile and adult fish populations in the river, and such huge

15

stocks had never before been subjected to such difficult passage anywhere in the world, the Bonneville facilities were a gamble. 'If you were a gambling man,' said Milo Bell, one of the designers of the fishways, 'you could have found some odds that the whole facility would not have been completely functional.'

The dam was completed in the spring of 1938 and the fish ladders were opened to the thronging hordes. The bulk of upstream migrants readily found the collection troughs leading to the long, curving ladders, and swam or flipped themselves from pool to pool until they arrived at the reservoir's gate. There an attendant recorded their numbers, by species, on a hand counter and permitted them to pass and head upstream for their spawning grounds. That year almost 500,000 salmonids, in addition to shad, lampreys and other fish, negotiated the ladders, and the numbers increased in later years. However, many fish failed to find the fishways and died without spawning. It was many years before studies could be developed to measure the extent of this mortality. It was estimated by the US Fish and Wildlife Service at between 10 and 15% of adults. For the fingerlings no exact estimate was possible but it was known that many were destroyed in the turbine blades or going over the spillways.

The success of the Bonneville fishways inspired confidence in the engineers that the hydroelectric potential of the Columbia River could be fully developed without undue damage to the anadromous fish. General Chorpening, Chief of the Corps, assured Congress in 1952 in testifying for appropriations for the Dalles Dam 'that with the experience gained in operation of Bonneville Dam, there will be no difficulty in the proper handling of this project.' However, the Corps' revised '308 Report' outlining plans for a series of dams on the Columbia-Snake Rivers told a melancholy tale of tributaries already dammed without ladders and lost to migratory fish. 'In only a few instances,' admitted the report, 'has any thought been paid to the effect that these developments might have on fish and wildlife.' About half the linear area of salmon spawning grounds in the entire basin had already been lost, thanks to dams without fish ladders, forest fires, pollution, and poor farming, grazing and logging practices. As industrialization and population increased in the Pacific Northwest pollution became an important factor in the decline of the runs. On the Willamette, one of the principal tributaries of the Columbia, most of the salmon were killed by pollution as many communities, including the city of Portland, largest in the state, dumped their untreated wastes into the river,

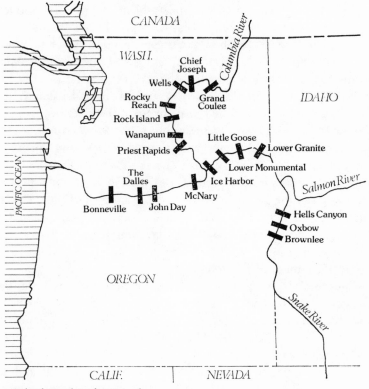

16 *Columbia and Snake River dams*

while pulp mills and other manufacturing operations treated the river as an easily accessible sewer.

The Corps' 1952 report envisaged the harnessing of virtually all the Columbia's free-flowing water above Bonneville for the generation of electricity and storage for irrigation and flood control, and much of the Snake River and some of its major tributaries as well. Some of the proposed dams were to be so high that no fish ladders were possible – these were never built. Eventually nine high dams, each equipped with Bonneville-type fish ladders, were added to the Columbia and four on the lower Snake, all but a few built by the Corps of Engineers. Three dams built by a private electric utility company on the middle Snake blocked off the anadromous fish runs from the rest of that long river.

Today the turbulent Columbia which periodically flooded the surrounding countryside and wreaked havoc on property and human lives, has been tamed under the control of a network of dams, and provides power for industries, homes, shops and farms at relatively low cost for much of the Pacific Northwest. But the impact on the valuable fish runs has been disastrous.

As the adverse effects of the dams on fish stocks became apparent Congress was asked to supply funds for a compensating programme designed to augment the wild stocks and safeguard their habitats. The Columbia River Fishery Development Program consists of five parts: (1) expansion of artificial propagation of salmon and steelhead trout; (2) removal of obstructions such as logjams in the streams, small abandoned dams, and the like; (3) laddering of waterfalls and screening of water diversions; (4) transplantation of some upriver runs to downstream areas; and (5) establishment of fish refuges.

The chief accomplishment of the programme has been the financial stimulus and technical aid given to artificial propagation that has permitted a great upsurge in breeding coho, chinook and steelhead. Thus the National Marine Fisheries Service estimated in 1970 that between 1964 and 1968 about 35% of the fall chinook taken by commercial fishermen offshore and in the river below Bonneville and 50% of those caught above Bonneville were hatchery fish. The Oregon Fish Commission estimates that over half the coho landed in the ocean troll fishery are artificially bred, and the Washington Department of Fisheries has published similar data.

Virtually all the imaginable consequences of damming a mighty river have befallen the Columbia River fishery. Nowhere in the world are the agile salmon required to overcome so many obstacles to reach the sea on their downstream journey and their spawning grounds upstream. Those who spawn in the uppermost tributaries of the Columbia, like the Okanogan River in Washington, must pass up to nine dams with a total elevation of about 850 feet. At each one they must find the entrances to the fish ladders, pass over them, and adjust themselves to the slack currents and other new conditions in the reservoirs, such as excessive temperatures and low flows in summer. Many of them die from fatigue, or from bubble disease induced by supersaturated nitrogen gas generated when water not needed for power generation goes over the spillways. Fish that spawn in the Snake River tributaries in Idaho such as the Clearwater, Grand Ronde or Salmon, must pass up to eight dams with a total elevation of over 800 feet. The progeny of all the fish who succeed in spawning must make the same perilous journey to the sea. In some years as many as 90% of the juveniles emanating from Idaho have been killed by bubble disease and other causes. In fact, nitrogen gas alone is believed to have killed up to 5 million salmon and steelhead each year since 1971, resulting in very small returns of adults to the upper rivers, and forcing severe curtailment of fishing seasons, especially in Idaho.

William E. Pitney, a biologist with the Oregon Fish and Wildlife Department, succinctly describes the difficulties of passing salmonids over so many high dams in a single river system:

Extensive efforts have been made to improve fish passage ever since Bonneville dam was built. The U.S. Fish and Wildlife Service, Corps of Engineers, private and public utilities, and the resource management agencies of the several states have struggled with the many problems. Improvements have been made, but for each gain an almost unending host of other problems has been recognized. Once it had been determined that adult fish could be passed over high dams it was quickly discovered that their young were ineffective in finding their way downstream through the many miles of slackwater. This resulted largely from the water being impounded at the time of year the migrants should have been carried by the freshets to the sea. Some of those which do leave the reservoirs find only the turbine systems as outlets and are killed by the pressure changes or spinning blades.

Often the downstream migrants are delayed because their built-in time clocks are disoriented and this seriously affects their survival. Thus, says Donald L. Park of the National Marine Fisheries Service:

> Historically most juvenile chinook salmon have migrated down the river in the spring when the environmental factors were most favorable for their survival. Flows were generally high, water temperatures were within optimal ranges for salmon, the river was sufficiently turbid to protect them from predators, and impoundments did not delay their migration to the sea . . . [Now] the juveniles have to migrate down to an almost totally impounded river during July and August, when environmental conditions . . . are far from optimum. By mid-July the spring runoff is usually completed, water temperatures begin to rise and the water clears up and affords little protection from predators.

In recent years emergency measures have been taken to safeguard downstream migrants to keep them out of the poisoned reservoirs by transporting them hundreds of miles from Lower Granite Dam on the Snake to below Bonneville and there releasing them in waters relatively free of nitrogen gas. Also, adjustments have been made to the spillways at some of the dams to reduce the amount of gas that is generated by the spills. Biologists believe that this has saved large numbers of salmon and steelhead and contributed to the catches.

Management of the fishery

The Columbia River fishery is under joint management of the fish and game agencies of Washington, Oregon and Idaho. Their job is to regulate both sport and commercial fishing. Biologists monitor the runs and on the basis of their data regulations are formulated each year for every run. Essentially regulations are designed to ensure an adequate escapement so that a perpetual crop may be obtained: this is accomplished by means of adjusting fishing seasons and restricting the types of gear that may be used. Salmon may be taken commercially inside the rivers only with gillnets and in marine waters by trolling. Anglers may troll for salmon offshore or in the river from boats or use rod and line on shore. The Indians, who have special status, use set nets strung along the banks. Because of the greatly depleted runs the commercial fishing season has been reduced from 272 days in 1938 to seventy-seven days in 1971 and much less in recent years. In Idaho no salmon or steelhead fishing was permitted in 1975 and 1976 because of the paucity of fish in the state's waters. Anglers take a sizeable portion of the total catches in Oregon and Washington, as the following table for 1976 shows:

	No. of Anglers	Total Salmon Catch	Total Steelhead Catch
California	unavailable	124,000	unavailable
Oregon	259,479	415,925	186,450
Washington	651,934	1,399,375	92,851
Alaska	unavailable	178,020	unavailable

Since the building of Bonneville Dam, almost $400 million has been invested in programmes to save the anadromous fisheries of the Columbia River including fishways, hatcheries and attendant research programmes, screening of irrigation diversions, cleanup of streams, and other projects, with the bulk of the money coming from the federal treasury. This is the most ambitious undertaking to save a fishery in the world, yet its future is by no means assured. The latest report, published by the Pacific Northwest Regional Commission, subsidized by the federal and state governments, issued in July, 1976, paints a melancholy picture.

The spring chinook runs consist of two major segments, a lower river run destined for tributaries below Bonneville Dam and an upper river run which spawns in streams above the dam. The former is holding its own although far below the levels of its heyday before the dam was built, while the latter is in a parlous state; no fishing in the upper river was allowed in recent years in order to protect the stocks. Spring chinook suffered a serious blow in 1971 when half the juveniles issuing from the Snake River tributaries were destroyed by bubble disease before they reached the Columbia. Further, considerable losses have occurred since, but a good run of spring chinook in 1977 permitted fishing for them again.

Summer chinook catches reached an all-time low of a few thousand in 1966 and now are so scarce that fishing for them is rarely permitted. The run consisted almost entirely of wild fish, for little success has been attained in breeding them in hatcheries. Their decline parallels the construction of main-stem Columbia and Snake River dams.

Fall chinook have fared much better thanks to successful hatchery production. River catches reached a low point in the years 1957–1961 but the trend has been upward ever since.

Coho stocks reached a low point around 1960 when less than 50,000 were caught, after which they made an amazing comeback as millions of hatchery-reared fingerlings were released each year in numerous streams and a large proportion returned from the sea. The run bounded to almost one million in 1970 but has since levelled off at about half that number. The report says that 'the outlook for the run is good ... supported by extensive natural production and massive hatchery releases in tributaries below and immediately above Bonneville dam.'

The estimated run in 1977, however, was only 200,000 pounds compared to the previous ten-year average of 533,000 pounds.

Sockeye, once caught in hundreds of thousands, have almost vanished from the Columbia, as their lake habitat has disappeared throughout the basin with the advent of high dams and their migration rendered difficult and at times impossible by the 'killer dams'. A similar fate has befallen the chums, of which 700,000 were harvested in 1928 and only 500 in 1975.

Steelhead trout, one of the Pacific Northwest's prime angling fish, with the fighting qualities of Atlantic salmon, offers a brighter picture, again partly because it can be produced in large numbers in hatcheries. The summer run has gone steadily downhill but winter steelhead are maintaining their productivity and in 1974–1975 between 200,000 and 400,000 entered the

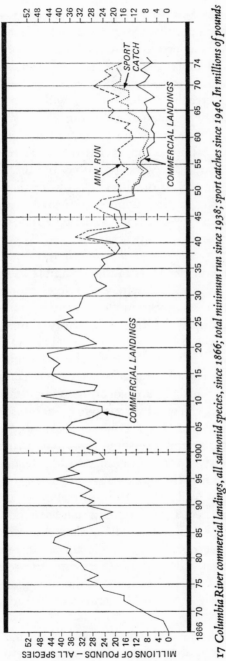

17 Columbia River commercial landings, all salmonid species, since 1866; total minimum run since 1938; sport catches since 1946. In millions of pounds

Columbia River. Steelhead may not be harvested commercially in either Washington or Oregon, except by the Indians, who are treated by the courts as citizens with special privileges.

Passage problems at the dams have affected all segments of the fishery. Thus in 1975 only 15,000 summer steelhead migrated up the Snake River into Idaho, along with 2,500 fall chinook, 7,735 summer chinook and 21,175 spring chinook. These meagre runs forced a closure on sport fishing, to the great dismay of Idaho anglers. Salmon canning has dwindled to a trickle. In 1976 only 8,600 cases were produced by the few canneries still operating in the Astoria area. In 1975 catches of all species totalled only 7.6 million pounds compared with five or six times as much in the 1880s and the period 1910–1920.

The Willamette River

One of the few bright spots in the Columbia River basin is the rehabilitation of the Willamette which flows entirely in the state of Oregon. Salmon stocks in this watershed were greatly reduced by municipal pollution and factory wastes until federal and state laws forced both to keep their muck out of the waters. The rehabilitation of the runs was therefore a feasible undertaking, assisted by the construction of eleven flood control dams on the tributaries which assure adequate water flows during the dry summer months, and by a massive programme of restocking suitable streams with hatchery-bred steelheads, coho and fall chinook. It was not till the summer of 1968 that the dissolved oxygen in the river rose in summer for the first time in many years to five parts per million, and as a result over 4,000 chinook were counted at Willamette Falls, increasing to 11,000 in 1972 and almost 40,000 in 1974. Steelhead runs have shown an equally remarkable improvement. As the outlook brightens for cleaner water and easier negotiation of the fish at the rebuilt ladders around the great falls of the Willamette, the restocking programme moves ahead to exploit the full potential of the watershed.

Coastal streams

Oregon has about a dozen coastal rivers which were originally well supplied with salmon. They were fished mercilessly in the last quarter of the nineteenth and first quarter of the twentieth centuries; habitats were also impaired by gigantic forest fires and reckless logging practices based on the cut-out and get-out principle which helped to ruin salmon streams by depositing debris and logjams. These rivers, open only to sport fishing, are now regularly stocked with juvenile salmon and have recovered some of their former productivity.

Some conclusions

Summing up, we can see that nowhere in the world have salmonids suffered greater effects from man's intrusion than in the Columbia River watershed. This, plus the customary greed of fishermen, who tend to exploit a resource until it is nearly exhausted unless restrained by law, has been responsible for the steady decline of the fishery. Innumerable studies have been made in recent years analysing the fishery's problems and offering solutions, and several hundred biologists and other analysts are employed by federal, state and private organizations working on the problems. Uncle Sam's treasury alone has been tapped to the extent of about $300 million for fish ladders at federal dams, construction of hatcheries, removal of blocks to fish migration in the rivers, research on every conceivable phase of the salmon's and steelhead's life, alteration of spillways at dams to reduce fish kills, etc. A symposium on the Columbia River Salmon and Steelhead held on March 5 and 6, 1976, in Vancouver, Washington, covered the entire gamut of problems afflicting this fishery. Papers read were published by the American Fisheries Society, Washington, D.C., in 1977.

The study by the Pacific Northwest Regional Council, already quoted, concludes that 'there are no short- or long-term solutions to the completely interrelated environmental, social, legal, political and philosophical problems contributing to contemporary Columbia Basin salmon and steelhead crises.

'Demand for the basin's salmon and steelhead resources has exceeded the supply for more than a century. The gap will continue to widen. Historic runs and geographical distribution are not recoverable within even the most distant foreseeable future.' Nevertheless, the report says: 'Given the tools, mandate and requisite public and political support the basin's fishery agencies can rehabilitate and maintain productive sport and commercial fisheries throughout the basin currently available to salmon and steelhead.' In other words, the biologists seem to be saying, 'Give us the money and we will make more fish available to both commercial interests and sportsmen.' This is an expensive proposition – already it seems that every salmon caught from the Columbia River stocks is almost worth its weight in gold – and in the light of the tremendous obstacles faced by migratory fish probably a dubious one.

I venture to suggest that the time has come to reconsider our values in developing and using our rivers. Americans destroyed the Atlantic salmon runs in New England and expensive efforts to restore them have so far brought relatively small results. The Columbia River stocks must not be allowed to decline any further, but this might require, for one thing, giving a higher priority to fish in the use of the waters. While low-cost electricity generated at the dams plus flood control, irrigation water and navigation benefits are tremendous boons, a high price has been paid in the staggering losses of valuable fish and wildlife, destruction of wilderness and much natural beauty.

Consider some of the social and economic aspects of the use of power generated at the federal dams. About 40% of the total output is sold to the aluminium smelters, equivalent to about all the power generated at the Snake River federal dams, and providing only some 40,000 jobs directly and indirectly. For the sake of such relatively small benefits the bulk of the great Snake River salmon runs have been sacrificed, a perpetual source of food and sport has been denied to us.

A great river like the Columbia is valuable to society for its fisheries as well as for the electricity which in a sense helps to kill them off. In contrast, the Fraser River in Canada, one of the last remaining major salmon producers on the continent, has been so far kept free of dams in order to preserve the fish runs. Fishery people in British Columbia point to the results of damming the Columbia, and so far their arguments have been persuasive, despite the continual efforts of Canadian power promoters to build a network of high dams that would destroy a large part of the Fraser fishery.

Perhaps some day Americans in their wisdom may decide that fishes, valuable for food and sport are more needed than electricity, which can, in any case, be generated from coal or other sources. When that time comes they may not only halt the building of hydroelectric projects on salmon rivers but perhaps they will destroy some of the 'killer dams' that now exist and return the free-flowing waters to the salmon.

CHAPTER 14

Washington and British Columbia

=====

WASHINGTON STATE FISHERIES

Indians and the land

IT is difficult now, when one visits the Puget Sound area, to imagine oneself back in the days before white settlement, when this was Indian country. The Sound, eighty miles long from the east end of Juan de Fuca Strait to Admiralty Inlet, with many branches from the Canadian border to Hood Canal, was a shimmering sheet of glass, roiled occasionally by strong winds, aquamarine in the sunlight, reflecting the towering snow-mantled Olympic Mountains, accepting the flow of numerous sparkling rivers laden with salmonid fishes. On a spring day an endless parade of migrating ducks and geese, mingled with snow-white swans, flew overhead towards their northern breeding grounds. Gulls, plovers, sandpipers, terns and other shore birds tripped along the white sandy beaches. Salmon plopped out of the water in their joy at nearing their ancient rivers; there were few fishermen to intercept them.

The Quinault, Makah, Nisqually, Skokomish, Puyallup and other tribes had the land to themselves and treated it with tender, loving care, as the late Clarence Pickernell, a Quinault, expressed it:

> This is my land
> From the time of the first moon
> Till the time of the last sun.
> It was given to my people . . .
> I took good care of this land,
> For I am part of it.
> I took good care of the animals,

For they are my brothers and sisters.
I took good care of the streams and rivers,
For they clean my land.
I honor Ocean as my father,
For he gives me food and a means of travel.
Ocean knows everything for he is everywhere . . .
He sees much and knows more.
He says, 'Take care of my sister, Earth,
She is young and has little wisdom, but much kindness'.
I am grateful for this beautiful and bountiful earth.
God gave it to me.
This is my land.

Puget Sound and western Washington comprise a land of mist and mountains. The climate is extremely moist, with grey days predominating during the year and sunshine comparatively rare and evanescent. The lowlands of western Washington obtain thirty-five to fifty inches of rain a year, the foothills seventy-five to 100 inches and the mountainous areas 100 to 200 inches, mostly in the form of snow. Such precipitation is responsible for the dense evergreen forests, including the unique rain forest of the Olympic Peninsula. Many rivers that flow to the Pacific originate in the snow fields of the high Cascades or the mountains of the Olympic Peninsula. They range from cold streams tumbling down rocky gorges to warmer ones meandering across the lowlands, and nearly all of them produce salmon and sometimes steelhead trout. Of great importance to the fishes are the estuarine areas where the mixture of semisalt and semifresh water provides the transition zone for juveniles and adults as they move from one environment to the other.

The white men came and peopled the land, pushing the Indians who survived their diseases and massacres on to the reservations. They began to chop down the forests, sliced the tops of the hills and removed the trees to make building sites. They ribboned the earth with asphalt and concrete roads, dumped raw sewage and factory wastes into the rivers, dammed some of the streams and brutalized the landscape around the Sound.

Wise old Chief Seattle of the Duwamish, after whom the

state's major metropolis is named, told the white men before signing the treaty of Point Elliott ceding their lands to the United States:

> Every part of this soil is sacred in the estimation of my people. Every hillside, every valley, every plain and grove, has been hallowed by some sad or happy event in days long vanished . . . The very dust upon which you now stand responds more lovingly to their footsteps than to yours, because it is rich with the dust of our ancestors . . . Even the little children who lived here and rejoiced for a brief season, still love these sombre solitudes . . . And when the last Red Man shall have perished, and the memory of my tribe shall have become a myth among the white men, these shores shall swarm with the invisible dead of my tribe . . .
>
> Dead – I say? There is no death. Only a change of worlds.

These sentiments meant nothing to the newcomers. They proceeded to pillage the forests and loot the fish-laden streams and tear up the countryside.

The Indians had a deep respect and veneration for the animals whose flesh and hides sustained them and also for others like deer, elk, cougar, raven, coyote, with whom they lived in friendly communion. The Chinook who lived on the lower Columbia, like other Pacific coast tribes, had a rather vague idea of the cosmos and the supreme being, but they believed in the immortality of the animals who were very important to them such as the salmon and around this belief they wove taboos and rituals.

The phenomenon of the salmon played an important role in the religion of all north Pacific tribes. The fish thronged the streams and returned with astonishing regularity every year to the bay or cove with which they were familiar. After a brief rest, they moved upstream and headed for their spawning grounds. After spawning, they died, and their lean and discoloured bodies lined the river banks, disintegrated and drifted back to sea. The very next year the same fishes appeared.

'What was more logical,' says the anthropologist Philip Drucker, 'than the concept that the salmon ascended the streams to benefit mankind, died, and then returned to life?' Thus the belief arose that 'the salmon were a race of supernatural beings who dwelt in a great house under the sea. There they went about in human form, feasting and dancing like people. When the time came for the "run", the Salmon-people dressed in garments of salmon flesh, that is, assumed the form of fish to sacrifice themselves. Once dead, the spirit of each fish returned to the house beneath the sea. If the bones were returned to the water, the being resumed his form with no discomfort and could repeat the trip next season.'

It was evident that the fishes' migration to the rivers was purely a voluntary act and therefore it behooved human beings to be extremely careful not to offend them. The new arrivals were greeted by the Indians with prayers and incantations to show their gratitude, joy and relief. Sometimes the first salmon caught in the spring was treated as though it were a visiting chief of high renown and was accorded due honours.

Vicissitudes of the salmon industry

Exploitation of the salmon commercially came with the advent of the salmon canning industry in Puget Sound in 1877; by 1890 there were ten plants in the Olympia area alone. By then the pack exceeded that of the Columbia River owing to the bounty of the numerous rivers emptying into the Sound, and also the rich Fraser River runs which had to pass through United States waters on their way to the home streams. All five Pacific salmon were found in Puget Sound and coastal rivers along with steelhead trout, but pinks and sockeye were the most plentiful.

Traditionally the Indians stopped fishing and removed their gear from the streams when they had caught their winter's supply – this is subsistence fishing. In contrast, the white men, to whom fish were a source of livelihood, fished as long as the runs continued unless restrained by law (which they often defied). Uncontrolled exploitation was the rule until the creation of the Washington Department of Fisheries in 1921 put somewhat of a halt to this practice.

As the stocks declined the owners of floating gear like gillnets and seines sought to curb the competition of those who used fixed gear like set nets, wheels and traps. The eventual result was the passage in 1935 of Initiative 77 by the state legislature which outlawed these fixed contrivances from all waters in the state. Subsequently fishing intensity increased. Salmon may now be taken commercially in Washington waters with purse seines, gillnets, trolling gear and reef nets.

The purse seine is the largest vessel used in the Pacific coast salmon fishery; fifty feet long or more, it usually carries a crew of three to seven persons. Speed is of the essence in such a vessel as it makes a large circle around a school of fish while the skiff remains more or less stationary. When the fish are surrounded the net is closed up. The catch is hauled aboard by means of power rollers and then brailed into the hold. A fifty-foot seiner using a net almost a mile long may take up to 5,000 salmon in a single haul.

The gillnetter, operated by one or two persons using a nylon net some 250 fathoms (1500 feet) long, is about half the size of a purse seiner, with a seven and a half foot beam drawing about four feet of water. It operates usually in a bay or estuary and also in a few rivers where gillnetting is permitted, as on the Columbia, Fraser and Yukon. An agreement between Canada and the United States forbids netting or seining outside marine waters (that is,

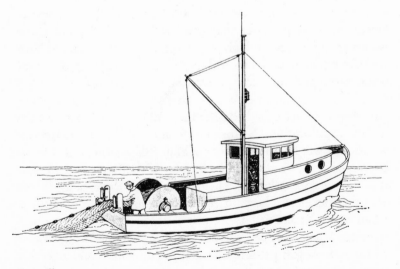

18 *A gill netter*

beyond the surfline). The gillnetter knows the river or bay he fishes like a book, and selects a channel where the salmon are believed to be, sets his nets and drifts with the current, usually at night. If the water is turbid, as during the spring runoff, he may fish around the clock. The net is retrieved by winding on a power drum and the catch may range from a half-dozen to a hundred salmon of legal size in a single drift, all other species being thrown back.

Trolling is a hook and line method of taking salmon. Trollers, operating offshore, generally range from twenty-five to forty feet and are fished by one or two persons, sometimes a husband and wife team, using two to four poles, each with up to six lines on which the bait, normally herring or other small fish, are attached. Trolling lines are pulled in by a power-driven winch called a gurdy. The boat moves at a slow pace, in daylight. Sport fishing for salmon on the west coast is by trolling; charter boats take anglers out to sea from various ports, the limit in Oregon being three fish per person. Some trollers can stay out for several days and have freezing facilities to keep their catches fresh.

A small number of reef nets, the invention of Indians, are now used in Puget Sound and off the mouth of the Fraser River. The net is set out from a boat among reefs in a narrow passage the salmon traverse to reach freshwater. To be successful the water must be clear so that the man in the watch tower can see the fish move over the net. When he thinks the time is right the lead line is raised and the fish are trapped and then brailed into the hold.

Fishing areas are chosen by the fishermen and each usually has his favourite location. A purse seiner may know one spot better than others and he can fish it best. Where several seiners wish to fish the same locality they may stay for a single setting and then turn it over to another vessel. Success depends on being in the right place at the right time. There are considerable dangers in fishing north Pacific waters. Squalls and storms come up without warning. Many lives are lost each year as frail craft go down in stormy seas beyond the reach of the Coastguard and men are swept overboard. At fishing ports along the Pacific coast, as at

Depoe Bay, Oregon, plaques remind one that fishermen left this quiet place in their little boats and were never seen again.

The Puget Sound salmon pack has declined in recent decades along with catches, from an average of 682,000 forty-eight one-pound cases annually in the 1950s to 283,000 in the 1960s, then rising to 350,000 in 1970–1975. However in 1976 only 195,000 cases were produced.

Summarizing their study of the Puget Sound fishery in 1969, Professors James A. Crutchfield and Giulio Pontecorvo said: 'Clearly landings are well below peak levels achieved in previous periods, and it seems unlikely that any economically feasible programme regulating fishing effort can restore fully the losses attributable to growth in population, industry and other elements of human society that impinge on successful propagation of salmon.' They conclude that better regulation in recent years 'has averted a disastrous collapse in landings, and has permitted some recovery in important areas, notably the Fraser River sockeye'.

Much of the decline in the stocks can be attributed to impairment of habitat. The forest products industry, one of the state's major industries, grew rapidly until it could boast of producing more lumber than any state except Oregon. But the impact on some rivers harbouring aquatic riches was sometimes catastrophic. 'Before the advent of modern logging equipment and practices,' say the biologists Henry O. Wendler and Gene Deschamps of the Washington Department of Fisheries, 'the most prevalent and economical medium for transport of logs to the mills was water. Logging and driving companies constructed a system of log dams to maintain ponds for holding logs to create a supply of water to move their cut timber . . . Since salmon were plentiful, little or no consideration was given to their passage over these barriers. Almost all of the structures were total blocks to anadromous fish and cut off considerable areas that had been utilized for the spawning of adults and the rearing of young.' When stream driving of logs was replaced by railroads and later road haulage, the dams became obsolete and were abandoned. There was no state law requiring their removal, so they 'remained until they rotted away, were washed out or eventually were removed by the Washington Department of Fisheries or other agencies . . .

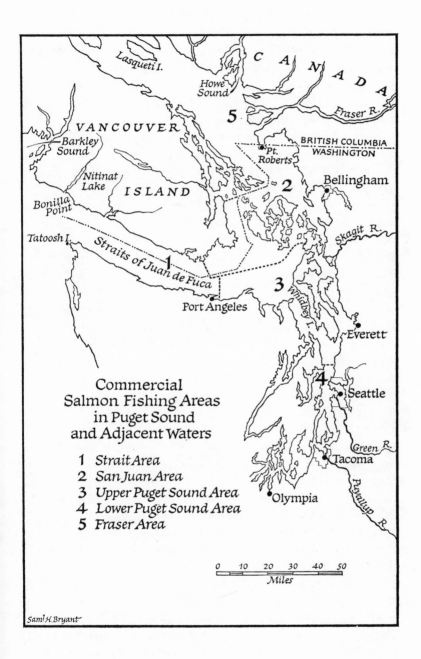

Commercial
Salmon Fishing Areas
in Puget Sound
and Adjacent Waters

1 Strait Area
2 San Juan Area
3 Upper Puget Sound Area
4 Lower Puget Sound Area
5 Fraser Area

0 10 20 30 40 50
Miles

Sam! H. Bryant

Some have endured in the streams and remain as total blocks or hindrances to fish movement.'

The Puget Sound area, which, a century ago, was replete with wetlands, streams curving inland around salt marshes and into the foothills of the Cascade Mountains, is now mostly a vast industrial-urban complex, lined with factories, mills, housing tracts, freeways, and shopping centres that consumed large acreages of once green farmland. The sound of moving waters is scarcely heard except around lakes which, bordered by attractive homes and spanned by floating bridges, still play host to valuable fishes.

'In the long run,' said Dr E. O. Salo at the Northwest Estuary and Coastal Zone symposium held in Portland, Oregon, in October, 1970, 'The greatest threat to optimal use of the Puget Sound system is not posed by direct effects of industrial and municipal discharges in water quality, but by failure to identify and evaluate estuarine effects of land use, not only on the water but upstream. All the important fish and shellfish resources of Puget Sound are vulnerable to this kind of careless development. Salmon, steelhead trout and cutthroat trout require extensive systems of small feeder streams that are being systematically destroyed by improperly regulated land use far away from Puget Sound.'

Sport fishing

Sport fishing for salmon and steelhead trout has increased more dramatically in Washington than in Oregon or California and is now an important economic and political force that often challenges the commercial fishermen. The largest concentrations of fishermen and charter boat operators outside the Columbia River area are around Seattle and Bremerton, the Narrows and Commencement Bay at Tacoma and off southern Whidbey Island. Considerable numbers of salmon are also caught by sportsmen off the Olympic Peninsula and around the San Juan Islands and Hood Canal. In summer the blue waters of Juan de Fuca Strait are crowded with sleek cruisers and yachts, many of which cross the international boundary and fish around the Gulf Islands, side by side with Canadian boats.

The number of fish available to sportsmen has been augmented by intensive artificial breeding. The Washington Department of Game operates nine rearing ponds as a supplement to its numerous hatcheries around the state, producing chinook and coho, the prime angling fish. A temporary bonanza for anglers was the revival of Lake Washington's sockeye run in the very heart of the Seattle metropolis. In its original state the area was replete with limpid waters and lakes teeming with fish but as population increased, thanks chiefly to the growth of the airplane manufacturing industry, the city spread in all directions usurping the shores of the lakes and rivers, and the sockeye runs tapered off, though never quite disappearing. In 1971 there was a sudden upsurge of sockeye and both commercial and sport fishermen benefited from it. Special dispensation was granted by the state legislature to permit both purse seiners and gillnetters to operate in fresh water. Altogether about 265,000 sockeye were harvested that year while some 180,000 escaped and moved to the spawning grounds. Since 1971 fishing for sockeye has been severely curtailed in these waters as the runs declined but the potential still exists for another bonanza in Lake Washington.

Indian fish wars

As in Oregon, the salmon fishing industry in Washington has been in a state of chaos since the federal judges decreed that the Indians who are descendants of those who signed treaties with the United States in the nineteenth century guaranteeing them access to their 'usual and accustomed fishing places' must have equal opportunities with non-Indians to take their share of the migratory fish in the Columbia River and many other Washington streams. In order to abide by the courts' decisions, state fish and game agencies have had to schedule separate fishing seasons for the small number of Indians benefiting from the generosity of the courts – on the Columbia River, for example, they are estimated to number 300 to 500 – and as a result fishing seasons for non-Indians have had to be curtailed. Strife has erupted on many occasions as state officials tried to prevent white men from fishing at forbidden times, and state legislatures have been besieged with angry fishermen.

On the Columbia River, at least, the fish war was at least temporarily settled, when on February 4, 1977, Dr John R. Donaldson, director of the Oregon Department of Fish and Wildlife, announced that Oregon and Washington agencies agreed with the tribes benefiting from the treaties on a management plan which allocates to each group specific portions of the runs. The plan stipulates that after escapement quotas are met and Indian ceremonial and subsistence fishing needs are satisfied, the fall chinook catch would be split 40% non-Indian and 60% Indian. Still hanging fire after this agreement was accepted by both parties, and implemented in the spring of 1977, was a division of the runs in western Washington and other waters. Here, as on the Columbia, federal judges ruled that the split should be fifty-fifty between white and red men, and the judges themselves were to act as arbitrators in case of disputes. A June 1977 decision by the Washington State Supreme Court, however, affirmed that federal court rulings on the fifty-fifty split were not binding if they interfered with the wise management and conservation of the runs, a decision that greatly heartened the thousands of commercial fishermen who had suffered considerable loss of income, or went out of business, because of the fish wars. At the end of 1977 chaos seemed to reign in the Washington state salmon fishery as the federal and state courts vied for jurisdiction and strife between Indian and white commercial fishermen became more bitter and enforcement of judicial decisions often erupted into violence and arrests.

How will the controversy end? As one official puts it, 'The more the Indians are given the more they want.' The sense of conservation which was inherent in their ancestors before the white man came seems to have vanished. They appear to be as greedy as the non-Indian fishermen, for salmon is now the highest priced freshwater fish in the United States and each one caught is worth a considerable sum of money. Only Congress apparently can solve the Indian fishing problems, which are spreading to California (where the Indians claim ownership of the mouth of the Klamath River, rich in steelhead trout, and have blocked off the area for their exclusive use), the Great Lakes and other states, by enacting legislation defining their rights to hunt and fish on lands they formerly inhabited, in the light of today's conservation needs, not those of a century ago. But Congress is slow to act and as the wave of pro-Indian sentiment sweeps the land, a reflection perhaps of the guilt complex Americans seem to have because of their brutal treatment of the red men in the nineteenth century, it is unlikely that legislation will be enacted in the near future to satisfy all parties.

BRITISH COLUMBIA FISHERIES

It is estimated that there are about 1,500 rivers and lakes in British Columbia that support regular runs of salmon, and sometimes steelhead trout. The Fraser, Nass, and Skeena are the most productive. All but a few of the major rivers flow into the Pacific Ocean.

Chum, pinks and sockeye are the most numerous species. Pinks are found in some 600 streams, coho in about 970, chum in 850, and chinook in 260. Prized for its savoury red flesh, sockeye is the mainstay of the fishermen's catch and canner's output. The Fraser, Nass, Skeena, Smith Inlet and Rivers Inlet and their hundreds of tributaries contribute the bulk of these fish. In the late nineteenth and early twentieth centuries the Fraser yielded annual harvests of 20 to 30 million sockeye (here called reds) every four or five years, in addition to huge runs of pinks. Numerous British Columbia rivers harbour steelhead trout, the angler's delight, deemed by American and Canadian anglers to give as good sport as *Salmo salar*. Chinook may reach 120 pounds in British Columbia; they push their way to the very headwaters of the undammed Fraser, 750 miles from the sea.

British Columbia is about 700 miles long as the crow flies, a land area exceeding that of Texas but with only 2.2 million people. Its fissured and jagged coastline covers some 16,000 miles while offshore are the Queen Charlotte Islands and Vancouver Island, longest in the eastern Pacific Ocean, and numerous lesser sea breaks. Rain and mist prevail a large part of the year along the coast and in the islands; in the interior the landscape ranges from dense forests where precipitation exceeds 100 inches a year to arid valleys that obtain only ten inches annually.

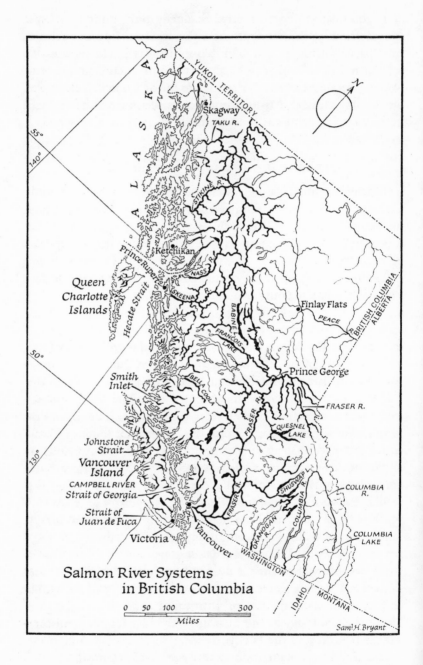

Salmon River Systems in British Columbia

0   50   100   300

Miles

Saml. H. Bryant

If you take a ferry in summer at Kelsey Bay on the north-east tip of Vancouver Island through the Inside Passage to Alaska, you pass a fjordlike coast resembling Norway's. The boat winds in and out of narrow sounds, in view of mountains tinged with snow. The sea changes from golden in the afternoon to blood-red in the long twilight. Opalescent clouds float across the sky and numerous islands glide by, mountainous or low and wooded, with steep rocky banks. Some of them are uninhabited except for a Coastguard station. There are few settlements until you reach Prince Rupert.

Salmon abound in these waters, going to and from their home streams. Many gillnetters may be seen, their orange floats bobbing in the clear water. A tug propels a barge heading for Alaska; occasionally a timber raft passes. In the morning the water has a glassy sheen, reflecting the rockbound coast. Probably more salmon are caught in the Inland Passage than in any similar stretch of saltwater in North America.

Canners and fishermen

Next to Alaska, British Columbia is the chief producer of salmon in North America. Intensive exploitation of the stocks began with the building of the first cannery in 1870, at Annieville below New Westminster at the mouth of the Fraser. The industry spread to other fishing centres on the coast such as Steveston, Vancouver Island and the Queen Charlottes. Output soared from 62,000 cases in 1880 to an average of 700,000 in 1900–1910, 1.2 million in the 1910s and 1.5 million in the 1920s, outputs exceeded only in Alaska.

The number of canneries increased from twelve in 1880 to a peak of eighty in 1913, of which forty were on the Fraser River, concentrated at Steveston. To supply this huge industry required an armada of fishing boats. At first Indians did most of the fishing, in rented boats, receiving as little as five cents for each fish, or at best $50 a month and keep. Later white men turned to salmon fishing, including Americans, British immigrants and Japanese who when they were not fishing tended their market gardens in the rich delta of the Fraser. Most of the fishermen came to be controlled by the canneries, an arrangement that benefited both because the packers were assured a supply of fish and the fishermen a market.

Commercial salmon fishing in British Columbia is now carried on chiefly along the inner coasts and estuarial waters. Channels and inlets are plied by the seiners and gillnetters while trollers operate in more open waters. A large portion of the Canadian and American fleets work the entrance to the Strait of Juan de Fuca, each carefully observing the boundary line. Such fishing is often dangerous. The veteran fishermen A. V. Hill says, 'The sea may become rough off the Canadian coast, and even the protected waters are not always kind to the men who seek to wrest a living from them.' Tides up to twenty-five feet roar through the narrow channels, causing treacherous rapids and whirlpools. Tides and waves can whip smooth waters into tide rips and even sturdy fishing vessels may be overturned by williwaws sweeping suddenly down the mountains; to escape them fishermen must seek shelter in the coves and inlets.

Fraser River fishery

The fortunes of the Fraser River have to a large extent determined the prosperity of British Columbia's salmon industry in the twentieth century. The year 1913 marked the apogee of the Fraser bounty, when a record-breaking sockeye run of 38 million permitted 31 million fish to be harvested, compared to an average of 9 million in the previous twenty years. The waters of Juan de Fuca Strait at the southern tip of Vancouver Island and Johnstone Strait at the northern tip, through which the fish had to pass to reach the Fraser, were packed with fishing boats. That year, however, passage through Hell's Gate, where the full flow of the mighty river rushes through a narrow defile, became impossible because of a massive rock slide induced by careless construction of the transcontinental Canadian National Railway. In this portion of the river the flow might vary as much as a hundred feet during the year.

As Cicely Lyons says in her book *Salmon: Our Heritage,*

The few fish that managed to penetrate Hell's Gate after mid-July in 1913 unfortunately found no quiet pools in the vicinity, where they could rest, all the little refuges being filled with rock. The strongest of these sockeye pressed on. Of their number a pitiable few reached their destination: the others, exhausted, perished in the struggle.

The sockeye and pink population was decimated by the Hell's Gate disaster and did not recover for many years. Although the Fraser is entirely a Canadian river, jurisdiction over the salmon stocks is a Canadian-American problem since the fish pass through either American or Canadian waters to reach their spawning grounds. It took about twenty-five years for the two nations to agree to a solution to the Hell's Gate impasse and meanwhile heavy fishing continued to deplete the runs. It was not till 1937 that a bilateral treaty was ratified creating the International Pacific Salmon Fisheries Commission, headquartered in New Westminster, B.C. It was authorized to investigate the status of the Fraser River salmon, to establish hatcheries if needed and take other measures to enhance the runs. Most important, it was required to regulate the fishery on the basis of dividing the catches equally between Canadians and Americans.

Restoration of the sockeye runs began in earnest with the construction of the unique fishways at Hell's Gate in 1946 and others at Bridge River rapids near Lillooet and Farwell Canyon on the Chilcotin River, permitting salmon readily to ascend to many streams in the upper watershed. These projects also facilitated the resuscitation of the pink salmon runs in the upper river, which had been virtually exterminated in 1913. Although the Salmon Commission has done a brilliant job in managing the Fraser the sockeye runs have not come back to anything like their pre-1913 abundance. But in recent years they have at times reached 60% of pre-1913 levels, though at others only 35%. Only one stream, Adams River, a tributary of the North Thompson, may be said to be in full production. In 1958 the Adams River sockeye run was 18 million; in 1930 3·5 million. Adams is seven and a half miles long with a drainage area of 1,600 square miles; its adjunct, Little River, is about two and a half miles long, and spawners concentrate on 160 acres. It is estimated that each of these acres is capable of producing fish valued at $150,000, probably the most precious salmon spawning grounds in the world.

The Fraser River is also a large producer of pink salmon, highly prized for canning, but bringing less money to fishermen.

Canadian salmon catches in the years 1971–1975 were as follows:

	Number (metric tons)	Value to Fishermen (thousands of dollars)
1971	63,252	44,476
1972	76,831	50,341
1973	86,861	100,216
1974	63,501	74,173
1975	36,384	48,973

Habitat protection

British Columbia now produces more salmon than any state in the Union except Alaska. The main reason for Canada's relative success in retaining its salmon wealth is its ability to protect their habitat. British Columbia is a vast and sparsely settled province with relatively little manufacturing outside the metropolitan Vancouver City area. The forest products industry dominates the economy.

There has also been somewhat better control of land-use in the province than in Oregon or Washington. The Canadian Fisheries Act as amended in 1970 strengthened the government's hand against polluters of waters frequented by migratory fish by making each offence punishable by a fine of up to $5,000 a day, a sum that deters even the richest corporation from breaking the law. The Department of the Environment requires all industrial effluents to be non-toxic before they can be discharged into rivers, although there seem to be exceptions, as with some mining wastes.

Sport fishing

Sport fishing is booming in British Columbia as it is south of the border, and salmon and steelhead trout are by far the most popular species. Unlike eastern Canada, where many salmon rivers are in private hands, rivers in British Columbia are in public ownership, so that all one needs to fish them is a licence and the proper gear. A study by the Department of the Environment published in July, 1972, estimated that about 390,000 residents of the province, or 14% of the total population, were sport fishermen. To them must be added up to 100,000 non-residents who fish the province's waters for salmon, mainly Americans from nearby states. In 1973 anglers reported landings of an estimated 335,000 salmon and grilse in tidal waters alone; coho accounted for 210,000, chinook (here called springs) and chinook grilse (called jacks) for 105,000; the remainder were mostly pinks. In 1971 a total of 540,000 salmon were caught by anglers in tidal and non-tidal waters.

As the number of anglers increases, pressure mounts on the provincial and federal governments to provide more fish. One of the measures taken to meet this demand has been a reduction in licences of commercial boats but of greater importance is the construction of hatcheries and spawning channels to augment chinook and coho stocks.

The sport fishery produces considerable benefits to the economy. According to the Department of Fisheries, 'a superficial estimate indicates an annual value in the Fraser system alone in excess of $40 million'.

The future

If we compare the Canadian experience with the American in handling the valuable Pacific salmon resource certain conclusions are evident. Thanks mainly to slower economic development and less population pressure, the Canadians have been able to save a larger proportion of their original stocks than the Americans did in California and the Pacific Northwest. The Canadian record is much better in the west than in the east.

In 1971 Rod Hourston, Pacific area director of the Department of Fisheries, reported that 'despite increasing catches by commercial fishermen, stiff regulations in some seasons and the recent complaints concerning threats to spawning grounds by industry and land settlement, British Columbia's salmon resources have increased by 13% during the past decade'. British Columbia is the second largest canner of salmon in North America, exceeded only by Alaska. In the decade 1966–1975 it produced an average of 1,270,000 cases, of which about 40% were pink salmon and somewhat less sockeye. In 1976 over one million 48-lb. cases were packed worth almost $100 million at wholesale.

As a wave of nationalism sweeps over Canada, especially in the western provinces, Canadian fishermen are pressing for a greater share of the salmon in national waters, particularly in the Fraser River. Here the catches are roughly divided fifty–fifty, a feat of management by the International Pacific Salmon Commission that is unique in the fishing world. The Canadians claim that the United States has been slow in providing money to rehabilitate the Fraser, and that Canada would be willing to take on more of this burden if it obtained a larger proportion of the catches. The dispute has been going on for more than a decade. If an agreement were concluded, said the late Roderick Haig-Brown, a member of the Commission, in a letter to the author of June 25, 1976, the Fraser River stocks 'could now be well on their way to doubling, entirely through the use of spawning channels. The Fraser system lends itself particularly well to this type of enhancement . . . It's all a great big unhappy mess.'

In April 1975 Romeo LeBlanc, Minister of Fisheries, announced in Ottawa the launching of a long-term salmon enhancement programme in British Columbia costing $250–300 million, including the building of hatcheries and spawning channels, and the restocking of available streams. Initial stages will be financed entirely by the federal government and later ones on a federal-provincial basis. This programme, he pointed out, is based on good business sense, because benefits include (1) a more even distribution of fishing effort resulting from a judicious selection of enhancement projects; (2) the supply of salmon will be stabilized at a higher level with the resulting reduced costs of catching and processing; and (3) since most of the increased production will be exported Canada's balance of payments in commodity trade will be improved. The programme is expected to double the value of Canada's Pacific salmon industry in the next fifteen years.

CHAPTER 15

The Alaska Fishery

IN every country where the salmon were once abundant, in North America, Europe and Asia, there have been heavy losses. The story of their fate in Alaska is perhaps the saddest of all.

Alaska covers 570,000 square miles, equal to over one-fifth the area of the United States. It stretches for 750 miles from east to west, bounded on the north by the Arctic Ocean, the south and south-west by the Bering Sea and the east by Canada. There are over 2,500 rivers supporting salmon runs (many are now depleted); their exact number, in fact, is unknown for many have not been identified or surveyed and have no names. Although the great majority are relatively short streams, some of the rivers are of great length and drain enormous areas. The Yukon flows from the region of Fort Selkirk in Canada for almost 2,000 miles to the Bering Sea and salmon ascend almost to the headwaters past Dawson City while the Kuskokwim comes out of the Alaska Range and empties into the Bering Sea some 600 miles distant.

From the air Alaska forms a vast mosaic of towering mountain ranges and glaciers with a scalloped coast similar to Norway's, creating deep and long fjords. The rivers flow in every direction through tundra and taiga, a vast coniferous forest region, bearing in their cold waters enormous schools of young salmon racing to the sea and adults returning to their natal waters.

Before the oil boom hit Alaska in 1970 and began to turn its economy and way of life topsy-turvy, fish and fishing were the mainstays of the economy. In almost every bay and inlet from Norton Sound to the Alexander Archipelago one may find a fishing village, occupied by Eskimos, Aleuts or Indians, or a larger settlement like Sitka or Ketchikan, or Kodiak on Kodiak Island, where fishing boats crowd the wharves in summer, fishermen tend their gear or mend their nets, getting ready for

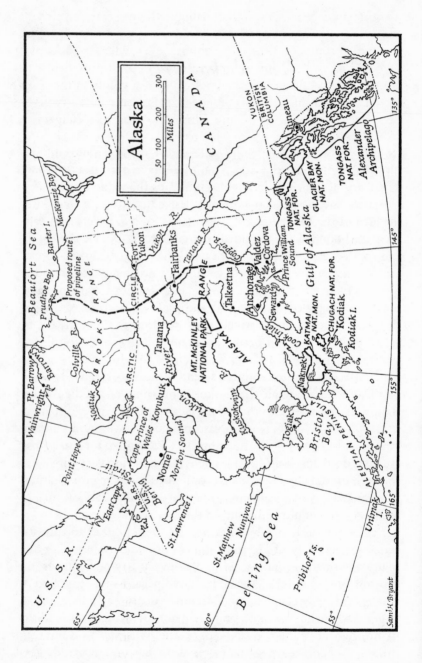

Sam H. Bryant

their next excursion in search of halibut, salmon, crabs or bottom fish.

One encounters fishermen almost everywhere; an angler standing in his boat trolling in sight of a glacier; a purse seiner in a quiet inlet with the spidery lines of his net visible in the pale-green water; a gillnetter, its orange float bobbing in the twilight sea; a scow laden with shining salmon moving to a cannery; a skiff drawing the end of the seine towards the purse vessel.

Flying in a float plane, the most common form of transportation in much of Alaska, the panorama of rivers unfolds beneath you. They curve and twist around bleak mountains on Kodiak Island, through the tundra of the Nushagak Peninsula, and around the dense forests of Baranof Island. Even a short river may be incredibly rich in salmon, like the sixteen and a half mile Karluk, which in its heyday produced up to 10 million fish annually.

Exploitation uncontrolled

Only Indians, Eskimos and Aleuts populated Alaska when Vitus Bering, commander of the Russian expedition, discovered it in 1841. For 120 years the Russians trapped furs, and used the fish only for their own food. Ivan Petroff, who took the first census for the United States Government in 1880, reported that the salmon fisheries around Sitka, headquarters of the Russian-American Company, used to supply the whole region. In 1867 Alaska was purchased by the United States.

The first cannery was built in 1878, at Klawak on Prince of Wales Island. Despite the remoteness of the territory and difficulty of moving workmen, supplies and machinery from ports like Seattle and Portland in slow moving sailing vessels and later in steamers, the industry developed rapidly.

All five species of *Oncorhynchus* are found in Alaska; pinks, sockeye and chum are the most abundant while chinook and coho are much less common than in Washington, Oregon or California. Probably nowhere in the world, except in Kamchatka and the island of Sakhalin, were the fish so abundant and in such readily accessible areas. In an age when *laissez faire* was the customary policy in exploiting natural resources, whether fish, timber or soils, and the concept of conservation was hardly recognized, they were exploited with unbridled ruthlessness. Many of the moguls who made fortunes in the 'lower 48' flocked to Alaska, like the Humes, the men who created the Columbia River Packers Association in Astoria, and others. In 1889 there were thirty-seven canneries that produced 720,000 cases of salmon; fifty years later when there were 156 canneries, Alaska was feeding millions in the United States and Europe with inexpensive nutritious canned fish. The prime canning species were sockeye (called reds in Alaska), pinks and chum.

Commercial landings reached a peak of over 100 million salmon in 1918, dropped for a number of years and shot up to 117 million in 1934 and 129 million in 1929; peaks over 100 million were again reached in 1937, 1938 and 1941. By then many of the bountiful rivers were exhausted and harvests began to decline. Numerous canneries were abandoned and their rotting remains can still be seen in coves and inlets in many parts of the state.

Since local capital in this outpost of the United States was scarce, outsiders monopolized the industry, taking the wealth from the rivers and leaving very little behind to improve the lot of the natives who worked for them in the canneries or as fishermen. In effect, this was a form of colonialism. Sometimes the cannery became the nucleus from which a community sprang up, like Ketchikan. 'A store to supply the workers, as well as the nearby native fishermen, and to run a sideline in the fur trade or in native curios – baskets, wooden implements, moccasins, silver and ivory handicrafts – was invariably the first step in such expansion, if the terrain was favourable,' says Ernest Gruening, historian of Alaska. Ketchikan was originally an Indian village on the banks of a stream emptying into Tongass Narrows, one of the principal channels for Alaska steamers. It boasts that it has processed more salmon than any community in the world (which may be true) and calls itself 'the world's salmon capital'.

After World War II the salmon industry steadily tapered off. Landings fell to an average of 92·5 million in the 1930s, 80 million in the 1940s, 41 million in the 1950s, and 51 million in the 1960s, after which Alaska's resources came under the management of the newly created state. The canned salmon pack followed suit, dropping from an average of 4·8 million cases in the 1940s – greater by far than in any other state or province – to 2·9 million in the 1950s, 3·0 million in the 1960s and about 2 million in 1970–1975. In 1976 2½ million 48-lb. cases were packed, worth about $200 million at wholesale.

What caused such a disaster in a state that was not industrialized and very sparsely settled (most of it was, and is, a pristine wilderness of mountains, glaciers, and unsullied streams)? There were only 226,000 inhabitants in 1960 and 302,000 in 1970, spread over an area twice the size of Texas. The answer may be quite simple: the fisheries declined because of ineffective regulation which failed to prevent the mining of the stocks. Until Alaska gained statehood in 1959 it was governed by an appointed governor operating under laws passed by the Congress. Its fisheries were supervised by federal agencies, such as the US Bureau of Fisheries which later became part of the Fish and Wildlife Service. In the earlier years there was scarcely any management.

In his report for 1897 the territorial governor, John G. Brady, described the problem of maintaining any kind of supervision over fisheries with a minuscule force of inspectors:

Now, here are 4,735 miles an agent must travel to reach the different canneries. But that is only half the story, for each cannery is supplied with fish from a number of streams, some of them more than 150 miles from the place of cooking . . . An agent is appointed . . . told to proceed to Alaska . . . and finding a folder of the Pacific Coast Steamship Company wrestles with the Alaska route until he believes he understands it. Finally he arrives at Sitka . . . He inquires how far is the nearest cannery, and how he can get there. It is forty miles and there is no regular boat running there. The only way to get there is to hire a canoe or wait until the cannery steamer, the *Wigwam*, happens to pass by. There is no boat of any kind belonging to the fish inspector, nor has the collector a boat he can loan; so all he can do is wait and take the next mail steamer for Karluk, seven hundred miles west of Sitka. When he reaches the cannery people will show him every courtesy and see that he has a boat to get around in. Can anything be more humiliating to a government officer appointed to carry out an important duty?

Corporate enterprise used the political power that money enjoys to pursue its goals of taking as much wealth out of Alaska as possible without any real restraint. For example, the J. P. Morgan-Guggenheim mining combine, one of the most powerful in the United States, at one time owned twelve canneries that produced one-eighth of the total salmon pack. The industry could easily persuade pliant congressmen to kill legislation that might interfere with their lucrative operations, or if such laws were passed, prevent the appropriation of adequate funds for their enforcement. According to Gruening, who became the first governor of Alaska, the packers fought nearly every conservation measure submitted to Congress and agreed to compromises only after bitter struggles. They subscribed to the popular philosophy in Alaska, 'Get in, get it, and get out!' Until 1960 all fishery regulations were shaped by congressional mandates and enforced by federal officials taking orders from superiors in Washington, DC, a system that did not lend itself to enlightened management or conservation. As late as 1913 there were only four agents in all of Alaska responsible for enforcement of fishery laws. From time to time Congress held hearings on the fishery problems but spokesmen for the industry invariably denied that there was any depletion of the stocks.

The situation was succinctly described by C. H. Gilbert and Henry O'Malley of the Bureau of Fisheries in their 1919 report on 'The Alaska Fisheries and Fur Seal Industries':

> The sequence of events is always the same. Increased production is accomplished by increase of gear. Fluctuations in the seasons become more pronounced. Good seasons will appear in which maximum packs are made. But the poor seasons become more numerous. When poor seasons appear no attempt is made to compensate by fishing less closely. On the contrary, efforts are redoubled to put up the full pack. The poor years strike constantly lower levels, until it is apparent to all that serious depletion has occurred.

In those days there was no real knowledge of the size of the runs, no attempt was made to balance catches with escapements. There were few fishery biologists in Alaska or elsewhere. The industry operated in the dark, without benefit of the vast research apparatus that is now available. Yet, as one looks at the past, one wonders if, had there been scientific guidance such as is now applied to fishery management in all salmon-producing states, the industry, obsessed with immediate profits, would have been willing to tolerate any restraint on its operations. This attitude is expressed in the remarks of Nick Bez, one of the leading Alaska canners, who testified before a congressional committee in 1936: 'I went to see Secretary of Commerce Roper [then in charge of the fisheries] and saw him right in his office . . . I told him to take his regulation book and throw it into the Potomac River.' Bez was a generous contributor to the Democratic Party then in power. It took Americans a long time to see the need for conservation of renewable resources and even now, when shortages of fish, timber, petroleum and other resources are apparent, many entrepreneurs are unwilling to accept regulations which might reduce their profits.

Impact on the natives

What the vagaries of the salmon runs mean to the natives of Alaska may be illustrated by the Bristol Bay fishery. In 1970, when I visited Bristol Bay, this fishery contributed about a third of the state's landings of 60 million salmon. The total run into the five major rivers that empty into the Bay was some 40 million, primarily sockeye, of which 21 million were caught and the remaining 19 million were allowed to escape. During the sockeye run from June 25 to July 15 biologists daily monitored the catches. Each of the thirteen canneries in operation reported twice a day on its output. On the rivers jammed with green-liveried fish, not yet showing their red heads which betoken they are near the spawning stage, biologists were taking samples of fish to estimate the strength of the run which had to meet the gauntlet of 900 gillnetters and hundreds of set nets along the banks.

So thick were the schools of sockeye, weighing on the average five or six pounds, that they hit the nets as soon as they were paid out – 4,000 could be taken in a two-man boat in a day, fetching about $1.25 apiece. Scows were anchored at strategic places in the Bay to collect the catches. A Japanese freezer ship was permitted to come in and purchase fish and take them back to Japan. Canneries could not keep up with the catches and had to limit their contract fishermen to twelve hours daily, or let them fish for twenty-four hours and rest for twenty-four. Fatigue was overtaking many workers as the canneries operated around the clock. Disappointed fishermen were everywhere because there were not enough facilities to process the run, although its magnitude had been predicted by biologists long before the season opened. A Quinault Indian said to me, 'I came to make enough money to put clothes on my children's backs but I had to dump some of my fish in the bay.' Another fisherman said, 'The fish are there to be taken but I have no contract and no buyer.' Emergency airlifts were organized to take the fish to other canning centres in Alaska, but still truckloads of gleaming sockeye could be seen rotting in the sun.

Alaska newspapers carried sensational headlines about the glut of salmon. Since this was an election year many politicians descended on Bristol Bay seeking to make political capital out of the mess. In the village of King Salmon, headquarters of the Alaska Fish and Game Department, men came into the res- taurants and bars with bleary eyes and unkempt beards. Some of them would make $20,000 to $30,000 during the three-week season while in a lean non-peak sockeye year like 1968 they did not earn enough to pay expenses. 'Feast or famine' is the saying up and down Bristol Bay.

How does the wealth of the rivers affect the natives? There are scores of Indian and Aleut villages in the Bristol Bay area dependent on the salmon. Naknek on Kvichak Bay is typical, an ancient Eskimo settlement now inhabited chiefly by Indians. In 1975 it had 335 inhabitants, probably more when I visited it in 1970. Naknek is a mean, dilapidated community, its unpaved streets following former caribou trails. The dwellings are chiefly tumbledown shacks with some Quonset huts. There are scarcely any lawns or plantings, no pavements, nor many street lights. In front of some homes lie old tyres, cannibalized cars, and other litter. Naknek in 1970 had several canneries, two liquor stores, a Russian Orthodox and a Pentecostal Church, a new schoolhouse and Borough Building that serves as a court house and administrative centre. There was one general store, owned by a cannery, and a rundown hotel housing one of the bars. A paved road runs from Naknek to King Salmon, fifteen miles; beyond in every direction is the tundra, and not far from King Salmon is a small military base and airport.

Nineteen seventy was a good year for the inhabitants of Naknek but succeeding years were less prosperous as the runs dropped in Bristol Bay rivers. Lael Morgan in *Alaska Magazine* (February, 1975) describes a visit to Naknek in 1974. 'A couple of years ago,' said Allen Aspalund, Council president, 'we had four or five open canneries. Last year we had only two and this season there was only a small floating cannery . . . We fished off the beach, [but] sometimes they wouldn't take our fish for a few days . . . It was a raw deal. We setnetters can deliver fish while they have the wiggle on their tails.' While many natives complained about the bad times a few did not. Dick Digh, part Aleut, part white, cleared over $12,000 in 1974. 'The fish were running so strong that for three or four days you could kick them out of the water,' he said.

Similar stories of declining incomes were told to Lael Morgan – in Ugashik, a dying cannery town, in Port Heiden, 'a wind-battered settlement around a defunct cannery and military base,' in Togiak at the far western corner of Bristol Bay where 'local fishermen coax a reasonably steady living from the fishing grounds', and in Dillingham, a ramshackle town, largest of all Bristol Bay communities with about a thousand inhabitants. Few canneries remained to provide summer employment and relatively few fishermen and their families were making enough money during the season to sustain themselves for the rest of the year without help from a welfare agency.

After many years of political pressure by the Alaska Federation of Natives, Congress in 1971 passed the Alaska Native Claims Settlement Act. Now any United States citizen who is at least one-fourth Eskimo, Aleut or Alaskan Indian is entitled to share in the settlement that includes 40 million acres of land and $1 billion in cash. Under the settlement about 220 native villages like those in the Bristol Bay area will receive title to the land on which they are located and every individual will be able to gain title to the land he lives on up to 160 acres. This generous settlement should alleviate the poverty of peoples dependent on the vagaries of salmon fishing.

The future of Alaska's salmon

Alaska's salmon fisheries are beset with increasingly complex problems. Most of them stem from the fact that, with the building of an 800 mile pipeline bringing North Slope oil to refineries in the lower forty-eight the state has been suddenly projected into the industrial age. Since the line was finished in 1977 over a million barrels of hot oil flows daily over the fragile wilderness terrain to Valdez, a port on Prince William Sound. Part of the pipeline is buried in permafrost and part is raised on stilts above the ground. This miracle of engineering, as it is described to Americans nightly on television commercials, is not only a gaping wound in the wilderness but a potential source of ecological disaster – it crosses several salmon rivers and lies in the path of the great caribou migrations, to mention but two vulnerable areas. While care has been taken to preserve the gravel beds of the rivers, a crack in the line spilling hot oil could irreparably damage the fragile terrain and whatever life it sustains.

The Valdez terminal on Prince William Sound is itself a major hazard. Some 300 salmon rivers debouch into the Sound where fleets of supertankers take the crude oil to Washington or California for refining or put it into storage because of inadequate refining capacity on the west coast and limited markets. In fact, much of the Alaskan oil is now a glut on the market. Since most of the chums and pinks spawn in the intertidal reaches of the rivers, any spills in the Sound would endanger whatever fishes are found in the vicinity. Young salmon that hug the river banks going downstream will be in particular danger if oil is washed on to the beaches, or the oil and water are emulsified by wave action.

The Department of the Interior's impact statement on the

pipeline, published in 1972, admits the inevitability of spills all along the Pacific coast during the transportation of Alaskan oil. Considering that, as it turns out, this oil may be a drug on the American market – there is talk of selling some of it to Japan – one wonders why the pipeline was built in the first place. Indeed, the pipeline has become for many people a symbol of the wanton development and use of petroleum resources and the burden it places on the world's oceans and landscapes. The consumption of gasoline in the United States for transportation alone jumped from 3·2 million barrels of forty-eight gallons per day in 1950 to 7·4 million in 1970, and has grown since.

Plans are under way by the federal government to lease marine areas for oil drilling at various places around Alaska, such as the outer reaches of Bristol Bay and the shelf of the Aleutian Islands, all rich in anadromous fishes. The possibility of adverse impacts on the fishes is great. And there are other sources of anxiety about the future of Alaska's natural resources. Most of the state's forest lands are under the control of the US Forest Service in the Tongass and Chugach National Forests. This agency, founded by the pioneer conservationist Gifford Pinchot, has in recent years adjusted its policies to meet the demands of the forest products industries for more wood, sometimes ignoring conservation and sound silvicultural practices. Cutting in the Tongass has been severely criticized by conservationists because it sometimes causes erosion and siltation of streams rich in fish life. In fact, evidence had accumulated that the Tongass was being vastly overcut before the federal court in 1975 halted clearcutting as a violation of the Organic Act of 1897 which then governed timber removal from the national forests. Louis S. Clepper of the National Wildlife Federation reported after a tour of Alaska in 1976 that 'some clearcutting on the Tongass National Forest has resulted in long-lasting scars, and the waste of wood (lying in windrows along the shorelines) is appalling'.

In an effort to bolster the declining salmon runs the state of Alaska has embarked on an ambitious programme of hatchery construction, mostly on a private basis, with some government help. A few state hatcheries are already in existence, but up to now their production has been limited since natural stocks were believed to be able to rebuild themselves. In 1974 the leglisature passed the Renewable Resources Act which commits a percentage of the considerable petroleum royalties expected by the state to the development of the fisheries; this will be a source of funds for loans to the hatcheries. The legislature also created a Fisheries Rehabilitation, Enhancement and Development Division in the Fish and Game Department, and passed a Private Nonprofit Salmon Hatchery Act which provides the legal basis for private aquaculture. Under this act a permit is required from the Department of Fish and Game that allows the hatchery to take salmon eggs for incubation. After incubation the juveniles are released into a stream for imprinting and migration to the ocean – the unique smell and feel of the stream thus becomes part of their mental apparatus and guides them back to it after a sojourn in the ocean. On their return the fish must pass through the common-property commercial fisheries before the hatcheries resume control and are permitted to harvest them and thus obtain revenue and brood stock. The state legislature has authorized $200 million in loans to such private schemes and at the time of writing, spring 1977, about half a dozen private hatchery permits have been granted. It is said in Alaska that up to 200 hatcheries will be needed to rebuild runs to historic levels.

Biologists, however, like William J. Wilson of the University of Alaska, point out that there are many technical problems to be solved before private hatcheries can be counted on to add substantial numbers to the state's salmon stocks. The major species that will be produced are pinks and chum, who go to sea soon after entering the fry stage and require only brief periods of stream feeding. Wilson identifies some of these problems as genetic, due to the potential mixing of wild and artificially propagated races, straying of hatchery fish, diseases that crop up in hatcheries and wipe out entire populations, etc.

While the fish farming programme gets under way, state officials continue their search for new salmon stocks. 'We had a tremendous run of chum salmon in the Yukon River in 1975,' says Wilson, 'a total surprise to the Fish and Game Department who have only three biologists in the area.'

In general Alaska's salmon resource has experienced the same kind of downhill trend as the Columbia's but whereas the latter's future is quite uncertain, despite the optimism of government agencies, Alaska's seems to have stabilized at a relatively high level, though greatly below its heyday. Allan C. Hartt of the Fisheries Research Institute of the University of Washington, an organization which has been involved in research on Alaska fisheries for many decades, sums up the views of knowledgeable biologists:

> There is no question but that there have been abuses to the Alaska salmon, particularly in the early days of exploitation, but by and large they are in a healthy condition and in many instances runs in recent years have rivalled those of some of the early more productive years . . .
>
> The salmon runs in Alaska can never be expected to match those of the pristine years before man was harvesting heavily, but most of them are producing at a level now that is probably what should be expected of a properly managed and harvested resource – that is, an optimum biological yield with escapements regulated to maximize the harvest without endangering future yield. Admittedly certain species in certain districts are at low levels. The causes of these low levels are known in some cases and unknown in others. In many instances sufficient knowledge is available that forecasts can be made for major district and major species . . .
>
> There is every reason to believe that Alaska is going to continue to be a large producer of salmon and in many cases the runs can be expected to increase or at least maintain their present level. I am optimistic that in due time research will reveal the causes of the low runs of pink salmon in recent years in the southern part of southeast Alaska and the low runs of reds in the Karluk River.

The full potential of what is left of the salmon's habitat in Alaska will not be reached unless there is better control over the use of the lands and waters. Much of the wilderness is being invaded, or threatened with invasion, as the profitability of oil, natural gas, minerals and other resources attracts entrepreneurs. For example, the Ramparts Dam which the Corps of Engineers

has had on the drawing boards for many years, a gigantic mono-
lith that would be built across the Yukon River, is being revived
by the agency which has been dubbed Public Enemy No. 1
of the American environment. This project, larger in its hydroelectric potential than Grand Coulee Dam, would seriously
endanger the salmon runs on Alaska's longest river.

The seas around Alaska are being scouted by oil drilling
companies, and some leases had already been announced for
auction by the Ford Administration, but the new Secretary
of the Interior postponed this action in order to make a study of
their impact on the sea and the fish. Oil drilling had actually
started in Kachemak Bay in 1976 when the state legislature
passed a bill which empowered the Governor to buy back the
oil leases the state sold two and a half years previously.

There are other sources of anxiety. Timber cutting and
processing is now Alaska's second largest industry. Logs for
sawmills and pulp mills come almost entirely from the Tongass
and Chugach National Forests. Much of the logging is around
streams abounding with anadromous fishes, and the fallers'
chain-saws do irreparable damage to the aquatic environment.
A letter from a resident of Petersburg to *National Fisherman*
spells out the problem:

> To my mind 'clear cutting' and 'efficient management'
> are conflicting concepts. One cannot exist in conjunction with
> the other.
>
> Clear cutting is causing severe damage to the environment
> in southeast Alaska.
>
> To continue clear-cutting for another two years while
> alternative solutions are being considered would be disastrous
> . . . One after another the salmon streams are being destroyed.
> The streams should continue to produce thousands of fish,
> years after the loggers have come and gone. But once a stream
> has been rendered useless by silt, erosion, fallen trees and
> destroyed 'cover', the salmon . . . are lost for all time.

About two hundred of Alaska's watersheds are now being
logged. The U.S. Forest Service, which administers the
forests lands, is now operating under the National Forest

Practices Act of 1976 that requires a certain amount of restraint in using the clear-cutting method of harvesting timber. Also, the new administration in Washington is not as subjected to the vested interests of the lumber industry as the Ford Administration seemed to be. So there is hope for greater consideration of the salmon rivers in the rush to get out Alaska's munificent timber supply.

CHAPTER 16

Asia's Salmon

THE WIDESPREAD RESOURCE

THE fate of the salmon in Asia has not been happier than in North America and this reinforces the belief that man and his environment and its flora and fauna may be on a collision course in the advanced countries where technology is running rampant.

Oncorhynchus species are found in Asia in rivers flowing into the Pacific and Arctic Oceans from latitudes 35 to 70 degrees north – from Korea to the Chuckchi Peninsula and in numerous islands. Chum, pinks and sockeye are the most prolific inhabitants of these streams while chinook and coho are of lesser importance. Cherry salmon, called 'masu', not found in North America, are an important species in Japan and Russia.

The great bulk of Asia's salmon are found in the Far Eastern region of Soviet Russia which covers about one million square miles, twice the size of Alaska, and comprises the former provinces of Amur, Primorje (including Sakhalin), Transbaikalia and Kamchatka (including the Komandorskiye Islands). The northern parts of this vast region are mainly tundra; most of the rest is mountainous, watered by innumerable rivers of considerable length flowing into the Pacific Ocean.

The major salmon rivers flowing northward to the Arctic Ocean are the 1,110-mile Kolyma, 850-mile Indigirka, 750-mile Yana, and the mighty Lena, longer than the Mississippi, which follows a course of 3,000 miles from the vicinity of Lake Baikal to the Laptev Sea. Among rivers flowing to the Pacific the Amur, 1,770 miles long, with numerous lengthy tributaries, is the most important for production of anadromous fishes. It drains an area of 1,299,000 square miles, five times the size of the Columbia, emptying into the Sea of Okhotsk. A large part of the Amur forms the border with China, thus giving the Chinese an opportunity to harvest the salmon that come up the Ussuri, a major tributary.

Almost everywhere in Asia's salmon world there are rivers containing chum salmon, called 'keta' in Russia. At times they are so numerous when they come up from the sea as to cause panic among fishermen. Thus the Russian ichthyologist I. F. Pravdin witnessed an amazing spectacle on July 30, 1926:

> Although the weather was calm and sunny, an extraordinary noise could be heard coming from the middle of the river between its main two channels . . . The population of the fishing camps rushed out to the river bank. Standing there, the fishermen feasted their eyes upon a tremendous school of fish which went up the river, making a very loud noise, as if a new river had burst into the Bolshaya; the fish jumped out of the water continually. The noisy stretch of water was at least one *verst* long (1·1 mile) and not less than 100 metres (330 feet) wide, so that the size of the school could be estimated at several million specimens, which all got to the spawning grounds upstream, having passed the fishing camps unimpeded.

Pinks or hump-backed salmon actually comprise the largest segment of world catches. Sockeye are found within a smaller range than chum or pinks – from the Gulf of Anadyr to Hokkaido, and only where lakes are available for part of the rearing stage. The Kamchatka Peninsula produces about 80% of these red fishes. They undertake extensive jaunts after spending a year or two in freshwater and may be four to six years old when they return to spawn. Sockeye from eastern Kamchatka sometimes go as far as the outermost Aleutians, where they mingle with fish from western Alaska. Chum and sockeye are the chief species produced in Japanese and Russian hatcheries. Landlocked sockeye (kokanee) are found in some of the lakes of Japan and Kamchatka.

Originally Japan, with numerous splendid rivers on the islands of Honshu and Hokkaido, offered ideal habitat for anadromous fishes. 'Before the Japanese began to lay waste their country in the name of Westernization,' Bernard Rudofsky says in his fascinating book *The Kimono Mind*, it was indeed a paradise

18

where the fishes could thrive and multiply. 'How inviting are the shores with their cheerful dwellings!' exclaimed the explorer Siebold when he entered Nagasaki Bay. Japan was blessed with groves of cedar, oak and laurel, windswept islands, rocky beaches and snow-capped mountains. The popular prints of Hokusai and Hiroshige depict a kind of lotus land of exquisite villages and manorial estates, sparsely-populated, undulating landscapes, and dreamlike valleys crossed by pellucid streams. The official narrative of Commodore Matthew Perry whose expedition in 1853–1854 opened up relations between Japan and the United States, noted: 'All the officers and men were in rapture with the beauty of the country; nothing could be more picturesque than the landscapes wherever the eye was directed . . . a scene of beauty, abundance and happiness.'

Now much of the beauty is gone, the dreamlike quality of the landscape has vanished, 115 million people are squeezed into an area the size of California. Only a small stock of wild fish is left in the rivers and the nation depends for its domestic supply on farming many species of fish and shellfish and ransacking the world's oceans.

Korea has some rivers where salmon were once indigenous. A team of American and Korean scientists who surveyed the salmon and trout resources of south Korea in the 1960s reported that 'fragmentary information indicates that two species of salmon, chum and masu, frequently occur in streams between the Demilitarized Zone and the Nakdong Kang near Pusan. In modern times the catches probably reached a peak in the 1930s. Following this period, overfishing and the destruction of spawning and rearing grounds have reduced the salmon populations to negligible numbers.'

In the northern part of the salmon world, as in Russia, the terrain is mainly tundra, where the subsoil is frozen permanently, and when the ground thaws during the short summer, bogs and shallows are formed, and plants, including dwarf trees, grow profusely. South of the tundra is the taiga, a forested belt stretching for 3,000 miles across Russia, and in some areas reaching a width of a thousand miles. In the northern taiga belt the stands are mainly coniferous, while in the southern part they are chiefly hardwoods. Salmon rivers flow through these gloomy forests. In northern Siberia eternal frost and ice mark the seasons except for the short summers. The coastal areas are shrouded in fog much of the year and throughout the region 70% of the days in the year may be sunless, snow lies on the ground for seven or eight months, and the temperature may drop to 50 degrees below zero Fahrenheit and stay there for weeks. Workers in this frigid region receive extra compensation. In contrast, in the lower Amur valley summers are quite warm and humid but, owing to the cold winds blowing from the north, winters are severe.

In rugged and volcanic Kamchatka Peninsula, rain, snow or fog occurs for about 320 days of the year and there are only two seasons, a short summer and long winter. The mountainous island of Sakhalin, 105 miles long and about sixteen miles wide, is one of the richest salmon producers in the world, second only to Kamchatka Peninsula, also sparsely peopled. Here the sun is a rare visitor, while cold currents from the Sea of Okhotsk, aided by strong winds, bring immense ice floes to the east coast even in summer. In such harsh climates the salmon thrive.

RUSSIA'S SALMON

Native fishery

Like their relatives who emigrated to North America the aborigines of eastern Siberia depended heavily on the salmon for sustenance. They built crude brush barriers across major spawning streams and caught all the fish they needed for themselves and their dogs. When a local supply failed they moved to a new location to take advantage of a better river. During the second half of the eighteenth and early nineteenth centuries the runs in Kamchatka Rivers, for example, declined so much, owing to natural causes, that famine broke out among the people. In contrast, Georg Wilhelm Steller, a German naturalist with the Bering expedition of 1740–1741 to Alaska, noted in his journal the fantastic number of fish clogging the streams, especially 'nerka' (sockeye), a favourite with the Kamchadales in Siberia as well as with the explorers. He tells how the natives fished the ubiquitous salmon with nets spread out from boats and also by means of weirs.

Sven Waxell, the Swede who took command of the expedition's boat, the *St. Peter*, after Bering and many of the crew died from scurvy, describes in his journal how the inhabitants fished for salmon under the ice: 'All that is necessary is to hack an opening in the ice and the fish come along of themselves, in such a way that they can be seized in the hand and thrown upon the ice. Each fish usually weighs six or seven pounds . . . In the spawning season . . . fish throng in such numbers that a short, sudden spate will leave the banks littered with large salmon, there to gasp, die and pollute the air. Fish! Even the lumbering Kamchatka bear wades out into the water with his hind legs and with his front paws scoops them up on the bank.' The Kamchadales lived almost exclusively on fish, and 'smelled accordingly', noted Waxell. Even at the present time some native peoples in the remoter parts of the Soviet Far East are heavily dependent upon the fishery for their existence. As late as the 1920s they are said to have harvested some 20 million salmon annually, $4\frac{1}{2}$ million for themselves and $15\frac{1}{2}$ million for their dogs.

The Communist Revolution of 1917 had profound effects on these seminomadic peoples. The Soviet Government brought them into the modern world and developed the natural resources of the region. It organized collective farms and fishing cooperatives, introduced modern fishing and farming equipment, built fishing stations, established game farms, and uplifted their economic and cultural levels, apparently at the price of making them, like other peoples in the USSR, loyal and submissive to the Communist regime.

Typical are the Evenki, the most numerous and widely scattered of north Siberian peoples. Much of the territory they inhabit, the Okhotsk coast, Sakhalin and Amur valleys, is rich in salmon and other fishes. Farley Mowat, a Canadian writer who visited Siberia in the 1960s, in his book *The Siberians*, describes life in the Magadan district on the Sea of Okhotsk, where the environment is savage. Roads are icy even in summer, while 'the sea is dark, cliff-girt, gale-whipped and fearsome'. There are

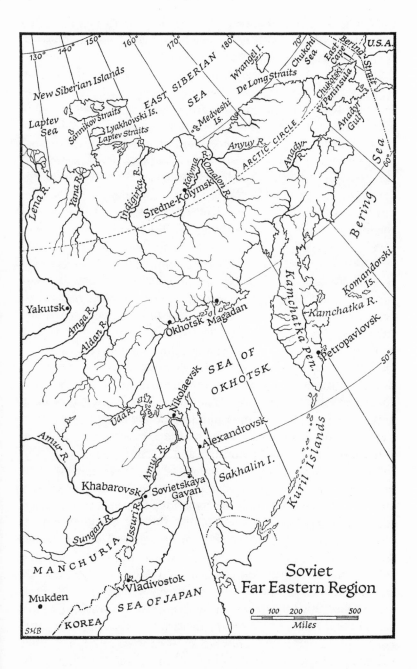

Soviet
Far Eastern Region

0   100   200   500
Miles

107 collective and state farms in this district where the natives engage in fishing, fur breeding, trapping, tending reindeer, raising cattle and hunting mammals in the ocean. 'The country-side belongs exclusively to the natives, the cities to the Caucasians,' Mowat observed.

He visited a typical village operated by the Magadan Fisheries Trust, which, in forty years, had grown from a primitive subsistence fishery to a thriving modern enterprise, exploiting mainly herring and some salmon and other fish. The workers are both Caucasians and natives, trained at the Fishery College at Magadan, and paid according to their abilities. 'The sea is a farm,' said the manager of the Trust, 'and we must farm it, and the farmers must be well rewarded for their work.'

The commercial fishery

It was the Japanese who first commercially exploited Russia's salmon. In the seventeenth century Japan claimed the Kurile Islands, Sakhalin and even Kamchatka and attempted to colonize these areas. In 1752 the feudal Baron of Matsumae had three fishing stations in Sakhalin and between 1773 and 1790 the third Baron of Fukuyama conducted large-scale fishing in this productive island, taking cod, herring and salmon. When the Russian-American Company established a post on Sakhalin in 1853 it found Japanese fishermen on the southern extremity of the island and offered them protection. When Japan emerged from its self-imposed isolation with the restoration of the Meiji dynasty in 1868 Japanese companies began to extend their exploitation of their neighbour's salmon stocks. In 1875 Japan ceded Sakhalin to Russia in exchange for the Kurile Islands but Japanese companies continued to fish there. Sakhalin was used by the Czars as a dumping ground for political dissidents and convicts.

When the dramatist Anton Chekhov visited the island in 1890 he found a lazy, demoralized and incompetent population looking to the fishery for much of its subsistence. 'They do not know how to fish or cure fish,' he wrote, 'and nobody teaches them. According to the present custom the prison takes over the best fishing grounds and the settlers are left with the shallows and rapids, where their cheap, home-made nets are torn to pieces by bushes and rocks.' The convicts were catching fish for the prison and fortunately one of them had been a fisherman in his home town of Tagenrog. He managed the saltery. 'It would seem,' said Chekhov, 'that if [he] had not happened to be convicted nobody would know how to handle the fish.' While the convicts were catching gaunt, half-dead salmon in the upper reaches of the River Tym, the Japanese were taking bright fish at the mouth of the river, after blockading it with palings, and loading them on junks for shipment to Hokkaido. In 1899 the Japanese had over fifty fishing stations on this island, using traps or set nets.

Expanding their activities rapidly in Russian territory, the Japanese companies entered the Amur district on the mainland, where they were permitted to lease salting stations below Niko-laevsk at the mouth of the river. They also contracted to buy salmon from the Russians. The Japanese dry salted their catches on crude bamboo mats in the open air while the Russians packed their fish in brine and shipped them in barrels. Most of the Japanese pack went to Japan or China and other Asiatic countries. It was a lucrative business.

A Russian company was the first to can salmon in the Far East, in 1899, using American machinery, but it ceased operations after two or three years. Meanwhile the Japanese fishery at Nikolaevsk grew from a catch of 8 million pounds in 1892 to over 105 million pounds in 1900, when eighty-five Japanese vessels were permitted to enter the port; the bulk of the catches were shipped to Japan.

Greater access to the profitable Siberian fisheries was one of the reasons for Japan's attack on the Russian Far Eastern garrison in 1904. By the Treaty of Portsmouth (NH) of September 5, 1905, Russia ceded the southern part of Sakhalin to Japan and granted Japanese subjects equal rights with the Russians to exploit the fisheries. The Japanese now had a firm hold on the lucrative Siberian salmon stocks and became a dominant factor in the world's trade in this commodity, a position it holds to this day (*see* Appendix) despite the fact that Japanese fishing for salmon has been severely curtailed in the Pacific by Russia, Canada and the United States.

Japanese high seas fishery

Finding themselves confronted with a resurgent Russia, with a government not inclined to give away its natural resources to foreigners as the Czars did, the Japanese in 1927 launched a mother-ship fishery on the high seas, taking huge numbers of salmon in gillnets on their feeding grounds and processing them in floating canneries. No other nation had yet begun to harvest immature salmon in the ocean. Russia, like the United States and Canada, the world's principal producers, forbade its fishermen to take salmon beyond territorial limits, and this policy is still in force. Japanese salmon catches in the ocean were mostly Russian fish supplemented by sockeye and chum from Alaska. Mother-ship fleets could stay out for months at a time.

In 1933 the Japanese also started a land-based drift gillnet and trap-net salmon fishery in the vicinity of the north Kurile Islands which they then controlled, and also fished in the rich waters around the coast of Kamchatka. Between 1933 and 1945 they took an average of 55 million salmon annually in this fishery, or about 40% of the total Japanese and Soviet Far East catch. Emboldened by their success, the Japanese in 1937 attempted to extend their mother-ship operations eastward and a fleet was actually sent to Bristol Bay, but American opposition was so fierce that it turned back. After Russia declared war on Japan in 1945 Japanese companies were no longer permitted to fish in its territorial waters. In fact, the Japanese fishing fleet was destroyed during the war.

The picture in the north Pacific changed once again as the Japanese, having recovered from the economic effects of the war, launched their world-wide fishing venture. In the process of rapid industrialization much of their freshwater fisheries were destroyed by polluting and damming the rivers. Salmon was only one of many species taken in Japan's ocean fishing; the bulk of the fish came from Russian rivers, and the remainder from Alaska and British Columbia.

Efforts to curtail Japanese exploitation were first made by the United States and Canada who forced Japan into signing a treaty in June 1952 requiring its fishermen to abstain from taking salmon (and other fully utilized species) east of a line drawn through longitude 175 degrees west, passing through Adak Island in the Aleutians. This was a provisional line subject to adjustment as more information became available on the migratory habits of North American salmon. The treaty was to run for ten years and could then be abrogated by each nation on one year's notice. As it turned out, large numbers of Bristol Bay sockeye and pinks migrate west of the abstention line and are taken in Japanese nets, but efforts by the United States and Canada to have it moved westward have met with stubborn Japanese refusal. In fact, the Japanese regard the 1952 treaty, which introduced the abstention principle, as humiliating, an infringement of the rights of nations to fish where they please beyond territorial limits. But they have so far not been willing to abrogate it.

A more humiliating restriction was imposed on the Japanese by the USSR after Nippon's high seas salmon fleet had grown from three mother-ships and fifty-seven catcher boats in 1952 to fourteen mother-ships and 407 catchers in 1955, when 162,000 metric tons of salmon were harvested and converted into 1,600,000 cases of canned fish, 19,500 tons of salted fish and about a thousand tons of roe (sold as a delicacy in Japan). In March 1956 Russia announced the closure of a large section of the international waters of the north-west Pacific to Japanese vessels and in May forced Japan to sign a treaty which banned its salmon fleet from additional areas and provided a bilateral commission to meet annually and set quotas on Japanese salmon catches west of the abstention line. Soviet patrol boats were to be allowed to monitor Japanese operations and Russian inspectors could inspect the catches.

The Soviet-Japanese commission meets annually and after lengthy and tough bargaining quotas are hammered out for the year's operations; being the owner of the fish, Russia has the upper hand. Thus in 1975 the Japanese quota for Area A on the map was 34,000 metric tons of salmon to be taken by the mother-ship fleet and about 8,000 tons in the land-based fishery which uses drifter boats coming from ports on Hokkaido and northern Honshu; in Area B the quota was 35,000 tons which could be taken by the land-based drifters and 5,000 in coastal waters. This

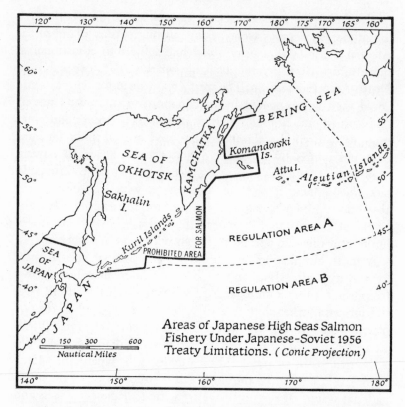

Areas of Japanese High Seas Salmon
Fishery Under Japanese-Soviet 1956
Treaty Limitations. (*Conic Projection*)

total of 82,000 tons was much below the Japanese quotas of the
1960s. In 1976 Japan licensed ten mother-ships and 332 catcher
boats in its high seas salmon fleet while 285 vessels were fishing
for salmon in the area south of 48 degrees north and 83 boats
south of 45 degrees north.

Impact on Russian stocks

There is considerable evidence that the huge Japanese landings
have adversely affected the Soviet stocks (and to a small extent
the Bristol Bay runs) and the Soviets are unhappy about it, as
their representatives on the Japanese-Soviet Commission make
quite clear. In a paper published in a Moscow journal in 1974,
Dr I. I. Kurenkov says:

The pressure on the salmon schools has increased sharply. The coastal catches of the U.S.S.R. decreased sharply and the ratio between the increase in Japanese catches and decline in Soviet catches was so closely related that the curves representing the catches looked almost like a mirror reflection. In 1955 the volume of catches was equal for both countries. In 1956 the international agreement was concluded limiting the industry where the deposit [mother] ships operated. Despite this, the catch by small boats [gillnetters] continued to increase and in 1958 the overall Japanese catch reached a maximum. After that there was a tendency toward gradual and almost steady reduction.

Kurenkov claims that the Japanese fishermen 'destroyed the largest schools of humpbacked salmon [pinks] which are the most numerous . . . found off the coasts of western Kamchatka and the Sea of Japan, while Soviet stocks of chum, while less depleted, were also hit hard by Japanese exploitation.' Sockeye, the next most important species, gradually decreased in both the Soviet and Japanese catches but Japanese fishermen annually take from three to twelve time as many sockeye as the Soviets. The statistical picture in the years 1956–1960 and 1967–1971 is given by Kurenkov in the following table:

	Pinks	Chum	Sockeye	Coho & Chinook	Total
		(thousand metric tons)			
		Average Annual Catch, 1956–1960			
USSR	57·7	43·7	3·7	4·5	109·6
Japan	83·6	51·8	27·9	7·5	170·8
Total	141·3	95·5	31·6	12·0	280·4
		1967–1971			
USSR	41·0	12·6	2·7	5·1	61·4
Japan	53·3	49·7	16·3	7·6	126·9
Total	94·3	62·3	19·0	12·7	188·3

Kurenkov concludes that the remedy for the deplorable state of the Russian salmon is to ban 'industrial fishing' both at sea and near the shore for at least one and perhaps two years in order to give the stocks a chance to recover. However, 'repeated proposals by Soviet specialists have unfortunately not been supported by the Japanese'.

Overfishing is not the only cause for the decline of the Soviet salmon hoard. As in the United States, habitat destruction seems to be fairly common in Russia obsessed with the wonders of mechanization and industrialization. R. S. Semko in a paper on 'The Stocks of West Kamchatka Salmon and Their Commercial Utilization', published in 1960, lists poaching, unfavourable land use and pollution as factors inimical to anadromous fishes in this rich salmon area:

> Experience indicates that settlement of people in the valleys of spawning rivers where there are no fish protective enforcement measures brings about rather quickly a decline in the number of salmon in those rivers . . . In the Kamchatka Peninsula striking examples are the more thickly settled areas of the Kamchatka and Avacha Rivers in which fewer and fewer salmon enter. Here . . . in addition to an intensive fishery, poaching is apparently widespread . . . Large numbers of fish are openly and secretly trapped throughout the length of the channels where substantial populations are found. Some of the spawning areas are polluted, indicating that 'the laws are not sufficiently enforced'. All these forces lead to a curtailment of breeding stocks. Also, 'water flow and fish habitat are impaired by cutting down the forests and the dumping of waste products from manufacturing plants. And sometimes the rivers are blocked by dams that prevent the fish from reaching their destination.'

In order to maintain salmon stocks at an adequate level, adjures Semko, 'the purpose of regulations should be to protect the fish against every agency and factor which is likely to adversely affect conditions in the rivers. Furthermore, measures must be undertaken to increase the productivity of the spawning grounds, particularly by increasing . . . the return of adult fish from the ocean feeding grounds.' The Soviets maintain numerous hatcheries for propagating chum and pink salmon and are considering breeding cherry, coho and chinook as well. There are eighteen hatcheries on the island of Sakhalin, including two in the Kurile Islands, two on the Kamchatka Peninsula, and four in the Amur Basin. The Sakhalin plants released 800 million pink and chum juveniles into the rivers in the spring of 1976, according to Dr William J. McNeill, an American fish-culturist who visited the Soviet Far East in 1976. 'The Soviets,' says McNeil, 'rely primarily on natural recruitment to support the pink fishery and on hatchery production to support the chum fishery.' They are not far behind the Japanese in the scope and quality of their salmon culture operations.

JAPAN'S SALMON

Japan consists of a chain of islands, really an archipelago, separated from the Soviet Union and Korea by the Sea of Japan. It has an area about the size of California yet contains 110 million people, of whom about half are concentrated on over 1% of the land, mainly along the narrow coastal strip of Honshu and on the less crowded islands of Hokkaido, Shikoku and Kyushu. The large cities on Honshu are so close together that they form a vast metropolis stretching from Tokyo to Kobe with little open land between. Away from the megalopolis the landscape unfolds in patterns of rice paddies and other crops planted in tiers, some-times in the cups of the hills, or cut out of a patch of woodland. Between the paddies there may be tobacco plantings, bean fields, or pear or peach orchards. Only one acre out of seven in Japan is arable but this acre must provide eight times as much food as the equivalent area in France. To supplement its own agricultural and fish production Japan relies on the harvests of the world's oceans – rice and fish constitute the bulk of the people's diet.

Salmon was originally plentiful in the 300 to 400 Japanese rivers supporting these fishes, most of which are on the island of Hokkaido boasting volcanic mountains, fumeroles, hot springs and other spectacular scenery. The 225-mile Shinano is the longest salmon river in Honshu, rising at the foot of Mt Kobushi and emptying in the Sea of Japan in Niigata. Most Hokkaido rivers are less than thirty miles long, a dozen or more about

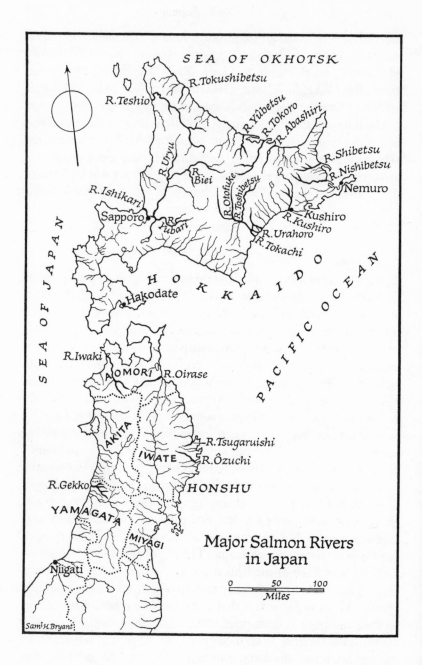

SEA OF OKHOTSK

R.Tokushibetsu

R.Teshio

R.Yûbetsu
R.Tokoro
R.Abashiri

R.Uryu

R.Biei

R.Shibetsu
R.Nishibetsu
Nemuro

R.Ishikari

Sapporo

R.Otofuke
R.Toshibetsu

R.Yubari

Kushiro
R.Kushiro
R.Urahoro
R.Tokachi

SEA OF JAPAN

HOKKAIDO

Hakodate

PACIFIC OCEAN

R.Iwaki

AOMORI
R.Oirase

AKITA

R.Tsugaruishi
IWATE
R.Ôzuchi

R.Gekko
HONSHU

YAMAGATA

MIYAGI

Niigati

Major Salmon Rivers
in Japan

0   50   100
Miles

Sam! H.Bryant.

fifty to sixty miles long; only six are longer. The Ishikari, longest river in Japan, follows a 275-mile course in south-western Hokkaido, dropping into Otara Bay. The most productive rivers in Hokkaido are the Tokachi and Nishibetsu, in each of which 100,000 to 200,000 fish used to ascend annually.

Japan has six species of salmon of which chum, pinks and masu (cherry) are the most numerous; coho, sockeye and chinook are rare. Chum and masu are widely distributed. Chum are found along almost the entire coast as far south as the island of Kyushu in rivers flowing into the East China Sea, but the densest populations are in the northern and eastern Hokkaido rivers. Masu are found mainly in Honshu and pinks in Hokkaido.

Early fishery

Salmon were regarded as valuable fishes by the daimyos of the feudal period. The Meiji dynasty, restored in 1867, encouraged their tenants and serfs to protect the stream beds and spawners, and severe penalties, including capital punishment, were inflicted on those who fished without permission. At first salmon were taken only inside the rivers but with the development of trap nets they were also caught with beach seines in estuarine areas. Introduction of the newly invented set nets around 1800 permitted the expansion of fishing along the rivers and coasts. Some feudal lords even experimented with artificial propagation of salmon.

Large-scale exploitation of fisheries began when Japan emerged as a modern nation and capitalist enterprises moved into neighbouring territories like Sakhalin, the Kuriles and eastern Siberia. At home too, the industry accelerated in the nineteenth century. The fishes streamed in from the sea and provided a livelihood and food for thousands of people. They were caught at the mouths of the rivers, such as the Ishikari, near the city of Sapporo, with huge seines that required many men to handle them. For example, Terry's *Guide to Japan* says that 20,000 or more salmon weighing at least ten pounds each were sometimes taken there in a single day around World War I. Sapporo was then the centre of an industry salting, smoking, canning and shipping salmon. No trace of this industry now exists.

From 1879 to 1893 the catch of chum salmon on Hokkaido, comprising the greatest portion of the nation's total, was between 6 and 8 million, with a peak of 11 million in 1889. This period was followed by a sharp decline for about forty years due to the deterioration of the rivers and then a moderate increase arising from large-scale fish farming. There was also a great deal of overfishing wherever the Japanese were permitted to exploit the resource, both at home and abroad.

Deterioration of the rivers

Dr Richard Van Cleve, former dean of the College of Fisheries of the University of Washington, was asked by the American Occupation authorities to survey the Japanese salmon industry in 1951. He saw nothing but neglect of the freshwater fisheries and apathy of local officials towards their preservation, despite their high productivity. 'In all areas visited,' he said, 'the record of at least one of the power companies is replete with instances of contracts made with fishermen and laws passed by prefectures, providing for proper operation of fishways and maintenance of flows below dams, only to have both contracts and laws disregarded in the interests of more electric power . . . As the company wielded sufficient influence to overwhelm any opposition, no effective maintenance of fish in many areas has been possible except by artificial production.'

In his tour of the islands Van Cleve found that where fishways existed they were often bereft of water so that salmon could not reach their spawning grounds while downstream migrants were killed by unscreened penstocks and diversion canals. A list of dams higher than fifteen metres on salmon rivers supplied him by the prefectural government showed that nineteen out of fifty-eight had fish ladders but only one was included in his itinerary and it was not in operation. 'Where fishes were able to negotiate the dams, fluctuations in reservoir levels made their ascent difficult,' he said. Officials in Hokkaido seemed to have the attitude that natural spawning was a lost cause and they argued that if the salmon were allowed to migrate up the rivers most of them would be pilfered by the local people. Hence they decided to pin their faith on artificial propagation by means of which populations could be protected, creating 'salmon culture rivers' owned by the government and reserved entirely for the hatchery system. Both commercial and sport fishing are banned in these streams.

Van Cleve found widespread pollution of rivers and noted that 'no effort was made by the government toward either preventing or correcting the misuse of the streams'. As an example, much damage was done to the Ishikari by starch factories, a sugar beet mill, and an alcohol distillery, while the entire upper watershed of the Sorachi River was rendered inaccessible to migratory fishes by coal mine pollution and unladdered dams. Yet both had excellent stretches of gravel which could provide ideal spawning grounds for substantial numbers of fish.

He came to the conclusion that the concept of conservation of natural resources was alien to the Japanese people, especially to the moguls who dominated the economy and in effect ruled the country. 'There is no record,' he said, 'that the Japanese have regulated any fishery for the purpose of maintaining yield. Restrictions of their fisheries have been primarily for economic reasons, and controls on fishing intensity seem to have as their primary purpose an adjustment of investment in gear and ships to the expected catch ... The overfishing of one species will result in its replacement by another species which will maintain the total yield at the same or higher level.' This policy has been followed by Japan in its global fishing and whaling operations to this day; however, in recent years extension of national fishing limits to 200 miles in the ocean has severely curtailed Japanese operations. To compensate for these limitations Japanese companies are forming joint ventures with American companies in harvesting and processing the salmon.

Salmon farming

As rivers were blockaded or otherwise rendered uninhabitable for anadromous fishes the Japanese turned more and more to hatchery operations. Artificial salmon propagation originated in 1889 when the first hatchery, modelled on the Craig Brook Atlantic salmon plant in Maine, was opened at Chitose on the Ishikari River in Hokkaido. It was called a central station because it was designed to supply eyed eggs for planting in other rivers and also to serve as a technical centre for disseminating knowledge and skills in salmon culture. It has been rebuilt in recent years and now has the capacity to incubate 13 million eggs.

By 1910 there were fifty-nine salmon hatcheries in Japan, usually small in scale, operated by the government or private bodies. In 1934 the Hokkaido government took over most of the private hatcheries on this island and incorporated them into its system. In 1962 salmon propagation was consolidated into a national development programme and administrative jurisdiction was transferred to the Japan Fishery Agency. Now salmon is propagated on a scale eclipsing that of the United States and is comparable to Soviet production. There are about 200 rivers where the fishes ascend for spawning, of which 123 are utilized for salmon farming. In 1976 about 750 million juveniles, mostly chum, were sent down to sea from Hokkaido hatcheries alone.

In Japan, salmon farming, as it is called there, is regarded as a system of sowing a crop and reaping a harvest, part of a vast national operation which includes the artificial mass production of prawns, lobsters, crabs, eels, sweet fish, trout, carp and other species. To meet the demands of a fish-eating nation Japan has to constantly expand its fish farming, concentrating on those species which offer the most promise yet always seeking new species that can be cultivated. In 1970 I found that even tuna was being studied as a possible object for fish farming. The Tokyo wholesale fish market, probably the biggest in the world, has more tuna on sale than any other species of fish.

A 1975 report on 'Fish Farming in Japan' by the Japan Fisheries Association notes that since 1962 'fish farming has been carried out as work commissioned by the national government. This was an experiment to increase fishery resources on a gigantic scale, and has attracted the attention of both the Japanese and interested foreigners.'

The extensive Japanese salmon hatchery production comes mainly from government-owned hatcheries, but there are thirty private hatcheries in Iwate Prefecture on the island of Honshu alone, and many elsewhere. The combined number of releases into the Honshu fish-culture rivers exceed 200 million fry a year.

The non-public hatcheries are usually owned by fishery cooperatives and operate under federal government supervision. Basic regulations, according to Dr McNeil, who visited the Japanese hatcheries in 1976, that govern private hatcheries are: (1) all the eggs are owned by the federal government; (2) eggs are stocked in private hatcheries in accordance with plans approved by the federal government; and (3) private hatcheries receive most of their income from sale of carcasses of hatchery fish, and in some cases from funds provided by fishing cooperatives or from voluntary assessments on catches.

At the 1975 Aquaculture Conference held by the UN's Food and Agriculture Organization in Kyoto a Japanese scientist said that in Japan 70 to 80% of all the salmon fry descending the rivers to saltwater are reared in hatcheries, a far greater proportion than in any western country. Adult fish are taken on their return from the ocean in sanctuary rivers with racks, traps, seines, wheels or gillnets. The eggs are incubated at field stations and when the fry of chum and pinks have absorbed their yolk sacs they are moved to outdoor ponds and fed crumbled pellets for about a month. They are released in April and May and sent down to sea where they remain from two to five years. Cherry salmon are held about a year in the hatchery before being released as smolts. On their return from the ocean the salmon are caught by the coastal fishermen and those who escape and reach the rivers are artificially spawned. All fish in excess of hatchery needs as well as spawned-out specimen are sold for food. The entire enterprise is designed not only to provide a fish supply for consumers but a profit for the hatchery system.

The Japanese claim that hatchery propagation is more efficient than natural production especially since the introduction of pellet feeding; there are few rivers left where natural spawning is permitted.

The eastern and northern coasts of Hokkaido are dotted with villages where small fishing boats ride at anchor, fish, mostly cod, are drying in the sun on racks, and old wizened fishermen are repairing their nets. As you drive along the highway facing the Sea of Okhotsk you pass numerous rivers marked by signs in Japanese and English identifying them as 'Salmon Culture Rivers'.

Since they belong to the government trespass is forbidden. There are also signs, in Japanese, saying 'Return the Kuriles!' which Russia took away from Japan after World War II.

The Hokkaido hatchery system has considerably expanded its operations in the past two decades, and as a consequence the runs of chum have increased greatly, from an average of 2,850,000 in the years 1954–1963 to 5,850,000 in 1964–1973. The bulk of these fishes are taken in the coastal fishery, a small proportion are netted on the high seas and less than 10% are used for brood stock. Runs totalled almost 10 million in 1973, 8,400,000 in 1974 and a record-breaking 15,200,000 in 1975 – this was a dominant year in the four-year cycle of the chum. It was estimated that the 1975 crop, worth $164 million, cost only $3·3 million.

In his 1951 report to the Occupation authorities Dr Van Cleve pointed out that the capacity of the Hokkaido hatchery system was being limited to that of the hatcheries, not to the potential of the island's salmon rivers. The Tokachi River alone, he said, if kept in its natural state could yield as many salmon as the Hokkaido government planned to introduce in its entire system in 1954. When the numerous rivers of the island are considered, 'the conclusion must be reached that the elimination of natural production and the placing of the entire future of the salmon stocks in the hatcheries alone are reducing the productive capacity of the prefecture to a small fraction of its potential if natural spawning was permitted and protected'. In the years since Van Cleve wrote his report destruction of Japanese rivers has continued at an increasing pace.

In 1974 Japan reported total landings of 134,000 metric tons of salmon, of which 45,000 tons came from domestic production and 89,000 tons were taken from foreign countries' stocks. A large proportion of the total was exported to earn foreign exchange but it also brought enormous profits to the cartelized companies that control the Japanese economy. Some of these companies are rushing into joint ventures with Americans as the United States implements the 200-mile fishing limits around its coasts, others have bought out American companies in Alaska and the 'lower forty-eight'. What share of the profits accruing from the catching and processing of salmon goes to the fishermen and factory-ship workers is hard to discover, but from our observations they do not fare nearly as well as their counterparts in the United States. The standard of living in Japan, probably the world's most industrialized, and also most polluted nation, is one of the lowest among the advanced countries. As before World War II, the nation's wealth is concentrated in the hands of a small and extremely wealthy group of businessmen.

In 1975 world catches of Pacific salmon were as follows:

	Japan	USSR	Canada	USA	Total
Pinks	46,400	69,000	10,200	26,400	152,000
Chum	33,200	6,700	5,400	15,000	60,300
Sockeye	7,700	1,500	7,300	24,400	40,900
Chinook	1,000	1,900	7,300	15,100	25,300
Coho	8,100	3,800	7,700	13,000	32,600
Total	96,400	82,900	37,900	93,900	311,100

The Appendix shows the catches from 1967 to 1975.

POSTSCRIPT

In a book published by the Canadian government for the delegates to the Law of the Sea conference in 1974, *Salmon*, the author, Roderick Haig-Brown, says: 'To suggest that the salmons of the world are an endangered group would certainly be misleading, yet it is true that, on a world-wide basis, their stocks are declining. As with all species of great natural abundance, there is a critical point below which recovery becomes extremely difficult, if not impossible. To say that Atlantic salmon are within sight of this critical point is no exaggeration.'

To keep *Salmo salar* from reaching that point, and to prevent the Pacific species from further drastic declines – world catches have fallen by about a third in the past thirty years – is a challenge which many conservation organizations and governments on all continents where salmon are native are facing.

Let us hope the challenge is well met and the future is brighter for the species of *Oncorhynchus* – as well as for *Salmo salar*.

Appendix

WORLD CATCHES OF PACIFIC SALMON, 1967–1975
(metric tons)

Species	1967	1968	1969	1970	1971	1972	1973	1974	1975
PINK SALMON									
Japan	70,100	46,700	74,600	35,300	55,000	28,800	49,800	29,700	46,400
USSR	51,100	16,600	63,500	16,200	61,100	20,400	66,400	32,000	69,000
Canada	23,400	25,200	6,300	24,000	17,600	18,200	13,300	11,200	10,200
USA	23,600	67,300	50,900	53,200	45,100	24,400	22,300	18,200	26,400
Total Pink	168,200	155,800	195,300	128,700	178,800	91,800	151,800	91,100	152,000
CHUM SALMON									
Japan	54,500	44,700	42,200	56,200	59,900	65,600	60,500	37,300	33,200
USSR	25,300	16,200	8,400	12,400	12,600	5,100	5,200	7,100	6,700
Canada	5,500	16,600	6,100	16,800	5,400	30,200	32,700	12,500	5,400
USA	15,600	27,800	11,300	26,000	25,900	29,800	26,000	19,200	15,000
Total Chum	100,900	105,300	68,000	111,400	103,800	130,700	124,400	76,300	60,300
RED SALMON (SOCKEYE)									
Japan	20,500	16,800	15,500	17,900	11,000	11,000	9,400	8,200	7,700

USSR	3,200	2,400	1,700	4,500	3,400	1,700	1,100	1,500
Canada	16,800	18,800	10,800	11,400	17,300	21,500	21,700	7,300
USA	30,000	24,800	33,600	72,400	48,100	22,200	22,100	24,400
Total Red	70,500	62,800	61,700	106,200	79,800	54,800	53,100	40,900
CHINOOK SALMON								
Japan	1,000	1,400	1,500	1,600	1,200	1,200	1,800	1,000
USSR	900	800	1,200	1,400	2,000	2,200	1,800	1,900
Canada	11,500	6,900	6,400	6,600	8,700	7,600	7,600	7,300
USA	12,100	12,000	13,000	14,700	14,200	17,700	13,200	15,100
Total King	25,500	21,100	22,100	24,300	26,100	28,700	24,400	25,300
COHO SALMON								
Japan	3,900	5,600	9,600	5,400	6,800	10,600	9,700	8,100
USSR	3,700	3,300	3,400	4,600	4,500	2,100	3,900	3,800
Canada	10,200	15,100	8,000	13,600	14,100	11,300	10,400	7,700
USA	17,200	17,300	9,800	19,900	18,300	15,200	19,200	13,000
Total Coho	35,000	41,300	30,800	43,500	43,600	39,100	43,200	32,600
Total catch	400,100	386,300	377,900	414,100	432,100	324,600	398,800	311,100

*Figures for Japan do not include catches by coastal fisheries which landed an average of 2,700 m./t. of pink salmon in 1970 and 1972 and an average of 26,000 m.t. of chum salmon annually during 1970–73. Catches of red, king and coho salmon by Japanese coastal fisheries during 1970–73 were negligible. 1975 figures are preliminary.

Select Bibliography

PART I. THE LIFE OF THE SALMON

Brett, J. R., 'The Swimming Energetics of Salmon', *Scientific American*, August, 1965.

Combs, Trey, *The Steelhead Trout*, Portland, Oregon, Northwest Salmon Trout Steelheader, 1971.

Foerster, R. E., *The Sockeye Salmon*, Ottawa, Fisheries Research Board of Canada, Bulletin 162, 1968.

Hasler, Arthur D., *Underwater Guideposts: Homing of Salmon*, Madison, University of Wisconsin Press, 1966.

International North Pacific Fisheries Commission, Bulletin 16, 'Coho, Chinook and Masu Salmon in Offshore Waters', Vancouver, British Columbia, 1965.

—Bulletin 18, 'A Review of the Life History of North Pacific Salmon', 1967.

—Bulletin 20, 'Sockeye Salmon in Offshore Waters', 1966.

—Bulletin 23, 'Spawning Populations of North Pacific Salmon', 1967.

—Bulletin 24, 'Distribution of Mature Western Alaska and Kamchatka Sockeye Salmon in the North Pacific Ocean and Bering Sea', 1968.

—Bulletin 25, 'Chum Salmon in Offshore Waters', 1968.

—Bulletin 31, 'Distribution and Abundance of Coho Salmon in Offshore Waters of the North Pacific Ocean', 1975.

Jones, J. W., *Atlantic Salmon*, London, Collins, 1959.

Le Danois, Edouard, *Fishes: Their Journeys and Migrations*, London, Routledge, 1933.

Pyefinch, K. A., 'A Review of the Literature on the Biology of the Atlantic Salmon', Edinburgh, Scottish Home Department, 1955.

Royce, William F., Lynwood S. Smith, and Allan C. Hartt, 'Models of Oceanic Migrations of Pacific Salmon and Comments on Guidance Mechanisms', U.S. Fish and Wildlife Service, Fishery Bulletin 66 (3), 1968.

Schultz, Leonard P., 'The Breeding Habits of Salmon and Trout', in *Earth and Life*, Vol. II, *Smithsonian Treasury of Science*, Washington, D.C., Smithsonian Institute, 1960.

Stuart, T. A., 'The Leaping Behaviour of Salmon and Trout at Falls and Obstructions', Department of Agriculture and Fisheries for Scotland, Edinburgh, 1962.

Tchernavin, V., 'The Origin of Salmon: Is Its Ancestry Marine or Freshwater?', London, *Salmon and Trout*, No. 95, 1939.

Went, A. E. J., 'Irish Kelt Tagging Experiments', *Irish Fisheries Investigation*, Series A, No. 5, Dublin, Department of Agriculture and Fisheries, 1969.

Wilimovsky, N. J., ed., *Symposium on Pink Salmon*, University of British Columbia, Vancouver, 1962.

PART II. THE ATLANTIC SALMON

Ashworth, Thomas, *The Salmon Fisheries of England*, London, Longmans, Green, 1868.

Breuil, Henri and Raymond Lantier, *The Men of the Old Stone Age*, London, Harrap, 1965.

Burgess, G. H. O., *The Eccentric Ark: The Curious World of Frank Buckland*, New York, Horizon Press, 1967.

Calderwood, W. L., *The Salmon Rivers and Lochs of Scotland*, London, Arnold, 1921.

Canada's Atlantic Salmon, Ottawa, Department of Environment.

Carlin, Borje, *Lectures Delivered for the Atlantic Salmon Association*, Montreal, 1969.

Defoe, Daniel, *A Tour Thro' the Whole Island of Great Britain*, London, Everyman's Library, 1928.

Elson, P. F. and A. L. W. Tuomi, *The Foyle Fisheries: New Basis for Rational Management*, Londonderry, Foyle Fisheries Commission, 1975.

Goode, George B., *The Fisheries and Fishing Industries of the United States*, Washington, D.C., 1887.

Goodspeed, Charles E., *Angling in America*, Boston, Houghton-Mifflin, 1939.

Grimble, Augustus, *The Salmon Rivers of England and Wales*, London, Kegan, Paul, 1913.

—*The Salmon Rivers of Ireland*, London, Kegan, Paul, 1913.

—*The Salmon Rivers of Scotland*, London, Kegan, Paul, 1913.

Herbert, H. A., *Tale of a Wye Fisherman*, London, 1953.

Jordan, David S. and Barton W. Evermann, *American Food and Game Fishes*, New York, Doubleday, Page, 1908.

McLaren, Moray and William B. Currie, *The Fishing Waters of Scotland*, London, Murray, 1972.

Netboy, Anthony, *The Atlantic Salmon: A Vanishing Species?*, London, Faber, 1968.

Nettle, Richard, *The Salmon Fisheries of the St. Lawrence*, Montreal, 1857.

Norris, Thad, *The American Angler's Guide*, Philadelphia, 1864.

Report of the Inland Fisheries Commission, Dublin, Stationery Office, 1975.

Scrope, William, *Days and Nights of Salmon Fishing in the Tweed*, London, Arnold, 1898.

Sosin, Mark, 'Greenland Salmon', *Field and Stream*, May, 1970.

Thoreau, Henry D., *The Maine Woods*, Boston, Houghton-Mifflin, 1893.

—*A Week on the Concord and Merrimack Rivers*, Boston, Houghton-Mifflin, 1893.

—*Walden*, New York, New American Library, 1960.

Vibert, Richard and L. de Boisset, *La Pêche Fluviale en France*, Paris, 1944.

Wells, Henry, *The American Salmon Fisherman*, New York, 1886.

Wright, Esther Clark, *The St. John River and its Tributaries*, 1966.

PART III. THE PACIFIC SALMON

Berg, Leo S., *Freshwater Fishes of the U.S.S.R. and Adjacent Countries*, Washington, D.C., National Science Foundation, 1962.

Clay, C. H., *Design of Fishways and Other Fish Facilities*, Ottawa, Department of Fisheries, 1961.

Columbia River Salmon and Steelhead, ed. Ernest Schwiebert, American Fisheries Society, Bethesda, Md., 1977.

Craig, J. A. and R. L. Hacker, *History and Development of the Fisheries of the Columbia River*, Washington, D.C., Bureau of Fisheries, 1940.

Dasmann, Raymond, *The Destruction of California*, New York, Collier Books, 1966.

Dodds, Gordon B., *The Salmon King of Oregon*, Chapel Hill, University of North Carolina Press, 1959.

Drucker, Philip, *Indians of the Northwest Coast*, Garden City, New York, Natural History Press, 1963.

Duff, Wilson, *The Indian History of British Columbia*, Vol. I, Victoria, Provincial Museum, 1965.

Gleason, George W., *The Return of a River: The Willamette River, Oregon*, Corvallis, Oregon State University Press, June, 1972.

Gruening, Ernest, *The State of Alaska*, New York, Random House, 1968.

Hallock, Richard J., Robert F. Elwell and Donald H. Fry, Jr., *Migrations of Adult King Salmon in the San Joaquin Delta*, California Fish and Game Department, 1970.

Hedgpeth, Joel W., 'The Passing of the Salmon', *Scientific Monthly*, Vol. 59, (1944).

Holland, G. S., J. E. Lasater, E. D. Neumann and W. E. Eldredge, *Toxic Effects of Organic and Inorganic Pollutants on Young Salmon and Trout*, Olympia, Washington Department of Fisheries, January, 1964.

Idyll, C. P., *The Sea Against Hunger*, New York, Crowell, 1970.

Krashnennikov, Stepan P., *The Natural History of Kamchatka and the Kurilski Islands With the Countries Adjacent*, tr. James Grieve, Quadrangle Books, Chicago, 1962.

International Pacific Salmon Fisheries Commission, *Annual Reports*, New Westminster, British Columbia.

Hill, A. V., *Tides of Change: A Story of Fishermen's Cooperatives in British Columbia*, Prince Rupert, 1967.

Kroeber, A. L., and S. A. Barrett, *Fishing Among the Indians of Northwestern California*, Berkeley, University of California Press, 1960.

LaViolette, Forrest E., *The Struggle for Survival*, Toronto, University of Toronto Press, 1961.

Laycock, George, *Alaska: The Embattled Frontier*, Boston, Houghton-Mifflin, 1971.

Lyons, Cecily, *Salmon: Our Heritage*, Vancouver, British Columbia, 1969.

McKeown, Martha F., *Alaska Silver*, New York, Macmillan, 1951.

McKervill, Hugh W., *The Salmon People*, Sidney, British Columbia, Gray's Publishing Co., 1967.

Netboy, Anthony, *The Salmon: Their Fight for Survival*, Boston, Houghton-Mifflin, 1974.

Nikolsky, G. V., *Special Ichthyology*, Washington, D.C., National Science Foundation, 1961.

Peoples of Siberia, ed. M. G. Levin and L. P. Potapov, University of Chicago Press, 1964.

Rostlund, Erhard, *Freshwater Fish and Fishing in Native North America*, Berkeley, University of California Press, 1952.

Rudofsky, Bernard, *The Kimono Mind*, Garden City, New York, Doubleday, 1965.

Uncommon Controversy: Fishing Rights of the Muckleshoot, Puyallup and Nisqually Indians, Seattle, University of Washington Press, 1970.

Van Cleve, Richard and Ralph W. Johnson, 'Management of the High Seas Fisheries of the Northeastern Pacific', Seattle, College of Fisheries, University of Washington, November, 1963.

—'The International Pacific Salmon Fisheries Commission and Conservation of the Fraser River Salmon Runs', *Transactions of the North American Wildlife Conference*, 1949.

Van Stone, James W., *Eskimos of the Nushagak River*, Seattle, University of Washington Press, 1967.

Index